GETTYSBURG
RELIGION

THE NORTH'S CIVIL WAR
Paul A. Cimbala, series editor

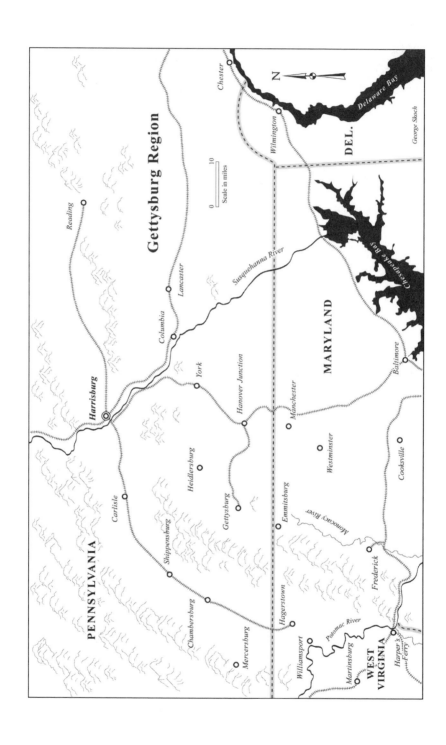

Gettysburg Region

Gettysburg Religion

Refinement, Diversity, and Race in the Antebellum and Civil War Border North

Steve Longenecker

FORDHAM UNIVERSITY PRESS
NEW YORK   2014

Frontispiece: Gettysburg region

Library of Congress Cataloging-in-Publication Data

Longenecker, Stephen L., 1951–
   Gettysburg religion : refinement, diversity, and race in the antebellum and Civil War border north / Steve L. Longenecker.
      pages cm. — (The North's Civil War)
   Summary: "Brings to life the religious history of a small and famous town and the surrounding area, the Border North. The theme is that Gettysburg religion reveals much about larger American society, often something unexpected and indicative of the Border North's advanced modernity" — Provided by publisher.
   Includes bibliographical references and index.
   ISBN 978-0-8232-5519-1 (hardback)
   1. Gettysburg (Pa.)—Religion—19th century.   2. Gettysburg Region (Pa.)—Religion—19th century.   3. Gettysburg (Pa.)—Church history—19th century.
4. Gettysburg Region (Pa.)—Church history—19th century.   5. Religion and culture—Pennsylvania—Gettysburg—History—19th century.   6. Religion and culture—Pennsylvania—Gettysburg Region—History—19th century.   7. Pennsylvania—History—Civil War, 1861–1865—Religious aspects.   I. Title.
   BL2527.G488L66 2014
   277.48'42081—dc23

                                                                                    2013017378

Printed in the United States of America

16 15 14   5 4 3 2 1

First edition

For peacemakers everywhere

Contents

Preface

The Civil War was my first interest in history, and Gettysburg is among my favorite childhood memories. The first book I remember was a child's biography of Robert E. Lee. I was a preschooler just before Christmas, and my mother was out for some reason. My father was looking after me and my younger brother, and we must have been a handful because at one point he said wait a minute, went upstairs, and came back with an early Christmas present, the Lee book. We read it over and over.

Gettysburg was an annual event in my childhood. Every summer my grandparents took me to the battlefield, and we did it all: Lee's Headquarters, Devil's Den, the electric map, and the souvenir shops. I got a hat, a bullet, and ice cream.

In 1961 my family attended the ninety-eighth anniversary of the battle, a "sham" battle, as it was called. It was a brutally hot day in July, and in those times nobody hydrated, hats were optional, and sunscreen, called "sun tan lotion," was for the beach. My seven-year-old brother barfed on the way home, probably from sunstroke, and both my father and his buddy, a tough-as-nails former Marine, got infected insect bites. But I was a bulletproof ten-year-old, and I thought the whole thing was wonderful: the uniforms, the noise, the smoke, everything. The only disappointment was that nobody died. None of the soldiers went down. Even as a child, I realized that spending the reenactment facedown in the grass would be bad, but a few guys biting the dust would have helped. The government banned these events in its parks for a long time afterward, and this was a memorable day in family history.

Our attendance at the Gettysburg celebration was ironic because we attended a historic peace church and were biblical pacifists. My father had an explanation for this obvious inconsistency, but popular thought is often irrational and it certainly was this time. Regardless, my interest in history was off to a start.

Years later, the Border North came to my attention as a graduate student in William W. Freehling's stimulating seminar at the Johns Hopkins University. As we discussed the Border South, it seemed that a Border North must also have existed, and I wondered why it received little attention compared to its counterpart. The Border North went on my list of questions to investigate.

This project, then, combines the nostalgia of revisiting historical sites first experienced in childhood with the joy of considering big questions first encountered as a graduate student. It has been a splendid adventure.

The dedication—"for peacemakers everywhere"—is a reminder of the imperative to mourn rather than celebrate the Battle of Gettysburg and to use rational conflict resolution instead of inflicting so much harm on so many innocents. Blessed are the peacemakers.

Acknowledgments

Many kind persons provided invaluable assistance for this project. One of the most pleasant tasks in the completion of the book is expressing appreciation for their contributions.

The staff of the Adams County Historical Society on the campus of the Lutheran Theological Seminary merits special appreciation. I spent many pleasant hours in their interesting and cozy building, and everybody was consistently helpful.

Similarly supportive were the staff of the Alexander Mack Library, Bridgewater College, Bridgewater, Va.; A. R. Wentz Library at the Lutheran Theological Seminary at Gettysburg (special thanks to Roberta Brent); Beneficial-Hodson Library, Hood College, Frederick, Md.; Carrier Library, James Madison University, Harrisonburg, Va.; Evangelical and Reformed Historical Society and the Philip Schaff Library at Lancaster Theological Seminary, Lancaster, Pa.; John T. Reily Historical Society, McSherrystown, Pa.; Lauinger Library, Georgetown University, Washington, D.C.; Library and Archives, York County Heritage Trust, York, Pa.; Library and Research Center, Gettysburg National Military Park; Library of Congress, Washington, D.C.; Millersville University Library, Millersville University, Millersville, Pa.; Musselman Library, Gettysburg College; the National Archives, Washington, D.C.; Phillips Library, Mount St. Mary's University, Emmitsburg, Md.; Presbyterian Historical Society, Philadelphia, Pa.; and State Library of Pennsylvania, Harrisburg, Pa. Robert Tout of the Bridgewater College library faithfully completed many requests for interlibrary loans.

The Gettysburg Presbyterian Church graciously opened its archives and allowed the use of a Sunday school room to read them. Jean Odom shared her collection of materials from St. Paul's African Methodist Episcopal Zion Church and was very generous with her time and hospitality.

Bridgewater College aided this project with two sabbatical leaves—one at the beginning of the venture and another at the end—and annual faculty research grants funded numerous research trips to Gettysburg and elsewhere. I am indebted to the college's President Philip C. Stone, President George E. Cornelius, Vice-President and Dean for Academic Affairs Arthur C. Hessler, and Vice-President and Dean for Academic Affairs Carol A. Scheppard. Carl Bowman, Pamela Cochran, Ann-Marie Codori, Bill Codori, Toviah Floyd, Nicholas Picerno, Jonathan Stayer, Larry Taylor, and Michael Utzinger assisted in a variety of ways.

Readers of parts or all of the manuscript were Paul Anderson, Edward Ayers, Steven Burg, Eric Campbell, Ruth Doan, Charles Glatfelter, Jennifer Graber, and Steven Nolt. They gave very generously of their time and expertise to spare me from embarrassing mistakes and greatly improved the manuscript with sensible and wise observations.

Lew and Carol, my grown children, deserve much appreciation for their continued conversation and interest and for being such good listeners. Finally, special thanks to Ada, my wife, for her support, patience, and understanding what I do with my summers, and, especially, for her love.

Introduction

"Some little town in Pennsylvania called Gettysburg," answered Rhett Butler when Scarlett O'Hara, anxious about her beloved Ashley Wilkes, inquired about the location of the great battle.[1] The dashing Mr. Butler can be forgiven for insinuating the insignificance of this modest settlement of over two thousand residents, known primarily for a great collision of armies. Yet this "little town in Pennsylvania," just seven miles north of the Mason-Dixon Line, remains among the strongest Civil War and American memories. In particular, religious sites such as Cemetery Hill and the Lutheran seminary belong to the core of this remembrance, and another Gettysburg memory, the Peach Orchard, though technically secular also has an intriguing religious story. A century and a half after the great battle, Cemetery Hill, the seminary and its ridge, and the Peach Orchard remain powerful memories, not just for three bloody days in July 1863, but for their embodiment of the small-town North and their ability to touch themes vital to nineteenth-century religion.

This book argues that religion represented by these sites and within their famous community reveals much about American society during the antebellum and Civil War periods. Like so many small towns, Gettysburg's religious life was vibrant but routine. As Christians nourished their souls on a daily and weekly basis, the priorities of congregational life, such as choir masters, fairs, debts, and pastoral placement, often preoccupied them. Historians want to know what the past teaches, and sometimes an honest resurrection of the past reveals that most persons in the pews were more interested in things small rather than large. Certainly, large political issues and grand reforms claimed attention, but, especially in their religious life, maintenance of the local societies was a very high priority.[2]

But despite the frequency of the humdrum, Gettysburg religion had direction, and during the period of this study three trends were particularly prominent: refinement, diversity, and war. Refinement—that is, the quest for improvement—became a groundswell, perhaps a tidal wave, among the American middle class through the nineteenth century and hardly distinct to a town in southern Pennsylvania. Books, print fabrics, shelf clocks, parlors, academies, inexpensive portraits, landscaped yards, and cast iron stoves were among the material marks of refinement, but attitudes, such as manners and beautification, were just as important in the reach for gentility. The religious version of refinement focused on improved facilities and polished worship. New buildings, often with steeples or cupolas, altered Gettysburg's skyscape, and improvement of church interiors was unending. Carpets softened the steps of worshippers as they entered and departed, and gas-lit chandeliers brightened sanctuaries when the sun was reluctant. Choir masters taught harmony, meter, and pitch, and a new community cemetery with garden-like surroundings upgraded burial and mourning. Additionally, the town's Lutherans bragged of a seminary to place polished men in their well-appointed pulpits, and Pennsylvania College (now Gettysburg College) prepared candidates for the seminary and sent other well-educated men into the secular world. As with worldly consumption, the components of religious refinement contributed to an image of conspicuous appreciation for dignity, polish, manners, and beauty. But paying for refinement stretched budgets, and the financial burden of dignity sometimes threatened to break the ties that bound, further evidence of refinement's high priority. If improvement seems commonplace and unremarkable, it nevertheless claimed time and energy from many.[3]

The quest for sophistication particularly touched two denominations—Methodists and Dunkers—although much differently. Antebellum Methodists changed more than any other fellowship, deemphasizing discipline and emotional conversion as they assumed middle-class respectability. A dignified, rational version of evangelicalism, initially associated with Charles Grandison Finney, a Presbyterian, grew throughout the nineteenth century, and the antebellum period caught Gettysburg Methodists somewhere along this transitional path with the emotional Methodism of earlier generations still evident but fading. Dunkers, as Anabaptists, conspicuously resisted refinement, and they opposed the sinful world with rigor and detail, specifically resisting the material trappings of middle class gentility, such as stylish clothing, fashionable furnishings, and stately church buildings. Where others saw improvement or sophistication, Dunkers saw worldliness, thereby demonstrating that the hunger for dignity was not quite universal. In sum, with enhanced church buildings, heavy mortgages, one denomination (Methodists) more noticeably sophisticated, another (Dunkers) conspicuously opposed to it, a college, a seminary on a ridge, and a new cemetery on a hill, refinement loomed large in this small town's spiritual life.

If refinement was routine in antebellum America, Gettysburg's diversity was more unusual and marked the town and region as uncommonly modern, especially for a rural area. The modernity of this region during the colonial period has drawn special attention from scholars. One historian of colonial Germantown, on the outskirts of Philadelphia, termed it an "urban village" for its diversity and market economy, and another for similar reasons proclaimed eighteenth-century Reading, Pennsylvania, "born modern." Michael Zuckerman, citing the old joke about the drunk who looked for his keys under a well-lit lamppost instead of the dark gutter where he dropped them, argued that the keys to America's past are in "America's first plural society," the Mid-Atlantic.[4]

In the nineteenth century this region's distinctively modern diversity continued to evolve. The Peach Orchard, owned and operated by a family of Dunkers, attracts immediate attention as an example of denominational variety, but antebellum Gettysburg had a long list of fellowships that included African Methodist Episcopal Zion (AME Zion), Associate Reformed, Catholics, German Reformed, Lutherans, Methodists, and Presbyterians. Presbyterians actually had two options: one congregation affiliated with the mainline Synod of Philadelphia and another, the Associate Reformed, descended from Scottish Dissenters. Ethnic diversity added to the mix. Catholics, Dunkers, Lutherans, and Reformed had German origins, and despite their long American roots planted deep in the eighteenth century, all still worshipped occasionally in their native tongue. German-heritage fellowships often disagreed internally on the balance between English and German, which resulted in another type of variety. Gettysburg Lutherans, for example, supported two congregations: A seminary-college congregation that was uniformly English and another that included German worship. Furthermore, a third German-only Lutheran group briefly flowered for immigrant Germans. Patches of doctrinal diversity further colored Gettysburg's religious quilt. Christians differed on whether the road to salvation passed through emotional, sudden conversion or through order, sacraments, catechisms, and time-honored church structures. Dunkers and Catholics added genuine doctrinal outsiderness to the community. Dunkers were unusually nonconformist to the world and especially stressed conformity to the faith community as an alternate source of authority. Catholics stressed human ability, hierarchy, ceremony, and mysticism much more than most Protestants. Education gave Gettysburg another layer of complexity as the seminary and the college contributed intellectuals and denominational leadership to the town's religious mix. Thus, with Methodists, two kinds of Presbyterians, Lutherans, including recent immigrants, German Reformed, Dunkers, Catholics, the AME Zion congregation, college and seminary professors, and worship in two languages (or three, counting the Catholic's Latin), this little town possessed denominational, ethnic, doctrinal, and educational diversity unmatched by many communities.

Indeed, the diversity of Gettysburg and the surrounding region was unusual compared to the rest of America, especially its rural regions. The rural South was much more homogenous than the Border North, and although other parts of the rural Mid-Atlantic also had some diversity, almost completely missing from these areas were obscure countercultural fellowships—especially German groups, such as Mennonites, Dunkers, and Moravians—who were native-born but with persistent ethnicity and who abounded in southern Pennsylvania and lived beside Baptists, Episcopalians, Methodists, Presbyterians, and lesser numbers of African Americans, Scottish Dissenters, Quakers, and Catholics. For an antebellum rural region, the "small town in Pennsylvania" and the surrounding Border North contained large variety, especially undersized, nonmainstream groups, and general but imperfect tolerance that signaled a coming pattern for all of the United States.[5]

Racial diversity added to the religious and ethnic assortment and makes the Border North even more instructive. Eight percent of Gettysburg's population was African American, which by southern standards was low but for a northern community relatively high. In Border North counties African Americans had numbers larger than in most other parts of the North and sufficient to establish community life in small towns, including Gettysburg. Admittedly, free blacks were a tiny minority in the Border North, but they nevertheless formed a visible thread in the social fabric and added to diversity.[6]

The small African-American community in the Border North faced numerous trials. Many whites were racist, slave catchers frequented the area, and blacks scraped along the bottom of the local economy. Black live-in servants for whites were common, and African-American property holding was so unusual that observers took note when it happened.

But the region still offered African Americans opportunity largely absent just south in slave territory. An underground railroad aided runaways, and antislavery whites contributed countervailing voices of support and encouragement for blacks. The most visible example of black achievement in Gettysburg was the AME Zion congregation, struggling but self-sufficient. Similar AME and AME Zion fellowships were routine in the antebellum Border North, but less prevalent just across the Mason-Dixon Line in Maryland and largely absent further South, including northern Virginia. Southern whites permitted black Christians to preach and discipline largely on their own but insisted on affiliation with white congregations and denominations, thereby providing nominal supervision. Truly independent black congregations and black denominations, including the AME, AME Zion, and Colored Methodists, did not routinely appear in the South until

Reconstruction. Consequently, race in Gettysburg and the Border North with free but besieged African Americans predicted national trends beyond the Civil War when blacks were no longer slaves and controlled their own religious organizations but otherwise remained second-class citizens.[7]

Finally, the seminary, Cemetery Hill, the Peach Orchard, and the other religious sites in Gettysburg shed light on the ability of the Civil War to change America. On the cautious side, historian George Rable observes that the influence of the war on veterans and their families "remains a matter of conjecture and perhaps some dispute," and in gender the Civil War also appear as something less than a defining moment. But popular thought, exemplified by writer Shelby Foote and filmmaker Ken Burns, considers the Civil War as one of America's greatest turning points. Foote believed that the conflict "defined us as what we are," and Burns used another Foote-ism—the war as "the crossroads of our being"—as the subtitle for an episode in his Civil War documentary. More serious scholars avoid this overblown language but nevertheless remain in the ballpark. James McPherson and William Cooper, for example, portray the war as the "most momentous event in American history" and as the creator of "fundamental changes that transformed the country." They cite the end of slavery, the permanence of the Union, and three constitutional amendments—the thirteenth, fourteenth, and fifteenth—as core shifts in American society brought by the war. One scholar has parsed Abraham Lincoln's Gettysburg Address as an "intellectual revolution" that permanently altered constitutional thought. For many the war was pivotal.[8]

Although students of religious history fall short of proclaiming a second American revolution, some nonetheless emphasize significant change in the form of army camp revivals, Lost Cause theology, or the rise of the southern black churches. Harry Stout has documented the growth of civil religion as a consequence of the conflict, and Drew Gilpin Faust and Mark S. Schantz identify the war as a turning point in how society viewed death. Others believe that religion changed more gradually or continued to evolve in familiar patterns, such as growing secularism, social reform, and denominational organization. But whether the "crossroads of our being" or something short of that, most agree that the Civil War altered American society in some way.[9]

For Gettysburg religion, the war brought moderate change. Undoubtedly, the battle was the experience of a lifetime for civilians. They evacuated or endured the conflict in their cellars. Their homes were trashed or worse—some were looted to the last scrap from top to bottom—and it took years to recover partial compensation from a stingy government. But congregations rebounded from the traumatic events of the battle, and the routine returned. The battle turned most church buildings into impromptu hospitals, which badly damaged the facilities, but fellowships repaired them as quickly as possible and resumed their quest for refinement. Two undersized, weak societies—the immigrant German-Lutheran congregation and the AME Zion—suffered the most from the battle and the war. The immigrant fellowship did not survive the war, and the AME Zion absorbed lasting injury because almost all of the town's black residents fled the invading Confederate army to escape enslavement. Some never returned, and the decline in the black population permanently damaged the AME Zion. The most conspicuous religious change was the growth of civil religion, the blending of faith with nationalism and a turning point in church-state relations. Even the Dunkers, who before the war were so far outside the political mainstream that they discouraged voting, caught a whiff of civil religion and lined up behind the Union, though still affirming their longstanding nonresistant principles. After the Civil War the marriage between religion and nationalism became a permanent part of American life, and in this way, too, Gettysburg religion belonged to the future. But with the exception of civil religion, admittedly a significant change, the great conflict only nudged faith, leaving intact refinement, diversity, and race, and making the war something less than a watershed in Gettysburg religion.[10]

In sum, refinement and war in Gettysburg and the Border North reveal American behavior, informing about national trends. Diversity, including race, in Gettysburg religion foretells America's future as the Border North's present would soon become the national norm. Religion among the memories of the Civil War in this famous but small place teaches big lessons about American life.

CR

This study defines the Border North narrowly as Gettysburg and the southern Pennsylvania region along the border with Maryland. The western Virginia panhandle, portions of New Jersey, and the Ohio Valley comprised other parts of the Border North, but to create a manageable project they lie outside this study. The racial composition and rich ethnic and religious diversity of the Ohio Valley especially suggest broad similarities with the Border North east of the Alleghenies, but it will require its own inquiry.[11] Additionally, this book concentrates on the rural and town Border North. Urban regions, of course, far outpaced smaller communities in modernization, but they were not typically American. Instead, the nation, even New England and the Mid-Atlantic with their growing industry, remained overwhelmingly rural. Consequently, this project studies a town and thinks of the Border North much more broadly than merely Philadelphia and Pittsburgh.

Moreover, the rural and small town Border North has been largely ignored. Studies of antebellum African Americans in the North focus on the large concentrations of blacks in urban areas, especially Boston, New York, Philadelphia, and Providence, Rhode Island. Yet 40 percent of Pennsylvania's African Americans lived in rural areas or towns of under 2,500 inhabitants. Additionally, the Border North's counterpart, the Border South, has received much more attention. Antebellum Virginia's politics and the struggle over secession have benefitted from several thoughtful studies, which include informative descriptions of western Virginia, an obvious borderland much less enslaved than east of the Blue Ridge.[12] Western Maryland, even more the Border South by virtue of its declining slave populations and location adjacent to the Border North, has attracted notice although the region's religion awaits a scholar.[13] On the other hand, the Border North has often been overlooked with the great exception of Edward Ayers's magnificent *In the Presence of Mine Enemies*, which compares and contrasts Staunton, Virginia, in the Shenandoah Valley of western Virginia, with Chambersburg, Pennsylvania, one county west of Gettysburg.[14] Even the town of Gettysburg, boasting battle books that consume forests of paper, lacks a history of its prewar life, and most of the battle accounts ignore the community to ponder instead tactics and movements. Margaret Creighton's *The Color of Courage*, a wartime study of blacks, women, and German American soldiers, and Gregory Coco's *A Strange and Blighted Land*, which discusses the immediate aftermath of the battlefield, come the closest to a history of the community.[15] In brief, antebellum Gettysburg and the Border North, which sent to Washington polar opposites James Buchanan and Thaddeus Stevens, have been surprisingly understudied.

This book defines Gettysburg as the battlefield, a convenient designation. If *Gettysburg Religion* excluded persons who lived just outside the town limits but whose property was in a combat zone in July 1863, readers would inevitably be curious about these missing persons. Moreover, the battle looms over everything in this community, past and present, and common sense, if not scholarship, argues for using the boundaries of the National Military Park as a marker. Consequently, all of the book's subjects lived on the battlefield, and, with the exception of the Dunkers, all of the meetinghouses were within the town limits. Dunker families, however, farmed on the battlefield, some in very strategic locations, and, therefore, they belong in the book.

Six chapters describe antebellum religion in this small town in the Border North. Chapter 1 introduces the community of Gettysburg, its region, and its religion. Chapters 2 and 3 explore the pursuit of refinement; Chapter 2 investigates the beliefs of those behind this mainstream trend and those opposed to it, and Chapter 3 describes refined facilities and worship and the impact of growing gentility on congregational life. Chapters 4 and 5 consider diversity; Chapter 4 covers ethnic and doctrinal variety, and Chapter 5 discusses racial diversity, focusing on the town's AME Zion congregation. The war and the battle are the subjects of Chapter 6, which looks at the impact of the battle and war on Gettysburg religion, especially continuity on the congregational level and the rise of civil religion.

Divertimenti, a musical term for light and entertaining pieces, introduce key topics by highlighting interesting individuals who exemplify them. Musical *divertimenti*, despite their amusement, can nonetheless be serious and difficult to perform, and the intent is that these little passages likewise inform.

ଶ

Gettysburg Religion portrays the faith in a modest-sized, bustling community on the borderland between freedom and slavery. In a form that follows the clutter of life, sometimes Gettysburg and the Border North marched in step with American society, but at other times they foreshadowed modern America. In both cases future American religion would look much like faith patterns in Rhett Butler's "little town in Pennsylvania." But, above all, in the spirit of the observation by James McPherson, a noted Civil War historian, that "one need not be a mystic to sense the presence of ghosts on the battlefield," this study aims to resurrect Gettysburg's religious life.[16]

Divertimento

Samuel Simon and Mary Catherine
Steenbergen Schmucker

amuel Simon Schmucker, according to one modern scholar, was the "most
prominent American Lutheran theologian of the early nineteenth century."
In 1826, with most of his career ahead of him, the twenty-seven-year-old
came to Gettysburg to serve as the first professor of the new Lutheran seminary. Schmucker had been an outspoken advocate and energetic fundraiser in
the founding of the institution, and the board of directors consequently selected
this bright young preacher and scholar as their first instructor. Schmucker left his
parish in Woodstock, Virginia, and relocated in Gettysburg while his teenaged
wife, Mary Steenbergen Schmucker, and infant daughter stayed behind until the
baby was old enough to travel.[1]

Schmucker was the son and grandson of Lutheran immigrants. In 1785 his
family arrived in Pennsylvania, and two years later they settled permanently near
Woodstock in Virginia's Shenandoah Valley, then backcountry. Schmucker's father, John George Schmucker, became a well-known Lutheran minister, a profession also followed by two uncles. In 1794 Schmucker's father accepted a call to
York, Pennsylvania, where Samuel was born. At age fifteen Samuel enrolled in
the University of Pennsylvania, Philadelphia, and two years later he accepted an
offer to teach the classics at the York County Academy. Then, he furthered his
education at the Princeton Theological Seminary and afterwards returned to his
family's roots in Woodstock to fill a pulpit. There the young preacher quickly
married Elenora Geiger with a son coming in two years, but Elenora died six
months later of complications from childbirth. In 1825 Schmucker, a widower
with a two-year-old son, remarried, this time to Mary Catherine Steenbergen,
the eighteen-year-old daughter of a wealthy local family with twenty slaves.
Schmucker had married up. The couple moved to Gettysburg and soon built a
spacious brick house near the seminary, located on a small but scenic ridge just
west of town.[2]

The Schmucker marriage was warm. When thirty-eight-year-old Mary lost
her teeth, Samuel proclaimed that their restoration would return her youthful

Samuel Simon Schmucker, first professor and president of the Lutheran Theological Seminary and prominent theologian. (Courtesy of Special Collections, Musselman Library, Gettysburg College.)

appearance, and he kindly added that "in every other respect you look as young as a *twenty one*."[3]

The slaveholder's daughter brought slaves to Gettysburg to lighten her domestic load. When Samuel arrived in town ahead of her, he learned that black servants were common in the Border North and that their status was identical to

Mary Steenbergen Schmucker, daughter of a Virginia slaveholder and a twelve-time mother. (Courtesy of Special Collections, Musselman Library, Gettysburg College.)

slaves in Virginia except that at age twenty-eight they became free. Consequently, he advised Mary to bring two sixteen-year-olds "or a little less" for servants, who could serve her for approximately twelve years. Then, when these servants came of age, Mary could repeat the process with two more adolescents. After a few years in Pennsylvania, Samuel became an abolitionist, and the 1840 and 1850 censuses show black servants but not adolescent pseudo-slaves in the Schmucker household. One can only imagine the conversations between husband and wife about the South's institution.[4]

Mary needed help, whether slaves or servants, because she spent most of her adult life either pregnant or recovering from pregnancy. In her twenty-three years of marriage, Mary gave birth twelve times with eight of her children surviving to adulthood. She died tragically. In 1847 at the age of thirty-nine, Mary was pregnant again. Returning home from a trip to town, she saw smoke from a fire kindled by a servant. Thinking that her house was in flames, she rushed to rescue a two-year-old son inside. Mary fell, miscarried, and developed an infection that claimed her life. Samuel had lost a second wife to childbearing.[5]

Together the Schmuckers represent several significant trends in Gettysburg religion. As Lutherans they belonged to the most prominent denomination in town. In addition to the seminary, its accompanying faculty, and its striking location on the ridge, Lutherans boasted of two congregations—and briefly three—plus a college. The Schmucker's middle-class household—including books, paintings, and a commodious home—and Samuel's prominence in higher education also indicate refinement. Moreover, the Schmuckers represent diversity. Although Samuel accepted the denomination's drift toward English-language worship, he also preached and prayed in German. And Mary was Virginian. Few other white Southerners lived in town, except for those born in nearby Maryland and a few students, but the Schmuckers nevertheless symbolize the diversity of the community. Finally, the Schmuckers with their African-American servants contributed to Gettysburg's racial diversity. Refinement and diversity, including race, formed powerful themes in Gettysburg's religion.

1   Community

The scenery of Gettysburg and Adams County impressed mid–nineteenth-century visitors and residents alike. A wide variety of deciduous and co-nifer trees, including oak, hickory, chestnut, walnut, elm, gum, birch, beech, pine, sycamore, poplar, hemlock, tulip, cedar, and maple, populated the forests. Blossoms from tulips, dogwoods, and redbuds, which actually produce a purple flower, colored the spring landscape. South Mountain, the local name for the Blue Ridge and the highest elevation in the county (2,100 feet above sea level), dominated the western horizon. A local booster described this modest line as "blue, distant, sweeping hills" and a sightseer called it the area's "great landmark." The farmland surrounding Gettysburg (540 feet) gently rolls and in the 1850s was "well-cleared" with more orchards than woods. The prosperous farms were typical of south-central Pennsylvania with fertile soil, large barns, and well-kept gardens. Closer to town the "most prominent spot" was a hill on its southeast edge with a cemetery and a commanding view.[1]

Although not as fertile as neighboring locales, the soil was productive enough to attract settlers in the early eighteenth century, mostly Scots Irish but also Dutch, German, and a few Catholics from Maryland. During the Seven Years' War (1754–63) the area remained frontier, and settlers suffered from occasional Indian raids. Warring Iroquois captured teenaged Mary Jemison and her family, and the account she wrote of life among them provides one of the best depictions of the period.[2]

The settlement of Gettysburg emerged from the enterprising spirits of Samuel and James Gettys. Just before the American Revolution, Samuel operated a tav-ern at the intersection of two well-traveled roads, but in 1785 he lost everything, perhaps because he dealt in too much Continental currency. At the sheriff's sale his son, James, bought 116 acres, including the tavern and the house. James then planned a town, divided the property into lots, and soon the settlement acquired the name of its organizer, "Gettysburg."

Gettys planned well. In 1800 the Pennsylvania legislature created Adams County, slicing off the southwestern part of York County to form a new political

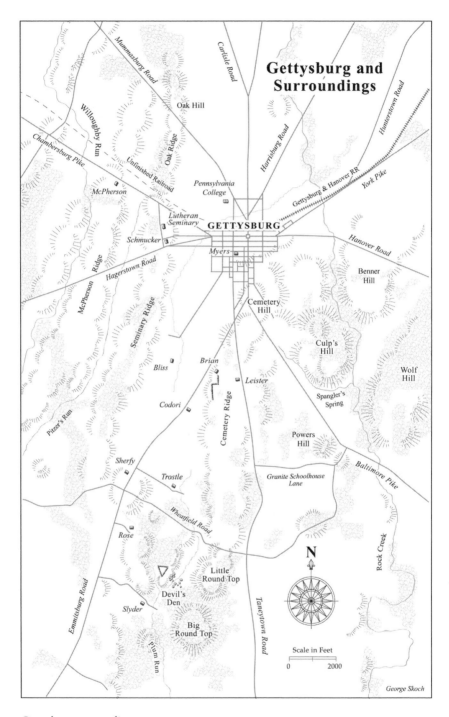

Gettysburg surroundings.

unit so that residents of a growing area could avoid the long trip to York for mail, court, and marketing. Legislators named the new entity after then-President John Adams and Gettysburg became the seat of the recently organized jurisdiction. A newly built courthouse proclaimed the town's status.[3]

The characteristics of community quickly followed, especially economic development. In the first decade of the nineteenth century James Gettys's community acquired a pottery, chair factory, brewery, printer, market house, two tanneries, and a stage connection to Baltimore and Chambersburg. The little settlement was on its way toward progress.[4]

Carriage manufacturing became the signature economic activity of the small town. Wagon making was common in south central Pennsylvania, most notably the famed Conestoga wagons from Lancaster County. Gettysburg produced carriages (large and comfortable vehicles), chariotees (four-wheeled with rear seats only), rockaways (light vehicles for two or four passengers with a fixed top and open sides), buggies (lightweight carriages), and jersey wagons (large with a cloth top). Approximately six shops plus subcontractors employed painters, cabinetmakers, upholsterers, blacksmiths, silversmiths, and lacemakers (for the interior trim). One local blacksmith and wagonmaker, John Studebaker, moved to Ohio in 1836, and then his sons built a large wagon-making business in South Bend, Indiana, that later crossed over to automobiles. Most of the customers for Gettysburg's wagon trade were Southerners, especially in Virginia's Shenandoah Valley, a somewhat distant market that suggested a modernizing economy. Every spring, after the weather had improved, trains of six to twelve wagons pulled by one horse or a team left town and formed processions headed across the Mason-Dixon Line. White muslin cloth protected the new paint, varnish, and trimmings from the rain, dust, and mud of nineteenth-century transportation. By the 1850s, however, decline had hit the carriage trade as shops closer to the Shenandoah competed with Gettysburg manufactories, and laborers moved south to follow the business.[5]

The railroad, the lifeblood of nineteenth-century economic development, came late to James Gettys's burg. In 1835 the state of Pennsylvania began construction of a line beginning in town and heading southwest to connect with the Baltimore and Ohio railroad. But the route was to include western Adams County and Thaddeus Stevens's iron furnace in Franklin County (immediately to the west), resulting in meanders that earned the route the nickname, the "tape worm line." Construction began, including cuts and embankments, but when state appropriations stopped, so did the work. Rail connection to the outside world did not come until December 1858, with completion of a fourteen-mile line from Hanover.[6]

As the economy advanced, respectability gradually overtook rawness. One curious step towards civic improvement came in 1806 when the town council prohibited swine from roaming at large. This was unusual because American towns and cities routinely welcomed pigs on the streets. Although aggressive, territorial swine shoved pedestrians off sidewalks and attacked little children, the remarkable scavenging ability of hogs—"walking sewers," according to one contemporary—kept garbage off the streets. Thus, for many towns and cities, porcine street denizens represented prosperity, cleanliness, and dinner, but, for some reason, not in Gettysburg. Once in 1832 the town council mysteriously suspended the swine-running ordinance for sixty days; perhaps the streets needed cleaning. Dogs were also a menace. In 1806 fifty-eight canines lived in the town's eighty-three homes; typical names were Liberty, Pen, Beaver, Pointer, Possum, Smart, Bull, and Forney. To regulate the animals, town officials registered them by size, color, and name without mentioning breed and imposed a forty-cent tax on males and two dollars, a large sum, on females. The dog situation persisted. In 1844 the town council placed a fifty-cent bounty on unattached, unmuzzled dogs loose on the streets. It was open season on man's best friend for sixty days. Moreover, owners of the roaming animals could be fined, and residents who tolerated homeless dogs about the premises were also liable for the fine whether or not they actually owned the animals.[7]

Other steps toward progress further improved the town. It became illegal to drive a wagon through town on the Sabbath. In the 1820s several paved sidewalks and large stepping-stones across the street at the town square kept pedestrian shoes and boots mud-free. A town clock provided order. Banker's hours in 1841 were from 10:00 A.M. to 1:00 P.M.[8]

Fire companies formed as early as 1808. In the 1820s the town constructed a new firehouse of white, painted weatherboard, the front lettered "Engine House," and in 1830 it bought a new fire engine, naming it "Guard." A waterworks, first begun in the 1820s, added another service. Pipes made of twenty-five- to thirty-foot yellow pine logs with a hole bored through their middle carried water pumped from a spring south of town to a reservoir on high ground. From there, gravity took the water into town, where hand pumps connected to the log pipes provided water to residents and four hydrants. In 1863, while Confederate General Jubal Early sat atop his horse in the town square and issued a series of demands to residents, his mount drank from a trough filled by a municipal hand pump.[9]

Religious leadership contributed to civic refinement. In 1822 three pastors— David McConaughy (Presbyterian), John Herbst Jr. (Lutheran), and Charles G. McLean (Associate Reformed)—joined Thaddeus Stevens's initiative to organize a Library Society of Gettysburg. They served on the Committee of Superintendence and Selection with McConaughy as president. Membership was five dollars initially and thereafter one dollar semiannually per share. Members could borrow two books per share; overdue charges were twelve and a half cents for the first week and twenty-five cents for each additional week. In 1841 Samuel Simon Schmucker (Lutheran) and James C. Watson (Presbyterian) became vice presidents of the newly formed Gettysburg Literary Association, which lent newspapers and magazines.[10]

In 1846 a travelling correspondent for the *Baltimore Sun* described Gettysburg as "good looking, well built, and considerable sized." Two streets formed the heart of the town, and "real, bona fide Pennsylvania Dutchers and Anglo Saxon" formed the bulk of the population of between 2,000 and 2,500. The reporter noted well-kept homes, and among the many businesses and shops he discovered "*two* barber shops," which, he complained, "were so uncommon in most country towns."[11] With manufacturing, a library, water works, swine-less sidewalks, dog ordinances, two barber shops, and at last in 1858 a railroad, Gettysburg could claim a measure of maturity. In seventy years—the life span of one individual—James Gettys's venture went from farmland to a successful community pursuing gain and refinement.

◌

In addition to material gain and civic sophistication, citizens of Gettysburg also sought eternal salvation, and they hewed a variety of pathways to heaven. From its earliest days, Gettysburg religion was diverse.

Scots Irish settlers built the initial religious organization in the area. The first congregation, Upper Marsh Creek, organized in the 1740s, and eventually Scots Irish Presbyterians founded eleven congregations in what became Adams County, most of them associated with the Synod of Philadelphia.[12]

Signs of institutional maturity for Upper Marsh Creek appeared in the late eighteenth century. In 1780 the congregation constructed a stone building, and the following year it hosted the presbytery. In 1788 the presbytery met there again, mostly concerned with the routine business of pulpit appointments and ordination but also deciding that David Williamson's marriage to his widow's niece was unacceptable and that dancing threatened the faith. In 1813 the Upper Marsh Creek congregation moved into town and became the Gettysburg Presbyterian Church. They met in the Associate Reformed building and the courthouse until 1816 when their place of worship was finished. This structure had a short life, and in 1836 the Presbyterians again used the Associate Reformed facility, this time for four years, until their new meetinghouse was ready. The best existing measure of membership for the congregation is pew rentals, which totaled 69 in 1853. Assuming that 5 or 6 persons occupied each pew, a conservative membership estimate is approximately 350.[13]

The Associate Reformed, a product a complicated schisms and mergers, provided variation to Presbyterianism. This minority Presbyterian connection came from the merger of two Scottish dissenter movements, Covenanters and Seceders, both seeking to safeguard traditional Presbyterianism and further Scottish nationalism, which they considered intertwined. Covenanters and Seceders immigrated to colonial America in small numbers, but in 1743 a formative moment for North American Covenanters occurred when Alexander Craighead led his congregation at Middle Octorara (Lancaster County) in a ceremony of crossed swords in celebration of "King Jesus" and condemnation of the British monarchy. The Presbytery of Philadelphia, the mainline Presbyterian organization, condemned Craighead for treason and he withdrew to Virginia and then the Carolinas, but the American version of Scottish dissent was underway.[14]

Scottish dissenters first arrived in Adams County in the 1730s and '40s when Covenanters settled there, and in 1751 a missionary minister arrived from across the waters to provide pastoral leadership. In 1776 another missionary, Alexander Dobbin, located in what is now the southern section of Gettysburg, and he became prominent. Dobbin built a large stone house that he used as an academy to train ministers, and he served as a trustee for Dickinson College. Three hundred books comprised his personal library, an indication of both wealth and education. For his entire life (d. 1809) this missionary minister wore breeches and a powdered wig, which denoted high social rank but also conservatism when this status-defining fashion fell out of favor. Dobbin represented early success for Scottish dissent.

Union between the two Scottish dissenting traditions, Covenanters and Seceders, seemed natural and transpired in 1782. The new denomination called itself the Associate Reformed, a combination of the formal names for the two movements (Associate/Seceders; Reformed/Covenanters). Dobbin, a Covenanter, favored the merger with the Seceders, and his Rock Creek congregation joined the new denomination. In 1805 the now Associate Reformed Presbyterians moved into town and built the first church in Gettysburg, a red brick building with high-backed pews, brick aisles, and a high pulpit with a large sounding board. Many of the members of the congregation were farmers, and the move indicated a desire to locate centrally. The Associate Reformed also attracted descendants of Dutch Reformed, fellow Calvinists whose denomination had withered locally. The Associate Reformed distinguished themselves from other Presbyterians by relying on a hymnody restricted exclusively to the Psalms and rejecting the use of musical instruments, including organs, in worship. They additionally practiced closed communion, that is, only members could receive the bread and cup, not visitors, and they opposed slavery and secret societies, especially the Masons.[15]

In 1821 the Associate Reformed preacher, Charles McLean, fell out of favor with the Presbytery and the Synod for his skepticism about creeds and confessions. Apparently McLean was a popular preacher because his congregation stuck with him and changed its name to Independent Church of Gettysburg, now without denominational affiliation, but several defectors left for the Gettysburg Presbyterian congregation. McLean gave the Independent Church a lengthy pastorate, but when he resigned in 1842, the congregation returned to the Associate Reformed, which could provide them with compatible supply ministers or fill the pulpit permanently. Congregational records for the Associate Presbyterians are thinner than for most other societies in Gettysburg, especially for the antebellum period, but the available documents indicate a small congregation. A subscription list for 1841 has a modest thirty-two names, but in 1859 the society nevertheless had enough vigor to remodel its meetinghouse. In 1858 the Associate Reformed denomination merged with the Associate Presbyterians, the remnants of Covenanters who had not participated in the union in 1782, and they formed the United Presbyterian Church. Scottish dissent, then, had a lengthy tenure in Gettysburg and Adams County, but growth was modest. (In 1890–91 the Gettysburg United Presbyterian congregation dissolved and sold its property to the United Brethren. In 1958 the United Presbyterians joined with the Presbyterian Church, USA, to create the United Presbyterian Church in the USA.)[16]

Methodism became another religious alternative for Gettysburg. Circuit-riding Methodist Episcopal preachers visited the area at the turn of the nineteenth century, and in 1815 Methodists in town formed a class. Classes were a division of the congregation into small groups with weekly meetings for hymns, prayer, examination of members, sharing of religious experience, and mutual support. Usually limited to congregational members, these gatherings provided intimate fellowship and individual spiritual growth. Attendance was mandatory although during the early years in Gettysburg attendance may have fluctuated for some reason. Gettysburg's first class had twenty-nine members, split equally between men and women, unusual for its intermingling of gender. Because classes did not require ordained leadership, they could serve as a forerunner to congregational organization, which happened in Gettysburg. Initially classes in Gettysburg met in private homes and preaching was in the courthouse, but in 1822, only seven years after the first class met, Methodists built a brick meetinghouse, forty-two and a half by thirty-seven and a half, with a gallery, boxed pews, upholstered pulpit furniture, and a cemetery, and the town became home to a circuit-riding preacher. Methodists in Gettysburg did not quite match the spectacular national growth of their denomination, but they gained ground quickly after a late start.[17]

Like many Methodists across the nation, Gettysburg's followers of John Wesley often came from the ranks of artisans and the modest middle class. An 1854 membership list counted 144, many of whom belonged to families headed by blacksmiths, coachmakers, painters, shoemakers, tailors, and farmers. Some were prosperous and solidly middle class, such as John and Hannah Welty, farmers (property value $4,000); Thomas and Ann Warren, an ironmaster and his wife (property value $10,000); and J. L. and Sarah Schick, a merchant and his wife (property value $15,000). Others were more humble. Elizabeth Lenzy, a fifty-four-year-old servant for the president of Pennsylvania College, was one of the poorest congregants, and several German immigrants also belonged to the fellowship.[18]

The first recorded, independent black religion in Gettysburg flowed from the efforts of Daniel Payne, a student at the Lutheran Theological Seminary. Payne, a free black from Charlestown, South Carolina, arrived in 1835 and quickly learned that the town's Methodist congregation was "pro-slavery." He attempted to organize an African Methodist Episcopal (AME) congregation, but a class leader whom Payne labeled "intemperate" doomed the effort. Then this active twenty-six-year old opened a Sunday school and organized women's gatherings "for moral and mental improvement." Other religious meetings and revivals followed, and at one service enthusiasm so overtook the young seminarian that he spoke for three hours, which, he said, cost him his voice for three weeks. Eventually Payne connected with the AME fellowship in Carlisle, Pennsylvania, and in 1839 he left town to pastor a Presbyterian congregation in East Troy, New York.[19]

Black momentum continued. In 1838 a fellowship of African Americans, perhaps the remnants of Payne's ill-fated AME society, perhaps blacks affiliated with the white Methodists, or perhaps a combination of both, appointed a committee to find a lot for a meetinghouse. (Although Payne had not yet left for New York, apparently he did not participate in this new initiative.) Instead, they acquired a structure from the white Methodists—a modest building, maybe a frame house—that the Methodists had for their black members. It was in bad shape, and repairs had consumed the meager resources of the small fellowship of black Methodists. White Methodists, still with title to the property, deeded it to Thaddeus Stevens, who held it on behalf of the new black society. Sometimes blacks cultivated wealthy whites by making them trustees, but perhaps the Methodist board felt better about giving a rundown building to needy African Americans if an influential white controlled the property. Within weeks white Methodists reported that their "colored class" had withdrawn and joined the "Bethelites," named after the first blacks to withdraw from Methodism in 1787. Twenty-one blacks remained with the white Methodists, but independent black religion in Gettysburg, an American-born variation of Wesleyanism, was under sail.[20]

Black Wesleyans in Gettysburg found a denominational home with the African Methodist Episcopal Zion (AME Zion), a fellowship resulting from the desire of black Methodists in New York City to escape white control. In 1796 the New York blacks began to worship separately, but they remained under white supervision until finally withdrawing in 1822, and three sympathetic white Methodist clergy ordained three black elders to supervise their congregations. The newly autonomous black Methodists quickly organized their own denomination and elected James Varick as the first superintendent. Well-known members of the AME Zion included Harriet Tubman and Sojourner Truth, and Frederick Douglass was a class leader and local preacher of the AME Zion congregation in New Bedford, Massachusetts. Douglass drifted away from the Zion to pursue abolition, but he affectionately remembered the "many seasons of peace and joy" with the congregation that left a "precious" memory.[21]

The AME Zion were different from the AME. True, their origins were similar. Like the AME Zion, the Philadelphia-based AME emerged from attempts of white Methodists to control blacks, and in 1787 Richard Allen led the Bethelites in separation. In 1816 Allen's group joined other black dissenters from the Mid-Atlantic to form the AME, but a pique over an alleged AME mission effort into New York City, which the Zion considered their territory, prevented the two black societies from merging. The AME and AME Zion left the white Methodists Episcopals over race, not theology, and after parting the two independent African-American connections remained thoroughly Wesleyan. Black Methodists, however, differed from white Wesleyans in two key areas: (1) they granted more authority to laypersons while stripping outsiders, including bishops and whites, of control the congregation, and (2) they barred slaveholders, a test of membership that white Methodists had considered but quickly abandoned.[22]

The black Gettysburg fellowship referred to itself in a variety of ways. Use of "African" reflected ethnic or racial pride, and although the term fell out of favor when colonization, a scheme to resettle blacks in Africa, became popular, the two oldest black denominations retained the term. Before 1848 what later became the AME Zion denomination did not officially use "Zion," and, therefore, an 1840 reference calls the congregation "African Methodist Episcopal." In 1854 the Gettysburg congregation identified as the "First African Methodist Episcopal Zion Society," and in 1859 it referred to itself as the "colored Wesleyan Society." While the different names offer minimal evidence of denominational affiliation, the congregation belonged to an AME Zion circuit, and pastors Abraham Cole and John D. Brooks appear on rolls of AME Zion preachers with Cole serving on a denominational committee, evidence that the Zion had an affiliate in Gettysburg.[23]

Throughout the antebellum period and Civil War, the AME Zion remained the smallest and most fragile religious society in town, except for a short-lived congregation of immigrant Lutherans. Although the AME Zion acquired a parsonage, a gift to an emancipated slave from her former owner, the meetinghouse was unassuming and, unlike the white fellowships, congregational records are silent about steeples, bells, and upholstered furniture. Membership numbered approximately forty-five adults, resembling a faithful remnant rather than a fashionable middle-class congregation. Although segregation kept the AME Zion from the larger religious life of the community, their thin institutional development would have made participation difficult even had racial barriers been nonexistent.[24]

German-heritage faiths contributed more entrees to Gettysburg's religious menu. The two largest German fellowships, Lutherans and Reformed, cooperated closely for the first several decades of their existence in Gettysburg. During the colonial period in what became Adams County, these two great religious traditions together founded seventeen union congregations, which shared a building and probably attended each other's services. This was commonplace in Penn's Woods, where between 1710 and 1800 Lutherans and German Reformed established over one hundred union fellowships, more than half the total number of congregations for each. In Gettysburg Lutherans and Reformed began by sharing a log schoolhouse, but the two congregations soon outgrew it and moved services to the new courthouse. They met on alternative Sundays, but for special occasions, such as a confirmation or communion, the German Reformed borrowed the Associate Reformed building. In 1814 Lutherans and Reformed jointly constructed a meetinghouse, which became known as the "old union church." At this time both traditions worshipped exclusively in German, but for the dedication Charles McLean, the Associate Reformed minister, preached in the afternoon in English. Associate Reformed laypersons had contributed significantly to the building fund, perhaps showing affinity for their Calvinist cousins, the

German Reformed, or perhaps a special relationship existed between the Associate Reformed and the congregation they hosted. Initially the union fellowship lacked funds for a steeple, but in 1821 they stuck a hundred foot tower onto their forty-five by fifty-five foot building, making it the highest spire in town. The following year the union church bought two bells in Baltimore for five hundred dollars, hauled this thousand-pound cargo overland by wagon, and hoisted the bells into their steeple. Not just the two bells, but German-language religion itself had arrived.[25]

In 1843 Lutherans wanted their own building, and their once-cordial relationship with the German Reformed quickly deteriorated. The two fellowships bickered over the division of the property with Lutherans complaining that their erstwhile partners left them with the choice of either cancelling plans for their own church building or going to court. "After much consideration and with much reluctance," Lutherans unleashed their lawyer. However, to the surprise of all litigants, the court dismissed the case because none of the trustees, neither Lutheran nor Reformed, had legal title to the property. As trustees died or otherwise withdrew, the congregations had appointed new trustees to take their place, but this was illegal. Instead, they should have created entirely new titles, and, therefore, none of the trustees had legal standing to sue. Lutherans then forged ahead and built a new church home, laying a cornerstone with preaching, praying, and singing in two languages. Meanwhile, hard bargaining dragged on. A nineteenth-century Reformed chronicler fondly reminisced that through the "skillful services of the attorneys, the whole matter was peacefully arranged without going to trial," but it took seven years of negotiations before a deal awarded Lutherans eight hundred dollars and the small bell for their interest in the union building. The Reformed retained the large bell, and, moreover, Lutherans had to remove the "small" bell, no simple task. Following the separation, the German Reformed also quickly built their own new facility. In 1851 a congregational meeting unanimously adopted a resolution calling for the "immediate erection" of a new meetinghouse on the old site, and within the year they laid a cornerstone. Lutheran and Reformed had gone their separate ways, but each was strong enough to stand independently, with new buildings as proof of vitality.[26]

Actually, Lutherans had two options. In 1836, when Lutherans and Reformed were still a heavily German-language union church, Christ Lutheran arose to serve the English-preferring seminary. This congregation became the spiritual home for professors, students, and a few prominent business persons, while St. James, the union congregation, had a heavier profile of farmers, artisans in the wagon-making industry, and recent immigrants. Christ Church added yet another new religious building to Gettysburg's streetscape. In total, antebellum German-heritage faith boasted of three strong Lutheran and Reformed congregations, all with relatively new meetinghouses.[27]

Roman Catholics stretched Gettysburg's religious quilt beyond Protestantism. Catholic settlers, many of German origins, arrived in Pennsylvanian early in the eighteenth century, and although small in number, they spread across the colony in Philadelphia, Lancaster, Goshenhoppen, Elizabethtown, and Lebanon. In the mid-eighteenth century Jesuits from Maryland visited the Adams-York County area when it was still frontier, looking after Catholic Hurons who had fled the Iroquois, and soon Jesuits developed a mission outpost at Conewago, near modern Hanover. A Pennsylvania census in 1757 counted 1,365 Catholics over the age of twelve with roughly equal numbers of German and English speakers, most of the latter presumably Irish, all visited periodically by Jesuit missionaries. Although anti-Catholic sentiments occasionally surfaced in colonial Pennsylvania—an arsonist burned the chapel in Lancaster—Catholics generally worshipped and built openly and enjoyed Pennsylvania's famed tolerance. In the nineteenth century numerous Catholic communities existed in south central Pennsylvania, including Bonneauville, Carlisle, Chambersburg, Conewago, Hanover, Littlestown, Millerstown, the Mountain, and New Oxford, and just across the Mason-Dixon Line in Maryland, Taneytown had a congregation and Emmitsburg a seminary, Mount St. Mary's. The region had a surprisingly sizeable Catholic presence given its stereotype as a Pennsylvania German and Scots Irish stronghold.[28]

Catholics in Gettysburg enjoyed a steady growth rate and created a flourishing parish. By 1830 the Catholic population, often German, was large enough to require its own parish, named St. Francis Xavier, after a Jesuit founder and the patron saint of foreign missions. A cemetery and a building soon followed, the latter completed in 1831, a thirty-by-forty-foot brick structure with a sixty-five-foot steeple gracing the front. In this building John McCloskey, who in 1875 became the first American Cardinal, received an early step in ordination along with several other seminarians from nearby Mount St. Mary's. Circuit riding priests based in Conewago provided pastoral leadership. The first was Michael Dougherty, an Irish-born Jesuit, who said Mass in Gettysburg once per month, but by the early 1840s priests came every two weeks. One of the most influential Jesuits to serve Gettysburg was James Cotting, a charismatic, brick-and-mortar cleric. In Missouri, where he had ministered before coming to Pennsylvania, Cotting told a German congregation reluctant to fund a cemetery that without it they would be interred "among the Yankees and the Irish" on Judgment Day. He added, "You know their tricks. They will jump up and steal your bones, and you will have none with which to appear at judgment." His humor worked, and the congregation created the burial ground. Cotting also built three church buildings in Missouri.

Gettysburg Catholics, whose building had become too small for their growing congregation, benefitted from Cotting's talents. In 1852 they gathered to watch John Neumann, bishop of Philadelphia and declared a saint in 1977, lay the cornerstone of a new structure. Reusing materials from the old, dismantled building, Catholics erected a larger structure, forty-eight-by-ninety and forty feet high with a cupola pushing another twenty feet heavenward. Inside were a pipe organ, choir gallery, sixty-four pews with room for more, and behind the main altar a painting of St. Francis Xavier raising a dead man to life. During the demolition of the old church, tragedy struck when a wall collapsed, killing two workers: Charles Buckmaster, an African American, and Henry Hollinger.

The last Jesuit to lead Gettysburg Catholics was Belgian-immigrant Francis Xavier DeNeckere, who established a library. Then the Jesuits gave the parish to the bishop of Philadelphia, and priests resided in Gettysburg rather than commuting from Conewago. The first resident priest, Basil A. Shorb, was born near Littlestown and educated at Mount St. Mary's but spent time in Ohio and Columbia, Pennsylvania, before returning to his home area. As non-Protestants, Catholics occupied an outer band in Gettysburg's religious rainbow and did not enjoy consensus tolerance, but with a resident priest and a new building St. Francis Xavier was just as vibrant as the Protestant fellowships.[29]

Faith communities in the surrounding Adams County supplemented Gettysburg's complexity. Dunkers, in particular, had congregants living on farms just outside of town. Dunkers were founded in 1708 in a remote part of Germany by a small fellowship that combined Pietism (conversion by choice and a direct relationship with Christ) with Anabaptism (separation from worldly sin and unity within the church). From the founding eight, they grew into several congregations, and by the 1740s the fellowship was completely relocated in North America, where their membership followed the German diaspora from southeastern Pennsylvania westward and southward. They preferred to call themselves simply the "Brethren," but they often answered to "Dunkers" for their unique baptismal mode: total immersion, three times forward, once for each member of the Trinity. Gettysburg-area Dunkers organized in 1805, and the congregation, called Marsh Creek, worshipped in private homes until 1830, when it built its first meetinghouse several miles outside of Gettysburg. In 1852 Marsh Creek Dunkers constructed a second house of worship to serve members who lived a bit distant from the original meetinghouse.[30]

Other traditions created more variety in Adams County. Two Mennonite congregations and two Quaker meetings worshipped there, and the United Brethren in Christ and the Church of God, both Methodist-like fellowships among ethnic Germans, held camp meetings in the area.

A few faiths were conspicuous by their absence from Gettysburg. Episcopalians were early settlers, and they created one congregation in York Springs, which became part of Adams County, but they did not worship in Gettysburg until approximately 1875. Baptists did not arrive until the mid-twentieth century.[31]

Thus, as religious life matured, it became more complicated. Presbyterians and Associate Presbyterians, black Methodists and white Methodists, German Reformed and German-preferring and English-preferring Lutherans, and Catholics, many of whom were German, gave Gettysburg's residents many religious options. Dunkers and other small fellowships in the county further muddied the area's mix, and the modest boom in church construction—antebellum Catholics, Presbyterians, German Reformed, and both Lutheran congregations built—provided physical evidence of the development of religion and of the town itself.

CR

Race added another dimension to the complexity of this community. Unlike religion, which seems responsible for relatively little strife, with Catholics arguably excepted, race created tension and occasional violence.

Racial distinctions were part of Pennsylvania almost from its inception, and before the American Revolution slavery was legal in Pennsylvania like everywhere else in the British Empire. In the first two decades of the eighteenth century African-American slaves amounted to 12 to 17 percent of Philadelphia's population, but in the 1720s a depression reduced the demand for labor and the proportion of slaves dropped to approximately 8 percent, where it remained until the American Revolution. Disease and high infant mortality prevented Philadelphia's slaves from sustaining their population, but imported human chattel enabled the slave population to expand with the economy. Rural colonial Pennsylvania required fewer bondpersons than urban Philadelphia, but large farms occasionally used slaves for fieldwork or chores in taverns, mills, distilleries, tanneries, and forges during breaks in the agricultural season. In 1776 the first African Americans came to Adams County as the slaves of Alexander Dobbin, the Covenanter missionary. Among the items in his estate was "Negro Becky," valued at eighty dollars and listed between crowbars and hackles. Founder James Gettys was also a slave owner. As in other border regions, most slave masters in Adams County had only a few persons. In 1783 the largest slave owners were William

Cochrane with sixteen and Robert McPherson with eleven. Only twelve others held six or more, and sixty-nine masters owned only one bondperson. Scots Irish possessed a majority of the human property in the area, and although Germans were disproportionally low in slaveholding, they nevertheless participated in the institution sufficiently to discredit claims that they fundamentally opposed it. Slavery, then, was a fixture of colonial Pennsylvania society but not essential.[32]

In 1780 Pennsylvania became the first state to ban slavery. A combination of factors motivated these early abolitionists, ranging from humanitarianism and Revolutionary rhetoric to the short life span of slaves and their growing rebelliousness, which made them poor investments. The Abolition Act of 1780 was notable not just for its originality but also for gradualness; it emancipated only those born after 1780 when they became twenty-eight years of age. Slaves alive when the act passed remained slaves forever, and those born after the law took effect had to wait twenty-eight years for freedom. The first emancipations would take place in 1808 and theoretically continue into the 1840s as children born into slavery after 1780 came of age. A further complication was that modest white families priced out of the slavery market could afford servants, and, consequently, newly freed slaves often became indentures, making bound service for a long but limited time an intermediate step to freedom. Though exceedingly moderate, the Abolition Act of 1780 was nevertheless a first step towards ending slavery in North America, and it set in motion other strides in that direction.[33]

In practice, gradual emancipation in the Quaker state gradually worked, and by 1820 only 211 slaves remained in the entire state, most of them in the counties bordering Maryland. In Adams County slavery peaked at 323 slaves in the 1790 census, but the next enumeration in 1800 counted only 111, under 1 percent of the total population. Dobbin and Gettys were among those still owning other persons. In 1820, 23 slaves still lived in Adams County, which ranked second-most in the state, behind Fayette in the southwestern corner with 41. Other counties with double-digit slave populations were all in the Border North region along the line with Maryland: Lancaster (21), Franklin (19), and Cumberland County (17). Interestingly, in 1820 Philadelphia had only 7 slaves, and nearby Delaware County had 1. Apparently localized economic reasons rather than ideology account for the minor fluctuations in slave population. Although in 1820 slavery remained very real for 23 persons in Adams County, for all practical purposes the institution had ceased to contribute meaningfully to the economy as bondage died a slow death just north of the Mason-Dixon Line.[34]

Slavery, then, was gone, but life in the Border North remained quite difficult for African Americans. Lancaster, for example, required blacks to register with the mayor's office, and when an AME congregation organized there, members publically expressed their expectation for "protection" when gathered for worship. Needless to say, no white faith community requested security, and the appeal was an ominous sign of the environment for African-American Christians in the borderland.[35]

Racism remained rampant in gradually emancipated Pennsylvania. Racist humor, for example, was common, especially in the *Adams Sentinel*, a local newspaper. "At a colored ball given the other evening," the paper reported, "the following note was posted on the door post: 'Tickets fifty cents. No gentleman admitted unless he comes hisself.'" Another account detailed the havoc created at a dance in Philadelphia when a prankster threw a large black snake onto the floor. In yet another example, once a "dusty-looking 'colored child,' about forty years of age" walked under scaffolding when a falling brick struck the man in the head and broke in two. He was stunned for a moment, then called out, "I say, you white man up dar, if you don't want yer brick's broke, jes keep 'em off my head." One story, titled "An Impatient Darkey," told of "Old Cuffey Longhead," a noted preacher and a widower, who became engaged to a "buxom and spicey damsel," descriptive words not usually applied to white women. At the wedding the preacher was white and spoke at length. As the ceremony dragged on, the "dusky couple," who were "dressed within an inch of their lives," began to sweat heavily, and finally old Cuffey burst forth, "Massa Trumbull, it 'pears to me you have too much preangulation. De company can't wait all night for de good tings—I neider."[36]

African Americans suffered more problems than bad jokes, and in 1838 they lost the right to vote. Several developments contributed to this. To begin, Philadelphia's black population increased noticeably, from 4 percent of the population in 1790 to 12 percent in 1820, an unsettling demographic trend for some whites. Most were poverty-stricken runaways from the South, but Haitian immigrants, fleeing their revolution-plagued homeland, brought foreign speech and lack of respect for whites, which must have unnerved the master class. Other new arrivals were large numbers of particularly racist Irish immigrants. Finally, state-level politics became a competitive two-party system with Democrats standing for white supremacy and blacks voting Whig, perhaps enough to influence the outcome. Black suffrage, therefore, came under pressure. In 1838 a state constitutional convention inserted "white" into its definition of citizenship, and in that spirit the Pennsylvania Supreme Court (*Hobbs v. Fogg*) denied the vote to blacks, concluding that Pennsylvania was from its inception a white republic. Pennsylvania anticipated *Dred Scott* by two decades, and African American civil rights stepped backwards.[37]

The economic outlook for African Americans was similarly bleak. Poverty plagued blacks, and the status and prosperity that flowed from self-employment often was elusive. The most popular occupation among Gettysburg's black men was day laborer and for women was domestic servant. (Seventeen of the 103 black women in the town claimed occupations). True, a few approached the lower middle class. A white acquaintance labeled Owen Robinson, an active member of the AME Zion congregation, as a "well-to-do Negro." Robinson earned this distinction because he operated a restaurant that served oysters in the winter and ice cream in the summer, but "well-to-do" though he may have been, Robinson nevertheless moonlighted as a humble sexton for the Presbyterians. Most other blacks in Gettysburg were less fortunate than Robinson. Only twenty owned real estate, and although African Americans represented 8 percent of the town's population, black realty accounted for less than 1 percent of the town's total property value. Obviously, African Americans looked up from the bottom rungs of Gettysburg's socio-economic ladder, and their predicament was typical for the Border North, as studies of Chester County, Lancaster, and Shippensburg have confirmed.[38]

The national debate over slavery added to racial tensions. In 1836 an abolitionist meeting five miles southeast of Gettysburg released a resolution appealing for the end of slavery in the District of Columbia, a cause popular with the wider abolitionist movement. A few months later a large crowd gathered at the Gettysburg courthouse to form a countywide antislavery society, but opponents defeated resolutions calling for the new organization. Resolution-less, antislavery activists then organized, and several months later a small group of antiabolitionists also came together.

Travelling antislavery lecturers escalated local emotions. Early in 1837 Jonathan Blanchard came to Gettysburg, assigned to central Pennsylvania by the American Anti-Slavery Society as part of a grand abolitionist strategy to spread the word in the towns and villages of America. As preparation for his campaign, Blanchard approached Thaddeus Stevens in Harrisburg, seeking entrée into Stevens's hometown, and Gettysburg's most prominent citizen responded with an unsolicited monetary gift and by arranging for three public meetings at the Gettysburg courthouse. All three events were loud and boisterous. At the first gathering, which was a debate, Judge William McLean, a Presbyterian elder, interrupted the proceedings, and at his urging Southern students from Pennsylvania College egged Blanchard while local bigwigs looked on passively. A resolution condemning abolition formalized the assembly's displeasure with the visitor's doctrine. In the second debate a resolve asserting abolition's threat to the Union failed; apparently the out-of-town activist had made headway. Stevens, absent from the first two events, appeared at the third. After quieting the "excited crowd," he pointed out that just a week or two ago a Universalist had spoken at the courthouse, denying "all the doctrines that Christ and the Apostles preached." Yet, Stevens declared, that speaker was unmolested. But, said Stevens, came Blanchard "to preach in favor of universal liberty," and he was met with "violence and rotten eggs! Oh shame! SHAME!!" When Stevens blamed the attack not on "the ignorance and refuse of our town" or "jail-birds escaped from the penitentiary," Southern students in the gallery hissed. Stevens looked at them and ascribed the misconduct to "some boys who have not yet been to the district school," a reference to the new public schools just established. According to Blanchard, the crowd, "roared and shouted with applause." Stevens's resolution appealed for free speech, repudiated the previous antiabolition statement, and invited Blanchard to continue his work, but it did not mention abolition. It passed overwhelmingly.

After the tumultuous days with Jonathan Blanchard, public debates and resolution-passing assemblages ended, but dispute persisted. The Adams County Anti-slavery Society still met, and in 1842 it hosted an antislavery convention in York Springs in northern Adams County that attracted representatives from central Pennsylvania. Antislavery lectures also continued; Blanchard, for example, appeared fifteen more times around the county. Blanchard and the other apostles of abolition considered rural Adams County listeners as receptive, if ill-informed, but Gettysburg was often hostile. Antislavery lecturers complained about small, somber audiences, an occasional egging, and little assistance in organizing meetings. One lecturer grumbled that sometimes he had to travel to the meeting place twice: once to set up the event and once to do it. In 1845 two speakers toured Adams County, but they found little support, perhaps because one was female or because Stevens, a powerful advocate, had moved to Lancaster. In 1847 another lecturer in Gettysburg was received very coolly, possibly because of the mistaken reputation that he favored disunion, and only the town's African Americans showed hospitality. Although abolition had some support, often it was a tough sell.

While whites exercised free speech, for blacks freedom itself was at risk. Kidnappers and slave catchers lurked, searching for runaways from nearby Maryland and Virginia or for free blacks who could be carried across the line and sold into bondage. A free black man in Columbia, for example, a town along the Susquehanna River, was lured into a shed, seized by four men, gagged, hand-cuffed, hurried across the broad waterway, and then taken to Baltimore. There he was recognized as free and provided with a pass and funds to return home. A free man in Carlisle was arrested but released by the magistrate who heard the case. Another in Philadelphia was mistaken for a runway, arrested, and carried to Elk-ton, Maryland. Slavecatchers nabbed James Phillips, who lived in Harrisburg for fifteen years and had a family, and took him before the U.S. Commissioner there who adjudicated runaway cases. At the hearing, which one account described as a "pretended trial," the magistrate ruled in favor the slave catchers, and as they handcuffed and shackled their captive to take him south into slavery, his wife, according to reports, "became frantic," an understandable response. Residence in free territory did not guarantee freedom.[39]

Border North blacks were not passive, and they resisted slave catchers when possible, sometimes violently. In Carlisle a group of African Americans severely beat James H. Kennedy, from Hagerstown, Maryland, as he moved three recov-ered fugitives from the courthouse to a carriage. Kennedy died several days later from the attack. Kidnappers in the Chambersburg area lured blacks to secluded areas outside of town, then, according to a Gettysburg newspaper, "clapped them into a carriage and drove them speedily over the Maryland line." Local blacks, however, set a trap when one posed as a "decoy duck," and just as the kidnappers were to make their getaway, a hidden "crowd of negroes" foiled their plot. One kidnapper escaped, but the self-defense initiative captured the other, who was released after a court hearing.[40]

In southern Lancaster County blacks organized against a group of slave catch-ers known as the "Gap Gang," named for the local hills and a tavern. One mem-ber of the band, a clock repairman, used house calls as an opportunity to find fugitives. Local blacks countered with an informal self-defense association, and Thaddeus Stevens, now a Lancaster attorney, employed a spy to aid their efforts. In one incident kidnappers took a black girl and headed for Maryland, but rescu-ers followed, overtook them, administered a severe beating, and then let them go. Two of the kidnappers, however, died from the assault, partly because many local whites refused assistance. The battered party finally found aid from a tavern keeper in Lancaster, an outspoken supporter of returning runaways, but his hos-tility towards fugitives cost the keeper his barn, burned by an arsonist. In other incidents, the self-defense group severely assaulted a black man who betrayed a runaway, and they burned the house of another African American who assisted slave catchers. The famed Christiana Riot occurred when a member of the Gap

Gang tipped off a Maryland slave owner that his runaway property was in the neighborhood, and he appeared to reclaim his people. The informal local black network gathered in defense, and the ensuing clash left the Marylander dead. After the Fugitive Slave Law passed in 1850 the legal scales tilted towards the masters, and resistance became more difficult.[41]

Kidnappers, slave catchers, and racial violence afflicted Gettysburg. In one circumstance, kidnappers captured an entire family, but white supporters rescued them. The victim was Catherine "Kitty" Paine, who was freed by her Virginia owner, a widow, and then moved to Gettysburg. But the widow's nephew claimed ownership of Paine and located her in Gettysburg. A midnight break-in surprised Paine and her children in their cabin, and the raiders carried them back to Virginia and slavery. Quaker activists followed the party into Virginia and appealed to authorities, who placed Paine and her children in the county jail for a year, but eventually the Virginia Supreme Court ruled in her favor. Paine returned to Gettysburg, where she found employment at Pennsylvania College. Meanwhile, the Maryland slave trader responsible for her plight was apprehended in Gettysburg and sent to the penitentiary. Who knew when the kidnappers would strike next?[42]

The famed Underground Railroad exacerbated racial tensions. Several locations in Gettysburg and the surrounding county harbored fugitives. Thaddeus Stevens and Samuel Simon Schmucker both provided assistance; Schmucker allowed runaways to sleep in his barn during the day. Basil Biggs, an African-American farm laborer and an active AME Zion, also gave shelter. McAllister's Mill, southeast of Gettysburg and operated by a Presbyterian family, was a frequent stop along a route that led north from Maryland. A thickly wooded hill and a rocky cavern that facilitated concealment bordered the mill property, but many of the escapees hid in the cog-pit, a room in the bowels of the mill underneath the interior water wheel. In addition to concealment, the McAllisters provided food and occasionally clothing. They claimed to have assisted the daughter of U.S. Senator Robert Toombs (Georgia) in her escape from Washington, D.C. The McAllisters remembered her as a beautiful, early twenty-ish woman light enough to pass for white, yet a slave because her mother, a bondwoman, had an illicit relationship with Toombs. From McAllister's Mill runaways went either east to York, Columbia, Lancaster, and Philadelphia or to York Springs, then further north. Another track in Adams County led along the South Mountain north into Cumberland Country and across the Susquehanna River.

Danger lurked along these routes. For runaways the Underground Railroad was a high stakes gambit between freedom or likely sale into the Deep South, separated there forever from family and with escape impossible. Those who assisted fugitives defied the U.S. government, which made such activity illegal, and risked severe punishment if caught. Because of the peril involved, frantic wagon chases and hair-raising escapes were part of the experience and legend. In one York Springs incident, a young slave mother hid in a closet while a white woman took the fussy baby to bed and told slave catchers that it was hers, at which the embarrassed men retreated without examining the child. Spies increased the risk. After the war the McAllisters named a prominent AME Zion member who tipped off slave catchers. Although much of the history of the Underground Railroad is white-centric and clouded with embellishment and folklore, the surreptitious effort to assist runaways nevertheless inserted tangible and very serious conflict into the community.[43]

Race, then, was a critical component of life in Gettysburg. Slavery had largely disappeared from the Border North, and blacks could point to the AME Zion congregation as evidence of progress. But poverty was endemic among blacks and racism among whites. Racial violence, injected into the Border North by runaways, and debate over national slavery roiled the community. The presence of an African American population and the proximity of slavery in Maryland put race relations on edge in Gettysburg and the Border North.

⚬⚬

Sometime in 1850, sturdy Lutherans, or, more likely, sturdy men hired by Lutherans, removed the small bell from the steeple of the old union church and lugged it a few blocks to their new building. According to the bargain Lutherans struck with the German Reformed, the obligation to remove the bell fell to them. The incident illustrates two trends: it indicates growing maturity of the town as the Lutherans and Reformed became strong enough to support independent congregations and the attention to the bell itself bespeaks of refinement. But this is just a small example of the growing maturity and complexity of this energetic town. Gettysburg's pursuit of material gain and improvement—from swine ordinances and distant-market carriage trade to new church buildings with bells—was typically American, but location along the border of slavery and the interesting mix of ethnicity, religion, and race was not. Additionally, non-English worship, African Americans, non-Protestants, and small, dissenting, nonconformist fellowships made Gettysburg religion unusually diverse and modern for small town and rural America. This little place was intriguing before it became famous.

Divertimento

Salome "Sallie" Myers

S alome Myers was a devout Methodist. On the morning of her eighteenth birthday, Sunday, June 24, 1860, she attended Sunday school, preaching, and a class meeting. In the afternoon Myers returned for more Sunday school. At 6:00 P.M. she made her third trip of the day to church for a "very interesting sermon" on Acts 16:30, "what must I do to be saved?" The following Thursday Myers attended prayer meeting. On Friday she wrote a composition, "When shall we meet again?," and baked cakes for a missionary fair, which she attended on Friday and Saturday nights.[1]

In her occupational life, "Sallie," as her friends called her, was a teacher. Gettysburg boasted of a new, comfortable schoolhouse with seven grades, a progressive system. The county superintendent considered the faculty well paid and superior and the facility a model for the state. Myers, of course, felt the frustrations of all educators. Once she described her attempt "to hammer subtraction into noodles" as a "mighty hopeless job." But this late adolescent was an effective teacher who controlled her large class of over fifty students with the standard techniques of the day. Commenting to a colleague about an especially difficult student, she remarked, "Just ask the young gent if I ever applied the rod of correction to his royal hide." She encouraged her friend to use this method "and see if he don't shake his head and scold, for which I always had to whip him the second time." Later she became quite fond of her profession.[2]

Death, depression, and romance complicated Myers's young life. In 1860 her grandmother and a close friend died within weeks of each other. Later that year a wagon accident claimed a student, and an "old and esteemed" local woman hanged herself in a stable. Myers took all of these deaths hard.[3] Simultaneously, a tumultuous romance tore at her emotions. In 1860 Thomas E. Snyder, a twenty-six-year-old tailor, was in love with the seventeen-year-old teacher, and the relationship continued for several years. "Snyder," as Myers refers to him in her diary, was a similarly active Methodist who sometimes led classes and prayer meetings. After one particularly inspirational Snyder-led prayer meeting, Myers confided to her diary that she had enjoyed this meeting "more than I have for a long time."

Salome "Sallie" Myers, teacher with a complicated romantic life and fervent religious life. (Courtesy of Adams County Historical Society.)

She continued, "I felt more of the 'awe that dares not move, And all the silent heaven of love,' than I ever did before." Perhaps her thoughts during this session were carnal as well as spiritual. In a poem she composed entitled "My Dearest," Myers described "eyes of liquid blue," "lips outspread with dew," "cheek of snowy white," and "hair so heavenly bright." But, she rhymed, the "charm around the whole" bound her "heart and soul." The eighteen-year-old was in love. Alas, Snyder suffered poor health, and at one point Myers thought that consumption (tuberculosis) would claim him. Perhaps worse, Myers's mother objected to the relationship—Myers does not say why—and demanded that her daughter choose between her boyfriend and her mother. Myers responded, "Of course, I will do neither simply because it is impossible." Her mother found the diary, and the ensuing stress weighed heavily on the late adolescent. She complained about the difficulty of "keeping my thoughts fixed on Religious subjects for any length of time." At the height of the torment between Snyder and her mother, she lamented, "I sometimes feel tempted to wish I were dead." Finally, she ended the relationship with Snyder, but she still loved him and the miserable young woman revealed her most troubled thoughts in a copybook, which her mother did not find:

> From sport-to-sport they hurry me
> To banish my regret,
> And when they win a smile from me,
> They think that I forget.

There was more: "This heart may throb and break and yet I'll not forget thee— *never*" (emphasis in original). Myers spent half of a school day in tears; then went home early. Yet she still enjoyed life, especially in a natural setting. An early April evening caused her to exclaim, "This is a glorious night. So calm and bright," and a late August night produced similar joy: "How I love such calm peaceful evenings when the moon shines so sweetly down on our beautiful earth, for the world is beautiful." A promotion at school made her "brimful and overflowing with happiness." Nevertheless, for the moment Myers faced emotional conflict.[4]

This young, pious, beleaguered educator participated in several large trends in Gettysburg religion. On the denominational level, as the late adolescent Myers began her faith journey, her Methodist faith system lost its earlier simplicity, both doctrinally and materially, and became more mainstream Protestant. But, more broadly Myers illustrates the liveliness of faith on the local level. Religion was vibrant and changing, and the brass tacks of congregational life, that is, the meetings, maintenance of buildings, and institutional progress, particularly in small steps, lay near to the heart of Meyers and to Gettysburg religion.

2   Refinement

In Theory

Early nineteenth-century Americans grew self-conscious about themselves and their surroundings. As never before, they gauged manners, dress, speech, possessions, bearing, pastimes, and homes for style, beauty, and refinement. Performance and evaluation became part of the daily pattern as they constantly evaluated themselves and others according to the new standards of behavior. Hints of rudeness and vulgarity quickly resulted in failing grades as the broad middle class, including those who sat in pews, now aspired to gentility.[1]

Refinement did not eliminate opposition to the sinful world, a traditional Christian attitude, and many still considered themselves in the world but not of it. Christians often drew lines against a variety of behaviors, including alcohol, Sabbath violations, the circus, theater, dancing, and sexual immorality, proscriptions that preserved the self-image of resistance to the world.

But often these boundaries had limited practical consequences. True, respect for the Sabbath was widespread and changed behavior one day of the week and temperance, too, was genuinely countercultural, but it always remained a minority viewpoint within most religious fellowships. Gettysburg congregations disciplined not for alcoholic consumption but for public drunkenness, a violation of basic manners and in many cases of public law. Discipline for sexual immorality likewise reinforced broad middle-class values and criticism of dancing and the circus had limited daily implications. Fashion was acceptable so long as it was not excessive, in bad taste, or outlandish, such as large feathers in a hat, or if it did not overly pursue rank and violate republican values. Although many Protestants never fully reconciled gentility and their faith—intellectual consistency is not a requirement for popular thought—those who yearned for the plainness of a previous generation and most vocally opposed the pursuit of worldly amusements, fashion, status, and luxury became a frustrated minority. Methodists in this camp acquired the unsympathetic nickname, "croakers." Clearly, the Protestant battle against worldliness fell short of total war.[2]

Benefitting from the limited assault on the sinful world, refined religion thrived. A double standard that practiced comfort and improvement at home but adhered to asceticism at church seemed wrong. Genteel Christians, therefore, no longer worshipped in the plain, austere meetinghouses of the eighteenth century, which in retrospect seemed cold, severe, and dingy. Instead, as described in the previous chapter, antebellum Gettysburg Christians were builders, and they put steeples and pediments on the outside of their new structures and carpets, drapes, organs, and stylish pulpits and altars on the inside. The beauty and taste of the setting suggested a kind and gentle God, and popular religion now assumed that a refined mind, capable of appreciating the improved surroundings, was more likely to receive God's truth.[3]

Refinement, however, became more than standards for church architecture and furnishings but guidelines for Christian life. An address delivered by Henry I. Smith, professor of German and French Language and Literature, to Pennsylvania College students stressed this. Although Smith exhorted his young listeners to build personal development on a religious foundation, he spent most of his effort on identifying the characteristics of development—"superior accomplishments, elegant manners, amiable deportment, and high moral worth"—and Smith only discussed the religious basis for these qualities in the last three pages of the thirty-two-page published version of his lecture. Throughout, however, Smith was self-conscious about refinement. He praised "refined and elegant taste" and "refinement of taste." He extolled "true refinement" in females and instructed the young men to "cultivate the society" of "refined" women. Although Smith concluded that piety provided the true path to an educated and refined heart, the emphasis he gave to taste, elegance, and refinement and the comparatively brief description of religion might have suggested priority to his young listeners. Taste and manners were Christian goals.[4]

Of course, improvement coexisted with other trends, movements, and impulses, including arguments about immigration and race described in later chapters. Scholars have especially noted the surge of interest in reform during the antebellum period, a development in which Gettysburg participated, especially regarding Sabbath-keeping and temperance. But much of the energy for social change came from interdenominational committees of like-minded individuals rather than from congregational efforts, and when people went to church, they usually got refined rather than reformed.[5]

Refinement, then, became a potent doctrine among the Gettysburg and Border North faithful. Two campuses, the Lutheran Theological Seminary and Pennsylvania College, polished religious leaders and two fellowships, Methodists and Dunkers, felt the power of refinement on their core beliefs—the former through change to become more respectable and the latter through resistance to it.

CR

The largest, most noticeable purveyors of refinement in Gettysburg were its institutions of higher education: the Lutheran Theological Seminary and Pennsylvania
College. First to arrive was the seminary in 1826 when Lutherans chose Gettysburg over several competitors as the location for their new endeavor. Gettysburg
was centrally located among American Lutherans, and twenty-six congregations
of Lutherans and Reformed in Adams County suggested a supportive local environment. Perhaps more importantly, Gettysburg outbid its competition. Carlisle
offered $5,000, including $3,000 for a building on the campus of Dickinson College, and a five-year residence for the seminary's professor. (In its first years one
faculty member would carry the entire teaching load for the institution.) Hagerstown, Maryland, bid $6,635. Gettysburg topped both with a pledge of $7,000
and use of the Gettysburg Academy building, an institution heavy with debt but
blessed with a spacious facility. Additionally, Gettysburg's first resident Lutheran
pastor, John Herbst, likely had a major role in the town's winning bid because
he knew Samuel Simon Schmucker, the first instructor, and Schmucker's father,
John George, who chaired the new seminary's board of directors. To fund the
new institution, Lutherans commissioned over twenty agents, including Benjamin Kurtz, who went to Europe for twenty-two months on a grand money-
raising tour. Kurtz's cup ran over with $12,000 and 5,000 books donated. Classes
opened on September 5, 1826, with seven students, and eight more arrived during
the academic year.

Perhaps Schmucker's young charges disappointed him because within a year
he wanted instruction to prepare students for his school. Consequently, the
seminary established a gymnasium or classical school, which in 1832 became
Pennsylvania College. (In the 1880s many began to call the institution "Gettysburg College" to avoid confusion with other institutions with "Pennsylvania" in
their name, but stubborn trustees did not approve the name change until 1921.)
Schmucker went to Harrisburg to plead for assistance, a visit that netted $18,000
of taxpayers' money for a new building.[6]

Pennsylvania College belonged to a national trend. Colonial America had
just nine colleges, but higher education exploded in the Early Republic with
the founding of over five hundred new schools, one of which was Schmucker's
preparatory school. Although only two hundred survived into the twentieth
century, the rate of growth was still remarkable. Most, like the Lutherans' new
college, were founded as denominational institutions, a sign of the openness of
American religion, but economic survival as only a denominational college was

The Lutheran Theological Seminary on the edge of town, refinement in the form of higher education. (Courtesy of Gettysburg National Military Park.)

difficult and limited the ability of colleges to stress the idiosyncrasies of their parent institution.[7]

Nevertheless, Pennsylvania College was very Lutheran. In the very early years students needed written parental permission to escape required attendance at Christ Lutheran, and periodic revivals stirred student souls, pre-empting classes and faculty meetings. One quickening emerged from the tragic death of a student, but at other times students joined in the revivals in town. A college historian recorded awakenings in 1837, 1840, frequently from 1842 to 1844, then again in 1849 and 1854, but then not until 1866 and 1868. Moreover, leadership of the college remained religious and denominational. In 1840 four-fifths of the presidents of church-related colleges and many of the faculty were clergy. This was true for Pennsylvania College, whose two presidents between 1838 and 1865, Charles P. Krauth and Henry Lewis Baugher, were ordained Lutherans and whose faculty were either Lutheran or had an acquaintance with the college prior to their hiring. Thus, as a relatively new institution and thoroughly Lutheran, Pennsylvania College was hardly unique; the German Reformed in Mercersburg, then Franklin College in Lancaster, and the Catholics in Emmitsburg were two more nearby examples of higher education in religion, and each contributed to a trend in American education.[8]

Denominations established colleges because they wanted educated preachers, especially for town congregations. Although demand continued for a populist style that delivered the gospel from heart rather than from notes, by 1850 this trend was in decline as even Baptists and Methodists opened colleges and seminaries. Preachers trained by these institutions often spoke from a text and adorned their discourses with quick references to their classical education. One wonders what John Wesley would have thought of Gettysburg Methodist J. H. C. Dosh's mention of Hamlet in a sermon. John Milligan, from nearby Cumberland County, in speaking to students assembled in Christ Lutheran, tested his listeners' Latin with *ex nihilo, nihil fit* (of nothing, nothing comes), a phrase first associated with the ancient Greeks, and Samuel Simon Schmucker informed the Female Bible Society of Gettysburg that the "ancient Paripatus," Democritus, and the Epicureans all had different views of the origins of the world. (Schmucker's point was that the Book of Revelation settled the debate.) All were more than men of faith; they were learned men of faith. Even when preachers from the seminary and the college stuck to sacred material, which happened more often than not, their sermons nonetheless displayed organization, structure, and a rational, persuasive approach that revealed their scholarship. Schmucker, the epitome of the well-read preacher, sometimes spoke from a carefully prepared text in tiny writing with occasional corrections for minor points or for just the right word, for example, replacing "would" with "will." ("It ~~would~~ will be a fearful thing, if God merely abandoned the sinner.") At times he relied on notes in outline form, but he also read in English or German from verbatim texts. Shakespeare, Latin, Greek, and sermons that smelled of the lamp marked educated preaching.[9]

Moreover, the college and seminary provided Gettysburg with the basic building blocks of refinement: books, libraries, concerts, lectures, and coterie of well-educated professionals who contributed prominently to town affairs. William M. Reynolds, a Latin professor, served as secretary of the Adams County Anti-slavery Society, President Henry L. Baugher was active in the temperance movement, several faculty and trustees were directors of the Evergreen Cemetery, and the weather observations of Michael Jacobs (math and science) appeared in the weekly newspaper. Jacobs and Frederick A. Muhlenberg (ancient languages) were among the organizers of the Gettysburg Gas Company, which brought new illumination technology to town in 1860.[10] An active faculty, then, provided another opportunity for the seminary and the college to disseminate improvement and education through the town and county.

In sum, the Lutheran Theological Seminary and Pennsylvania College belonged to a national movement toward an educated ministry, and they contributed educated minds to Gettysburg's civic community. These two institutions of higher education were conspicuous centers of refinement.

∝

The quest for refinement, however, reached far beyond higher education to touch most American Christians, even those with a heritage of standoffishness toward the high and mighty and badges of status. Methodists, in particular, had a tradition of resistance to fashion and gentility, yet by the antebellum period they valued sophistication just as highly as other Protestants. Whether refinement transformed Methodism or whether other Methodist adjustments made sophistication acceptable may be a chicken-and-egg question, but without a doubt the fellowship of John and Charles Wesley traveled a greater distance towards refinement than most during this period.

English Methodists at their birth were distinctly nonconformist, and the first generation in North America followed in these footsteps. Early American Methodists dressed simply, refused to swear oaths, flirted with pacifism and antislavery, disciplined for alcohol abuse, challenged authority, and created a tightly organized community that supported and reinforced members in a countercultural daily walk. But in the early nineteenth century Methodists migrated into the mainstream, and historians still argue about why. Perhaps revolutionary movements like Methodism naturally lose momentum and evolve into something more conservative and mainstream. Perhaps success doomed Methodism to the mainstream. According to this argument, Methodists enjoyed spectacular growth, but outsiderness and majority status are mutually exclusive. Religion cannot be simultaneously popular and nonconformist. Another line of thought suggests that Methodists borrowed so much from popular culture that it finally overcame them. Or, perhaps Methodists made strategic concessions to popular opinion to fuel their growth. One recent study encourages scholars to "follow the money." Perhaps as Methodists became wealthier, they replaced their egalitarian system of aesthetic circuit-reading preachers with a more stratified system of residential, town pastors, who naturally favored refinement over nonconformity.[11]

Most notably, the Methodist fondness for sudden conversion in revivalist settings discouraged converts from considering the alternative lifestyle that came with the new birth. Hence, the pews gradually filled with members born again in the spirit but not in the lifestyle. True, Methodists had a probationary system that guided new converts and theoretically denied them full membership until they convinced the congregational leadership of their commitment to a Methodist way of living. But clergy complained that this scheme had lost effectiveness, and they lamented that revivals produced converts less willing to walk the Wesleyan walk.[12]

Regardless of the underlying causes, early nineteenth-century Methodism changed and grew comfortable with the American mainstream. At the local level, three waning practices—revivals, camp meetings, and classes—marked drift from emotional conversion and discipline and the corresponding increase in Methodist polish.

Revivals sprang from the core of traditional Methodist theology: the doctrine of the new birth, or evangelicalism. In brief, evangelicals taught that salvation came from a free will choice to receive God's infinite forgiveness for sin, and the process typically involved three stages: awareness of and struggle with sin, acceptance of Christ, and entrance into the new life with Christ, commonly called a "new birth." Conversion included a direct, intimate, and emotional relationship with Christ—the new life was very tangible—and evangelicals spoke often of the heart. Revivals were special times when congregations and communities experienced spiritual awakening together and sinners were born again in bunches. Emotion poured forth as worshippers wept, shouted, swooned, and leaped for joy. At the most Spirit-filled moments, order broke down as preachers continued to speak while the born-again confronted those who were not. Some cried in anguish over their sins, and still others shouted for joy as they entered into new life. Revivals, closely related to the conversion process, could be chaotic, but they were integral to early Methodism.

The first known revival in Gettysburg occurred in 1826, reaping sixty souls, although other awakenings likely occurred earlier. The next began on Christmas

Day 1835, and another took place in 1840; both won approximately one hundred converts. In 1847 Methodist leaders gave thanks for a "gracious revival of religion at which 65 persons joined the Society and a new class formed." Other seasons of grace occurred at approximately three-year intervals through 1858.[13]

Camp meetings provided a special setting for revivals. These large, outdoor events featured preaching and singing from dawn into the evening for several days consecutively, and the harvest of souls was often bountiful and emotional. Camp meetings appeared among Methodists in the early 1800s, when quarterly meetings (gatherings of leadership from bishop to class leader) grew too large to meet the administrative needs of clergy and simultaneously feed the souls of laity. Hence, ministers still gathered quarterly, but large harvests of souls now took place in camp meetings. Although these gatherings acquired a reputation as a stereotypical frontier Methodist activity, in reality the congregations in the woods predated Methodism, outlived the frontier, were employed by other denominations, and were often interdenominational. That said, camp meetings were a powerful spiritual weapon in the Methodist arsenal. The first camp meeting in the Gettysburg area came at a quarterly conference of the Gettysburg circuit in 1827, long after Adams County ceased to be frontier, on a farm about three miles north of town. Subsequent Methodist camp meetings in the Gettysburg area became near-annual events through 1844, always in August, a convenient moment in the agricultural calendar. Camp meetings brought innumerable souls into the Methodist fold.[14]

But towards the late antebellum period revivals in Gettysburg and Adams County declined, and the Methodist camp meetings ended. As a member of the Gettysburg congregation, Sallie Myers experienced a significant revival in 1858 at age sixteen, when fifty were saved—perhaps part of the "businessman's" awakening that swept the nation that year—but thereafter revivals became less prominent in her faith walk. Of course, some Methodists still hoped for periods of mass conversion. For example, in 1860 the congregation met for a week consecutively following a quarterly meeting and a Love Feast. Counting the quarterly meeting, Myers attended services for seven consecutive days and nine out of ten. (Myers was home on a rainy January Saturday when she complained of a severe headache and worsening sore throat, but she does not actually say that she missed a service and perhaps there was none.) This was a protracted meeting, a classic sign that the spirit was about to descend and stir, leading Myers to surmise that the "prospects are brightening for a revival." But after a week of waiting upon the Spirit, only two persons had responded to altar calls, and the last service, on a Monday, faced competition from a fair and was poorly attended. This revival ended, ingloriously. Methodist revivals continued in Gettysburg after the Civil War in 1866 and 1875 but now less frequently and less essential. Camp meetings, purveyors of revivals, passed from the scene more visibly. In 1852, when Myers was eight, area Methodists held their last camp meeting, noted primarily for heavy rain. Thereafter, only the United Brethren and the Church of God, both ethnic German fellowships, held camp meetings in the area. Revivals and camp meetings with their emotionalism and disorder had become increasingly unappealing to the refined middle class, and these two opportunities for emotional conversion faded from the Methodist scene, one partially and the other completely.[15]

If revivals and camp meetings were the gateway to Methodism, classes were the fence. From the inception of American Methodism, these subgroups of laity, sometimes meeting on weekdays, contributed significantly to individual spiritual growth, assimilation into Methodism, denominational identity, and expansion. In particular, classes required converts to subscribe to the Methodist lifestyle, to some semblance of nonconformity to the world. In other words, classes defined Methodist boundaries with the world and screened out those swept up by the revivalist moment but unable or unwilling to conform to long-term Methodist expectations. In early Methodism classes maintained regular meetings while the preacher was elsewhere riding circuit, and they formed a key building block in explosive Methodist growth.

But increasingly class lost its allure. Sharing intimate thoughts and exposure to admonition, perhaps from a collection of artisans and farmers like those who occupied Gettysburg's Methodist pews, had little appeal to the aspiring middle class. This trend began in the 1830s and 1840s, and Methodist leadership noticed. In 1848 the Baltimore Conference, which included Gettysburg, complained about the decline in class meetings, especially for discipline. The assemblage of preachers noted that too many of their peers neglected class meetings for the pulpit—they spent too much time on preaching—and, consequently, the church had admitted many that had not truly been converted. They had "little or no profession of experimental godliness." The Baltimore ministers added that now in communities where "Methodism commands respect and influence" faithfulness had declined, and they asked elders to report whether preachers actually expelled delinquents. Sallie Myers contributed to the decline of classes. Despite her deep commitment to Methodism, her attendance at class meeting was sporadic. "Did not go to class," she matter-of-factly recorded in her diary. When Myers was there, many others were not, and attendance was low. Moreover, her class did not meet for weeks or months at a time. Although Myers enjoyed class when present, this once-critical Methodist institution had little impact on her congregational life or the faith of others in her fellowship.[16]

Instead of class, Myers attended Sunday school. This institution, which basically replaced classes, won her allegiance. Sunday Schools for children grouped students by age with a small student/teacher ratio; student groups of six to ten per teacher were common. The program included persons on the peripheries of childhood with infant classes for ages four to six and Bible sessions for adolescents. The first Sunday schools, appearing in the 1790s and the early nineteenth century, focused on children of the white poor and African Americans and sometimes mixed the ABCs with religious instruction. But as public education became more common, Sunday schools enrolled significant numbers of the middle class—in 1826 eighty "scholars" attended Gettysburg Methodist Sunday School—and shifted to religious education exclusively. The Baltimore Conference frowned when some Sunday schools closed for the winter because if children could still trudge to common school through the week, then the two-hour meeting of Sunday school should also be possible, and the loss of the nurture-time disappointed the Methodist clergy. (Gettysburg's Sunday school was not among the slackers and met through the winter.)

The Baltimore ministers considered Sunday school important because of its expanding role in conversion. Conventional wisdom held that children were pliable, persuadable, and capable of holding religious sentiment, and, therefore, educating them in religion made sense. By 1830 Methodists expected a student's Sunday school career to end with conversion, and by 1840 Methodists required Sunday schools in all congregations. In the 1850s, middle-class attitudes about children continued to evolve, and now instead being latent sinners or sharing in Adam's fall, children were innocent and possessed the ability to grow up in the faith without having a sudden, singular moment of conversion. Consequently, Sunday school teachers nurtured their pupils along a path of gradual new birth. In the early years instruction consisted of scripture, songs, and catechism with a heavy dose of memorization, but increasingly catechisms dominated. New child-friendly editions appeared with short, simple answers, and pastors routinely ran the children through their paces while an appreciative congregation looked on. Sunday schools and the related changes in conversion advanced gradually; emotional conversion and nurture coexisted in many settings, just beginning in Myers's time and accelerating after the Civil War.[17]

Most likely, Myers's immersion in Sunday school was unusually intense, but following her through a Sabbath nevertheless reveals the role of this institution in Methodism and the larger community. "To S.S. at 9. To preaching at 10 ½" is a common entry in her diary, and she also participated in the Methodist infant Sunday school, taught a class of children, and occasionally attended union Sunday school meetings with the Lutherans and Presbyterians. Frequently Myers attended Sunday school twice on the same day. On one Sunday, for example, when her congregation held no meetings, Myers visited the German Reformed Sunday School and their infant school in the morning, then in the afternoon she went to the Lutherans and also their infant session. Snyder, her beau, sometimes led one of the Methodist sessions, which may have contributed to her sparkling attendance record, but, on the other hand, imagining this fervent, young Methodist missing Sunday school is difficult, even when Snyder did not preside. Her adult Sunday school provided a small group experience, similar to her class but with less fervor, less baring open of the soul, and no discipline. Additionally, for Myers, as with other young women, Sunday school may have represented more than a moment of spiritual growth but a rare opportunity to contribute talent publicly, albeit with children. Regardless of her motives, the young woman's participation in Lutheran, German Reformed, and Presbyterian Sunday schools plus her own congregation's infant, children's, and adult levels shows just how common Sunday school had become in antebellum Gettysburg.[18]

Almost gone were the old-style classes, once the bedrock of local Methodism but now sometimes barely functioning in Gettysburg. Instead, Sunday school, with less intimacy and enthusiasm and more dignity, became indispensable.

Discipline and nonconformity followed classes into the Methodist twilight. In the 1830s Gettysburg Methodist congregational leaders took actions when members went to the circus, bet on an election, or engaged in "foolish plays" at a quilting party. Some of these countercultural tendencies persisted into the late antebellum period. Sallie Myers probably shunned playing cards if the stakes were higher than "Old Maid," and she angered a gathering of friends and relatives when, in her words, she "left in disgust" as a fiddler arrived and dancing began. But this was a personal decision, shared by some but certainly not all Methodists. Myers left, but everybody else stayed, offended, no less, by her high nonconformist standards.[19] Moreover, young Myers had a worldly side, after all; she published sentimental love poetry. In "My First Love," for example, Myers portrayed a lovestruck man who could "no longer live/Unless we were united." Then, her fictional swain recounted that

I breathed my love—her hand I pressed—
    While she, her eyes adverting,
Returned the pressure and confess'd
    That she was only flirting.[20]

Surely Methodism's founders would have disapproved of such sensual thoughts
as frivolous and inappropriate for the born again. Even the dutiful Myers embodied changing Methodism.

Accordingly, enforcement of nonconformity through discipline declined.
True, members could still be denied their privileges for very bad behavior. C. W.
Hoffman received suspension for involvement in a bitter fight in which he used
a club and threw stones while his opponent, John Barrett, a nonmember, was
armed with an iron. Hoffman, a thirty-nine-year-old coachmaker, served on a
congregational building committee, and Barrett was a sixty-year-old shoemaker.
The two middle-class property owners injured each other badly. For "highly improper and immoral conduct" Hoffman, an influential Methodist, lost his membership, but after confessing before the congregation, he was reinstated. Discipline for brawling, however, does not mark outsiderness but merely conforms
to broad middle-class values and basic civic law and order. Myers's diary, which
documents her faith journey in detail, does not mention church discipline, and
the semi-extant Methodist records for the 1850s have no other cases besides the
Hoffman-Barrett scuffle. The complaint of the Baltimore Conference ministers
that discipline accompanied classes into disuse had validity.[21]

For Methodists, then, significant change accompanied their passage to refined
doctrine. Once known for emotional conversion and discipline, they gradually
discarded the means by which previous generations had achieved these ends—
revivals, camp meetings, and classes—and replaced them with Sunday school
and catechisms. Methodists were now in greater control of their emotions, less
nonconformist, and less accountable to their fellow members. All represented
sophistication and made Methodism increasingly indistinguishable from mainline Protestantism. Methodist thinking, not just in Gettysburg but throughout
the denomination, drank deeply from the cup of refinement.

CR

As Methodists became more refined, another fellowship, the Dunkers, rejected
the entire concept. If Methodists noticeably accepted mainstream standards,
Dunkers just as conspicuously avoided them. Their firm nonconformity to pre-

vailing aspirations of fashion and respectability demonstrated that refinement had become so mainstream that nonconformists could use it to define themselves. True, Dunkers were not self-conscious foes of refinement, and they did not use the word. Instead, they framed their conflict with the mainstream in terms of separating the faithful from the sinful world. Nevertheless, as Dunkers drew boundaries against worldliness, they became determined bystanders in the pursuit of refinement.

The Dunker faith community, not individual judgment, defined unacceptable worldliness. Although Dunkers believed that the Holy Spirit wrote God's laws on each member's heart, they disdained individual interpretation of these commandments. To illuminate God's word, Jesus provided the church, and truth came from its collective discernment, not from individual insights. In practice, the denomination's collective wisdom flowed from annual gatherings called Yearly Meetings. During the early nineteenth century the Yearly Meetings grew increasingly formal, resembling a legislative branch of the fellowship that laid down guidelines on matters large and small. Congregations sent one or two delegates, but the floor was open to all in attendance and decision making was by consensus. This remarkably democratic arm of the denomination guided the Brethren as they maintained their "ancient order," as they called their tradition, amidst changing larger society.[22]

Safe-guarding the ancient order required innumerable lines against the world. Dunkers, for example, had no use for a seminary like the Lutherans' imposing institution on the ridge, and Pennsylvania College was similarly worthless. According to Yearly Meeting, colleges were "unsafe places for a simple follower of Christ," and college students rarely returned "to the humble ways of the Lord." Instead, Dunker ministers were self-trained or guided by informal mentors, and they had no more education than the rank-and-file members. At Marsh Creek the elder, often called a "bishop," was David Bosserman, a well-to-do farmer. Even high schools were questionable, and Yearly Meeting advised parents to be "cautious" about sending their children to them. In the shadow of the Lutheran Theological Seminary and Pennsylvania College, Bosserman and the Dunkers' disdain for higher education appeared especially out of step with the mainstream.[23]

The building in which the Dunkers worshipped represented another line against the world and reminded the devout of their contempt for the fashion and taste of the world. Eighteenth-century Brethren had generally met in private homes, one more example of nonconformity, but in the next century Yearly Meeting permitted congregations to build, provided that they avoided "unnecessary ornaments," including bells, which were specifically proscribed. In part, meetinghouses emerged from membership growth and the need for more space. Marsh Creek Dunkers followed this pattern. Organized in 1805, they gathered in residences until 1830 when they built their first meetinghouse on land donated by their first minister, David Pfoutz. In 1852 the congregation constructed a second house of worship, called "Friends Grove" after land leased from the Society of Friends, to serve members who lived a bit distant from the Pfoutz meetinghouse. Plainness dominated this modest, roughly finished building. Interior walls were plastered, and the room had a ceiling but otherwise the décor was minimalist. Worshippers sat on "common benches," with backs, according to the church book, while preachers faced them from behind a ten-foot table on a simple platform, raised one or two steps above floor level. Absent were rented pews, which emphasized status among worshippers, and a raised pulpit and communion rail, which enhanced clerical rank. The building was also without a steeple and decorations, which further separated Brethren meetinghouses from the other religious buildings in Gettysburg with their curtains, carpets, and cupolas. A four-hundred-pound bell was unthinkable.[24]

When Dunkers left the meetinghouse and went into the world, they remained similarly plain in their individual lives, opposing fashion and consumption and thereby maintaining their highest walls against the mainstream. Yearly Meeting denounced "building and ornamenting houses in the style of those high in the world" as a "dangerous and alarming evil." The annual gathering put teeth in its warning with bans on specific items, including carpets, stylish furniture, and sleigh bells. "The tinkling of bells are [sic] improper," decided the delegates. Dunkers gave special attention to clothing and appearance, which provided daily reminders of identity. Men, especially ministers, wore beards because "God made man with a beard," and this facial hair went untrimmed because Yearly Meeting took literally Old Testament law that commanded priests "not to mar the corners of the beard." For added evidence, Brethren were convinced that Jesus and his disciples wore untrimmed beards. While fashionable gentlemen wore their hair in a casual, natural look with short curls close to the head, reminiscent of ancient Romans, Brethren men parted their hair on top of the head and combed it straight down or back in what today would be called a "bowl" haircut. During the eighteenth century, a clean-shaven era, bearded Dunker men had been nonconformist, and in the next century when men of stature grew facial hair, Dunkers reinforced the line between themselves and style by condemning those who trimmed beards "in conformity to the fashion of the world." When stylish men started growing mustaches, Yearly Meeting adjusted again with its disapproval unless with a beard. Apparel also merited close scrutiny. "High and fashionable clothing," Yearly Meeting determined, equated to "conformity to the world," a "great evil, which is not to be tolerated." Specifically, stylish caps for men and fashionable bonnets for women were out, and so was jewelry. When hoop skirts became popular, they, too, were off-limits. One annual meeting ruled out two suits of clothes, one plain for church meeting and another "after the fashion of the world" for other occasions. Apparently a few wavering Dunkers had attempted to straddle the wall separating them from the world. Yearly Meeting also admonished members to keep their children from "high fashions." With converts typically baptized in their twenties, children were not members and, therefore, unaccountable to congregational discipline, but Yearly Meeting wanted them supervised anyway. Few could mistake the bearded Dunker brothers and plain-bonneted sisters as pursuing respectability.[25]

Yet not even the Dunkers could completely avoid refinement. Tobacco, for example, earned their scorn. Yearly Meeting denounced the addictive custom as a "shamefully bad habit, and everything bad" and banned farmers from raising the crop. The delegates pointed out that "so many men (and women too)," an interesting comment on gender, were "led captive" by the addictive plant. Yet Yearly Meeting's antitobacco campaign met resistance from the rank and file. In 1864, an inquiry to the annual meeting observed that the effort to "suppress the excessive or intemperate use" of tobacco, both smoked and chewed, "has virtually proved a failure." In response, the gathering "counseled," not ordered, members to abstain from it in worship "so as not to be filthy or offensive to others." Apparently, some worshippers chewed or maybe smoked during the services. Yearly Meeting added that tobacco usage offended some members and that "excessive" use was an "evil." Evidently, a total ban on tobacco was unenforceable, and Yearly Meeting now limited its censure to consumption during worship. Whether Dunker opposition to chewing, spitting, and smoking when assembled as Christ's gathered community was a step toward refinement or simply a battle for cleanliness and against addiction, the effort brought mixed results.[26]

Despite stumbling over tobacco, on balance the Dunkers starkly contrasted with Gettysburg's Lutherans, Methodists, Presbyterians, Reformed, AME Zion, and Catholics with their explicit and detailed resistance to the sinful world and refinement. Plain households, plain dress, opposition to higher education, and unadorned meetinghouses presided over by uneducated ministers confirmed Dunker nonconformity to the genteel standards of the mainstream. Ironically, the

Dunkers testify to the power of refinement. Had the drive for dignity and fashion been less pervasive among most fellowships, the Dunkers' resistance to refinement would have been less detailed, less determined, and less conspicuous.

☙

Refinement, then, was integral to Gettysburg religion. The college and seminary prepared refined Lutheran men to go forth into all the world, or at least the region, spreading polish through word and deed. Among Methodists, revivals, camp meetings, emotional conversion, classes, discipline, and nonconformity waned while Sunday schools, catechisms, nurture, and dignity waxed. Middle-class respectability moved to the center of Methodism. Meanwhile, Dunkers went the other direction, redoubling efforts to resist refinement at home, in their garb, and in the meetinghouse, paradoxically bearing witness to the ability of refinement to define the mainstream. In sum, the Lutheran Seminary, Pennsylvania College, Methodists, and Dunkers illustrate the power of refinement in Gettysburg religion and in American thought.

3

Refinement

In Practice

Refinement was more than educated leadership, a marker of denominational transformation, or a foil for nonconformists. In practice, it permeated the daily and weekly rhythms of congregational life.

The house of refinement was built on a rock of economic growth, sometimes called the "market revolution." Basically, this involved a shift from a localized, agricultural, barter, preindustrial economy in which relationships mattered to a large, complicated, industrialized, competitive, impersonal, cash-oriented economy. For many, especially in the middle class, a new standard of living, facilitated especially by the widespread availability of consumer goods, was a very tangible and positive consequence of the changing economy. This trend began in approximately the 1830s and was apparent to a casual reader of Gettysburg's antebellum newspapers. "Lost and Found," read one advertisement, "at the Cheap Corner, Fall and Winter Goods of every description." Some used political developments to court customers, demonstrating the need for creativity in the competitive marketplace. In one issue of *The Star and Banner*, eye-catching headlines in neighboring columns proclaimed "'Know Nothing' Meeting" and "Know Nothings," references to fast-rising political party for nativists. Actually, one of these headlines advertised a general store and the other a harness maker. Both claimed that the new party, recently organized in town, met on their premises, not to "tear asunder former parties," as one ad put it, but to "examine the [proprietor's] stock of new spring and summer goods." Another retailer boasted of "Anti-Nebraska Hats, Caps, Boots & Shoes," a reference to the controversial Kansas-Nebraska Act. In truth, the availability of advertised consumer goods was impressive, including bonnets, carpets, clocks, coffee, cravats, cutlery, figs, frock coats, gloves, handkerchiefs, hats, hosiery, jewelry, lace, lemons, looking glasses, molasses, monkey jackets, oranges, overcoats, pantaloons, parasols, pistols, queensware, raisins, ribbons, sack coats, sugar, umbrellas, and vests. Historians argue about whether consumerism came to American society quickly or slowly and whether it brought traumatic change, including mysterious, painful economic cycles, class conflict, and altered gender roles or simply a basketful of goodies for those with cash. But regardless of the specific characteristics of the market revolution, by the antebellum period the broad middle class undeniably had the coin to purchase the nuts and bolts of refined life.[1]

Yet refinement was more than store-bought goods, which often functioned as mere means to a refined end. In addition to their utilitarian function, individual objects represented values, and the collection of goods sent a powerful message that demonstrated participation in an elaborate set of rules governing Victorian daily life. Umbrellas, for example, which became available to the middle class in the nineteenth century, in addition to keeping dry the head and shoulders, conveyed orderliness and Victorian concern with appearance. Likewise, hallstands transcended their practical purpose and signified participation in the Victorian system. Hallstands held umbrellas, hats, coats, and canes and provided a mirror to reflect light. But with their unnecessarily intricate woodwork, occasional marble, larger than necessary mirrors, and grandiose size, they were conspicuous consumption and indicated status. Further, as one scholar has suggested, hallstands "ceremonialized coming and going" as hats and coats either missing or present showed who was in and out. Hallstands were large, the first object noticed by a visitor, and the first information imparted about the residents of the home. Thus, hallways were more than just an extended doorway and communicated important messages. Further inside, carpeted and wallpapered parlors formed the center of the home and its values. Here, where adults pursued refinement and children learned it, material objects also signified participation in the Victorian system. Rocking chairs, a new staple of the parlor, suggested ease, a new concept. Well-stocked parlors with books, china, family portraits, pianos, pillows, stands, tables, a wide variety of specialized chairs, draped windows, and a curtained entrance informed about the occupants—according to another scholar, a "miniature museum thick with meaning"—and through it the owners demonstrated their self-control, management of the surrounding world, and appreciation of comfort, beauty, taste, polish, and manners, all treasured concepts without a price tag. In short, goods represented values, and the total was greater than the sum of the stuff.[2]

Victorians brought their passion for refinement with them to church. They improved their buildings and grounds, most noticeably the cemeteries, upgraded worship in general, and applied specialized skills, especially in music. All of this infused religion with the values of refinement. Many congregations, however, could barely afford their appetite for improvement, and funding it absorbed them.

Downtown Gettysburg, Baltimore Street, and the courthouse, ca. 1865. (Courtesy of Adams County Historical Society.)

CR

Gettysburg religion took a big communal step towards refinement when it joined the rural cemetery movement. Nationally, this new approach to death and mourning began in 1831 when Bostonians dedicated Mount Auburn, and the concept quickly spread to all sections of the country as countless communities moved their final resting places from churchyards to garden-like surroundings on the edge of town. Gettysburg's contribution to this fashionable trend was Evergreen Cemetery.

From a small churchyard to a large community cemetery represented a significant cultural shift. On the practical side, maintenance of church burial grounds and family plots had grown wearisome. When Presbyterians, for example, moved into Gettysburg, they retained their old cemetery, called "Black's Graveyard," several miles outside of town. By the 1840s the stone wall surrounding the plot was in disrepair with cattle grazing and leaving part of themselves amid the tombstones. Managers of the cemetery finally secured a wooden fence around it.

Perhaps with situations like Black's Graveyard in mind, a resolution adopted by the organizational meeting of the Evergreen Association delicately hinted that the "present state" of cemeteries in town made improvement in burial facilities "expedient."[3]

But the rural cemetery movement involved more than dilapidated fencing or cattle among the markers, and contemporaries cited numerous rationales for planting their dead in community gardens. On a basic level, they noted that memorializing the departed was part of human nature. In 1855 at the laying of the Evergreen cornerstone, Lutheran preacher Reuben Hill commented that even the "lowest races of men," including the "degraded Hottentot," cared for their dead. On another level, cemetery boosters argued that these new graveyards inspired and educated visitors. Patriotism, for example, emerged from the celebration of civic heroes, including war dead, a lesson taken from the revival of the ancient Greeks that immersed antebellum America. Social conservatives viewed cemeteries as a way to improve public morality. In this pensive environment sinners became aware of their faults, and the profligate thought twice about the consequences of sin. Finally, rural, garden cemeteries represented human-improved nature, not the raw variety, and consequently contributed to refinement. Hill was self-conscious about this; "civilization and refinement," he pointed out, "add new charms to this lovely virtue" of caring for the dead. Cemeteries were about more than mourning and memorializing; they inspired.[4]

The market revolution added momentum to the rural cemetery movement. The growing hustle and bustle of the new economy produced heightened desire for pastoral solitude for the departed, a trend noted by Evergreen's planners, and winding cemetery lanes contrasted with the right-angled grids of urban and town life and encouraged contemplation. Thus, Evergreen's organizers sought an aesthetically appealing landscape, a perceived departure from the growing commercial world, as they pledged to erect "neat and substantial fencing" and to "render the place attractive and beautiful." Samuel Simon Schmucker approved and termed the new grounds "elegant." The market revolution also influenced what grew in the cemeteries. As America urbanized, flowers, orchards, shrubs, and greenhouses developed into hobbies or businesses, and gardening and horticulture became distinct from agriculture. Garden cemeteries, then, were a refuge from the market revolution but a consumer of it.[5]

The growing popularity of freewill, born-again religion at the expense of Calvinism also contributed to the movement. Evangelicalism increasingly convinced Protestants that everlasting life was available to all and that death was but a peaceful sleep or a journey to a better life rather than an encounter with a mysterious, judgmental god. Rural cemeteries reflected this by casting aside the foreboding ambiance of the old churchyard burial plot. J. H. C. Dosh, a Methodist minister who delivered an address when construction of Evergreen began, emphasized quiet rest in a natural setting by reciting a few sentimental lines from Caroline Elizabeth Sarah Norton, a contemporary English poet:

> Weep not for him who dieth,
> For he sleeps and is at rest;
> And the couch on which he lieth,
> Is the green earth's quiet breast.[6]

In death, Dosh said, the faithful merely wait for life after death; they "*fall asleep* in Christ—they shall awake again to immortal life."[7] (Poetry demonstrated Dosh's refined preaching.) Additionally, cemeteries expressed the optimism of free will conversion. Hill, the Lutheran, suggested that when believers "adorn the garden of the Lord"—he expected Evergreen's patrons to improve on the natural setting—they would express the best in human nature and testify to what humans were before the fall and to what they might become again through Christ. The cemetery, he remarked, reflected "a high and holy principle of our nature," an unmistakable expression of optimism about human behavior. Rural cemeteries, then, mirrored the evangelical god, forgiving and within reach of all, and conveyed human capacity.[8]

More than anything, however, cemeteries provided knowledge gained from experience and feelings rather than rationalism, a popular intellectual trend. Insights acquired by the heart had become as valuable as wisdom obtained by the head. Pennsylvania College students, for example, learned not to focus exclusively on the intellect but that those with truth "not only know and have, but feel." Likewise, at the dedication of the Mount Auburn burial ground Supreme Court Justice Joseph Story argued that truth comes not just from reason but that it "must be felt, as well as seen. It must warm, as well as convince."[9]

Warm wisdom abounded in rural cemeteries. In cemeteries two worlds—life and death; the past and the present—came together. As individuals left their ordinary lives to stroll among the markers and greens, they experienced nature, eternity, and death, and then returned to their world wiser. Dosh in his dedicatory address extolled the beauty of the location, a nearly unanimous choice of the stockholders, as he described the impressive vista before his listeners: "the vast chain of Blue Ridge mountains in the west—an unobstructed horizon in the east—Round Hill and other prominent points in the south—and a beautiful view of Gettysburg in the north." Indeed, the Cemetery Association chose wisely, although Dosh, perhaps carried away with the moment, pronounced this as "one of the most magnificent landscapes in the world." But beyond aesthetic appeal, the location instructed in matters of faith, a notion that achieved wide acceptance. Samuel Simon Schmucker, for example, noted that "the royal Psalmist" drew deep inspiration by contemplating nature. A Pennsylvania College commencement speaker praised the "maternal wisdom" of nature, and another drew attention to the majesty and goodness of God in nature. From "gigantic wonders" to "microscopic beauties," nature had lessons. Like "nowhere else," the natural world revealed God, and special knowledge and unlimited truths emerged from the innumerable variety offered by the nature, including its "hidden recesses." Thus, Dosh emphasized that Evergreen was more than a "pleasant" spot to "sleep" until the "last trump" but a place of "study" and a natural setting that divulged "nature's God." Here God was revealed, and visitors drew a variety of religious lessons, including God's goodness, the fickleness of life, resurrection, and eternity. Cemeteries and wisdom went hand in hand.[10]

To maintain the quiet dignity requisite for the absorption of truth, trustees hired a custodian and regulated behavior inside their burial park. The custodian was Peter Thorn, who lived with his wife, Elizabeth Möser Thorn—both German-born immigrants—in the cemetery gatehouse with their family as Peter performed routine duties and care for the facility. Custodial rules to enforce the solitude were part of the movement, but enforcement proved difficult in Gettysburg. "Friends of the dead" complained about buggy racing, drunkenness, desecration of the Sabbath, flower-stealing, and obscene graffiti inside the cemetery. Evergreen's board denied the charges, and a testy exchange of notes, all published in the *Adams Sentinel*, ensued between David McConaughy, president of Evergreen's board of managers, and Robert Harper, the editor, over the identity of a critic of Evergreen, whom Harper had not revealed. Proper maintenance of the park and its rules were important.[11]

Given the widely shared assumptions behind rural cemeteries and their general popularity, ecumenicity and egalitarianism flowed easily from the movement. Although the Evergreen Cemetery Association was an independent company with a board of directors that sold stock and family plots, all of the congregations in Gettysburg, except the AME Zion and Catholics, quickly become involved in the planning of the new grounds. A fair involving most of the town's congregations raised cash for the project, and the two dedicatory ceremonies celebrated local ecumenicity. At the laying of the cornerstone, Dosh and Hill, the Methodist and St. James Lutheran ministers mentioned previously, spoke. Schmucker, of Christ Lutheran and professor at the Seminary, laid the cornerstone. The president of Pennsylvania College, also from Christ Church, prayed, and the Presbyterian pastor pronounced the benediction. Placed inside the cornerstone along with the act of incorporation and a list of stockholders, lot holders, and officers were a Bible, copies of local newspapers, and the *Kirchenbote* and the *Evangelical Review*, both Lutheran journals published in Gettysburg. The ceremonies included Gettysburg's Germans, represented by the German-language periodical, and Hill, whose congregation still worshipped occasionally in German. Explicitly extolling inclusiveness, Dosh pointed out that in Evergreen "members of all sects, and inhabitants from every clime may lie." He even predicted that Jews, Gentiles, Calvinists, Arminians, Europeans, and Americans—a hodgepodge of doctrine and ethnicity—would "rest together as brothers." Or, as Evergreen's planners suggested, "all sects may mingle in the dust." God's acre also stripped away class distinctions. Dosh proclaimed that in Evergreen "the rich, the poor, the great, the small, Are levell'd." In his enthusiasm for tolerance and democracy, however, Dosh overlooked several groups missing from the new burial grounds. Conspicuous by their absence were the AME Zion and St. Francis Xavier Roman Catholic fellowships; not quite all would rest together as brothers and sisters. Nevertheless, Evergreen was a self-conscientious, if imperfect, display of tolerance and cooperation.[12]

Somewhat less conspicuous by their absence were the Dunkers. Marsh Creek's location just outside of town probably eliminated it from the Evergreen project, which involved only congregations inside municipal limits. But the Dunkers, nevertheless, would have been out of place in the trendy garden cemetery. In 1855, just as rural cemeteries penetrated small towns, Yearly Meeting decided that "large and expensive tombstones" contradicted "principles of the gospel, such as humility, nonconformity to the world, etc." The rural cemetery movement proceeded without the plain Dunkers, and their nonparticipation indicates how fashionable Evergreen was.[13]

Indeed, the new burial plots struck a chord with the community. "Hundreds of Ladies and Gentlemen," according to the committee, viewed the grounds prior to the cornerstone-laying ceremony, and a local undertaker, A. W. Flemming, offered to move coffins and markers from old burial spots to the new cemetery for a "moderate charge." Sallie Myers took pleasure in the pastoral graveyard, strolled through it, and penned a composition, "An Hour in Evergreen Cemetery." Others must have agreed. Refined burial in rural gardens had become popular.[14]

CR

Not just afterlife but daily religious life also benefitted from refinement. Whether structural improvements, enhanced décor, polished manners, or dust-catching knick-knacks, a step-by-step path to refinement was a regular part of the spiritual walk in Gettysburg.

Some steps forward were very ordinary. Gettysburg Methodists, for example, decided to place offerings in baskets rather than bags. In an affirmation of cleanliness, their trustees denounced the "filthy practice of spitting tobacco spittle on the church floor," and they requested those desiring nicotine high during worship to stay away. To emphasize the point, the trustees wanted their statement read to the congregation. Sinners welcome, but not if they chewed or dipped. (The Dunkers' Yearly Meeting, mentioned previously, gave ground on tobacco.)[15] Christ Church Lutherans acquired a clock, placed a fence in front of their building, and repaired stones in the lecture room.[16] St. James Lutheran experienced "some disorder" in the vestibule, (the vestibule was another example of refinement); apparently some came but not to worship. To create order, St. James hung a curtain around the banisters leading to the gallery, restricted the gallery to the choir, and prohibited standing in the vestibule during worship. Council further authorized "whatever improvements might be necessary." While the St. James decisions might be explained simply as an elimination of distractions during worship, they also fit the pattern of increased dignity and order.[17] Late 1858 or early 1859 the bell in the German Reformed spire cracked, and the congregation had it recast in a foundry in Baltimore. In the process the bell lost thirty-eight pounds, but approving listeners noted that it gained in volume and had a clearer tone. When in 1822 the Lutherans and Reformed jointly purchased the bell, it had arrived via horse and wagon, but this time it returned by rail. Refinement came in multiple forms.[18]

Structural enhancements further improved several congregations. Catholics renovated their basement. Methodists pondered whether to build a new church or to enlarge their present facility, but they opted instead for repairs. Perhaps the modest wealth of their membership determined the decision. They added a basement and collected donations for a new roof although records do not say whether this fundraising campaign succeeded. Presbyterians resolved to build a new lecture room, asserting that the current one was in "unhealthy condition." But their fundraising failed, and the project remained uncompleted. St. James added a cupola and a railing around the pulpit, quickly spending the proceeds from the Reformed buyout when the union church dissolved.[19]

Christ Lutheran Church, English-only for the seminary and college; three gaslights on each chandelier. (Courtesy of Gettysburg National Military Park.)

Gaslights were particularly tempting but expensive. In the 1830s innovators began to distill gas, that is, kerosene, from coal, and this burned with superior illumination. By mid-century gas-lighting had moved beyond large urban centers, and in August 1860, Gettysburg's street corners and homes with the required fixtures glowed in the dark. Sallie Myers was intrigued; she pronounced the corner lights "very nice" and toured the gasworks, which produced the kerosene. Gaslighting was trendy and exciting technology, but congregations struggled to fund it. Christ Church Lutherans appointed a committee to look into gas, and then held a congregational vote on whether to put two gaslights or three on the chandeliers. Three lights won. The congregation granted the committee discretion on

St. James Lutheran, mostly English but lingering German. No standing in the vestibule during worship. (Courtesy of Adams County Historical Society.)

the other fixtures, either less important or less expensive. St. James Lutherans took subscriptions for the new illumination, but when members proved reluctant to dig a little deeper, the council permitted the "Ladies of the Congregation" to hold a fair to raise money for the gas. (Use of "Ladies" when some fellowships might refer to "sisters" shows a genteel tilt.) Apparently the women succeeded because soon after the event, St. James installed this latest refinement, seven months after it first became available. Financially struggling Presbyterians were a year late in installing gas, and ultimately it took another one hundred dollars added to their debt to illuminate their worship more brightly. The seminary likewise borrowed to acquire gas, then asked each congregation in the synod to contribute to the liquidation of the obligation. Catholics had to wait until 1871 to worship in a gas-illumined sanctuary. Gas-lighting was a big but difficult step forward.[20]

Improved music, another sure sign of refinement, was one more high priority. British Protestants, much under the influence of Calvinist austerity, had little musical ability, a deficiency they imported into North America. Usually they lined hymns—a leader called out a line or two—and the congregation repeated it. Lined hymns could be moaned, spoken, chanted, or sung, either in unison or a multiplicity of pitches; intonation was not important. Every word had a note, and the tempo was slow as worshippers lingered on each note to contemplate the meaning of its word, including *and* and *the*. In the nineteenth century a new trend in hymn singing required significantly improved musicianship, including intonation, lively tempos, and parts or harmony. Singing schools or classes led by a paid singing master, either local or traveling, taught the new style, and, according to an announcement touting one in Gettysburg, promised to fix "sadly deficient" congregational singing owing to inadequately instructed younger members. Singing schools typically lasted a week or two and taught notation and harmony, including singing in syllables (do, re, mi, etc.), and shaped notes (each shape representing a different pitch). Some questioned whether singing schools were appropriate for the Sabbath, but generally they became popular and congregational music became more sophisticated. As Samuel Simon Schmucker urged, the "more generally good tunes can be introduced, the better."[21]

The new musical skills led to choirs. Methodists restricted participation in their choir to church members, a limit suggesting lingering reservations about this innovation, but other congregations showed no inhibitions about the musical upgrade. When St. Francis Xavier got a choir, organized by a priest, Catholics now could hear Psalms and a "high" or sung Mass, further uplifted by the new organ acquired in 1852. Choirs rehearsed, which required a time commitment from members. Presbyterians, for example, granted its choir the use of the gallery to rehearse "as often as desired." Choirs were typically situated in the gallery, removed from the common worshippers, and their harmonies drifted down into the pews, heard but not seen.[22]

Refined music even crept into plain Dunker meetinghouses. True, the Dunkers held back from the new singing style, choirs, and paid choir masters, and the Marsh Creek church book is silent about these innovations. Instead, Brethren approved of "correct singing" done solemnly without distracting from "serious contemplation" of the text, and Yearly Meeting discouraged tunes that encouraged merriment rather than sobriety or the "tickling of the outward ear." In 1825 Yearly Meeting denounced singing schools—they "have nothing to do with the service of God"—and the delegates were especially concerned about members teaching them. Nevertheless, singing schools made inroads into the Dunker fellowship. Later annual gatherings deliberated on the teaching of singing schools, implying that attendance was now acceptable. Then Yearly Meeting said that Brethren were not to instruct in the evenings or on the Sabbath, suggesting that daytime, non-Sunday leadership passed the test. By 1862 the Brethren openly accepted singing schools but warned, especially to the young, about "abuses," and added that the schools should be "conducted orderly." Gradually, then, Dunkers began singing music that tickled the outward ear, and improved musicianship became part of their worship, too.[23]

Only the Associate Reformed resisted upscale music. From their inception they believed that the only acceptable hymns were from the Book of Psalms, and when the mainline Presbyterians adopted the new trends in music, the gap between the two branches of Presbyterianism widened. Otherwise, refined music enjoyed general popularity, except perhaps for the Dunkers, whose ancient order gave it a grudging reception.[24]

Undoubtedly, offering baskets, spittle-free floors, hymns sung in tune, and decorous choirs perched in the gallery, all illumined by gas, represented progress. With the possible exception of the new lighting, all were relatively minor adjustments, but they combined to create a significant priority, plainly visible on Sunday mornings.

CR

Alas, refinement was expensive. When the St. James Lutherans laid the cornerstone for their new worship house, a splendid ceremony with six pastors including college and seminary presidents, they collected an offering, not wishing to miss an opportunity. This small gesture exemplifies the difficulties presented by the high cost of sophistication.[25]

Choirs, for example, usually required a salaried director, but because the ensemble "better[ed] the singing," as the Methodists put it, most congregations in town reluctantly accepted this financial obligation. Presbyterians fought a losing battle in their attempt to find free musical leadership. When their choir director requested remuneration, the trustees, already burdened by a building debt, directed the choir to find someone who would do it without payment. Quickly, however, they yielded, and a few years later the Presbyterians paid their chorister thirty dollars, although they soon dropped him for failure to perform his duties.[26] St. James Lutherans agreed to pay their choir director twenty-five dollars annually because the others received small salaries, and the council felt obligated. For another twenty-five dollars St. James added a young woman to play the melodeon, a small organ powered by foot pedals, on Sundays and at choir rehearsals. A few years later the choir director asked for a pay increase to fifty dollars, which the council denied, claiming that the added cost was unaffordable. After the director made a counteroffer of forty dollars, he lost his job, and the hard-bargaining Lutherans hired someone else. When the St. James choir asked for music books, congregational leadership permitted them only to take a collection upstairs. In other words, the choir received permission to pass the hat among itself and others in the gallery, who were probably there because downstairs pews were unaffordable. Moreover, when the books were paid for, the collections had to end because the congregation was broke and disliked the competition for scarce donations. Even relatively modest burdens for choirs were uneasy yokes.[27]

Raising cash, in fact, was a permanent thorn in the flesh. Fundraising options were limited. Offerings placed in collection bags or baskets went to the deacon's fund to assist the poor. Annual subscriptions and pledges supported the pastor, building projects, and other major expenditures, such as an organ. But a donation pledged was not necessarily a donation paid, and subscription campaigns often fell short of their goals. Thaddeus Stevens promised two hundred dollars to a Presbyterian building fund but actually gave fifty dollars, which the committee eventually accepted and considered the pledge met. A few years later, Presbyterians ran a newspaper notice requesting payment of subscriptions for their building fund, then appointed a collector to dun those owing pledges. For his efforts, the collector retained 10 percent of the cash he collected and 5 percent of notes, which were IOUs. Offerings and subscriptions, then, were inadequate and fell short of paying all the bills.[28]

Fairs, however, returned immediate cash. Women organized these events, and they donated countless hours to produce fancy needlework, such as watch cases and pincushions, and food, including ice cream, floating islands (meringue on custard), pound cake, cold turkey, and oysters, all for sale. Fairs also supported rare public and commercialized roles for females, and the women themselves were part of the attraction. John Nevin of the Reformed Seminary in Mercersburg disliked this. He was disturbed that the "charms" of young women generated sales as much as the value of individual items and that men of all ages had an opportunity to flirt with the "fair actresses." It would be different, he thought, if "only elderly matrons" staged the affairs.[29] Nevin had a point. Most coordinators were married women, but salespersons were usually young and single. "Fair actresses," however, did not feel exploited and, to the contrary, freely noted their ability to pry open manly wallets to pay for penwipers and the like.

The nearly universal assumptions about sex and fairs were secondary, Nevin notwithstanding, and the priority was charity. Fairs raised serious money. One event, a fifty-cent dinner plus "other eatables and fancy articles," held two evenings before Christmas for Christ Lutheran, collected three hundred dollars for "fixing up the church." Samuel Simon Schmucker took his grandchildren to another Christmas fair and instead of surprising them with gifts on Christmas morning, gave them money for purchases at the bazaar. The event ran for four days, and Grandpa Schmucker reported that his grandkids spent several hours per day "feasting their eyes and palates." This occasion involved most of the congregations in town and produced eight hundred dollars income, much of which was profit. Doubtless had Schmucker considered the sexuality of the event awkward, he would have kept his youngest generation home, but the flirtation remained within very limited bounds, enabling young women pushing pincushions and ice cream to reap profit for their favorite causes.[30]

Given that church debts often amounted to several thousand dollars and that one fair could return several hundred, why did congregations not rely on them more? Several consecutive fairs might put a serious dent in debt. Perhaps the number of fairs the town could support had a limit, and the intensive labor involved probably imposed a ceiling on these affairs. But more importantly, men could not imagine significant female contributions to finance, which fell in the male domain, and regardless of the success of fairs, this moneymaker had gender boundaries.[31]

Thus, despite their usefulness, fairs did not pay for large construction projects or retire big debt, and the responsibility of financing refinement fell on pew rent, especially when subscriptions fell short, which was often. As St. James instituted pew rents, it simply explained that "present income is not sufficient to meet the annual expenses." Presbyterians gave their pastor a significant salary increase, but the subscriptions to fund it fell short and they raised pew assessments by 20 percent. When Christ Church Lutherans revalued pew rents, the proposal provoked discussion and amendments, indicating its importance. The German Reformed, who adopted pew rentals relatively late in 1859, simultaneously had a building that needed repair. Catholics also used the pew system. Moreover, the pew system gave refined worshippers a chance to display their finery in choice locations, and the system itself supposedly represented improvement. St. James's leadership asserted that many families sought pews "for their greater convenience and comfort," and they observed that pews were "highly promotive of good order in the house of god." Pew rents paid for progress and were progress.[32]

Pew rents, like subscriptions, were hard to collect. The same collector hired by Presbyterians to chase down unpaid pledges also went after long overdue rents. St. James Lutherans threatened pewholders in default for one year with loss of their seats, then placed a 10 percent surcharge on deadbeats. Christ Church appointed George Swope, president of the Gettysburg Bank, to collect rents and decided that those in arrears for a year's payment would surrender their pew. Unpaid pew rents were a running problem for congregational leadership.[33]

Because fairs, though successful, were supplementary and subscriptions and pew rents often fell short, the steep price of refinement burdened several congregations with debt, especially Presbyterians. In 1843 Presbyterians had a half-finished building, and the building committee informed the trustees that without more funds construction would end. They borrowed $600 from the Bank of Gettysburg. When the sexton wanted extra pay to open the lecture room for choir rehearsal, the trustees rejected the request, claiming that "our funds are required to meet our indebtedness." In 1858 Presbyterians with diminished income from pew rents called a congregational meeting to determine the pastor's wages and how to raise them. A few months later a committee charged to raise $100 towards the pastor's overdue salary reported failure and requested dismissal. The trustees somehow found the amount, but the church still owed more and a bank note due in sixty days made up the difference. Debt became a dominating motif for this congregation.[34]

Both Lutheran congregations also struggled with finances. Christ Church faced an especially difficult situation because it served the seminary and the college, both of which filled seats with students who had no means to pay for them. Some relief came from the seminary, which forgave a debt of $1,000 in exchange for the pew rents along the western side of the building. Basically, the Seminary bought pews for its students and faculty. Additionally, several synods contributed $2,000. The congregation also appealed to seminary alumni, who responded that the debt of $4,000 appeared insurmountable and suggested that Christ Church ask somebody else—the college, the seminary, and the synods—for assistance. Because of ailing finances, tight-fisted economics prevailed at this college church, and the congregational meeting stipulated that all repairs over ten dollars required its approval, an unwieldy requirement that lasted for five years. In 1853 the trustees grandly resolved to eradicate the congregation's remaining debts but two months later faced a crisis over payment on interest due in just one week. Three days prior to this deadline Henry Lewis Baugher asked the congregation to pay his travel expenses to the synodical meeting, where he would request the gathered ministers to assume another portion of the church debt. Baugher received a ten-dollar allowance. In 1858 the congregational meeting authorized a subscription campaign of no less than $250 for three years annually to pay off debts, and in 1861 they agreed to raise another subscription of $1,500 to cover obligations. In a complicated scheme, subscribers would give notes, payable within a few years, with interest paid semiannually, but none of the subscriptions would become due unless the goal of $1,500 was reached.[35]

St. James Lutherans were also mired in red ink. To lighten the load, the congregation sold its parsonage and applied the proceeds to debt. The minister had been renting out the house rather than living in it, so the congregation's action did not create a homeless pastor and he received compensation for the lost income. In 1850 St. James's financial burden increased when its pastor, Benjamin Keller, asked to relinquish congregations in the county (Flohr's and Arendt's) so he could preach in town every Sunday: three Sundays per month in English and one in German. At the moment Keller preached in town twice per month— once in English and once in German—and the two rural congregations heard him on the other two Sundays. Keller claimed that young Lutherans in St. James preferred English and sought it elsewhere on the two Sundays he missed plus his German Sunday. In other words, young St. James Lutherans worshipped with other fellowships three out of four Sabbaths, which was unacceptable. But leaving the two rural congregations would lower Keller's income, and as compensation he asked St. James for another fifty dollars annually, adding that this did not fully make up for lost salary and he desired more. St. James, already in debt, needed another fifty dollars.[36]

But St. James's financial health was anemic, and, accordingly, the congregation struggled to fill its pulpit. During one vacancy two candidates declined offers, and James R. Keiser, who accepted, requested a parsonage, which meant more debt.[37] Nevertheless, Keiser's stay was short. The congregation fell behind in its payments to him, then took a loan of $375 to pay his back salary. Perhaps lost income from the departure of German-speaking congregants, described in a following chapter, added to the financial crisis, but the defectors were low-income and St. James's treasury was always small. In May 1861, Keiser resigned, reminding the congregation that he had warned them of this possibility. He quipped that "I would simply add, that my reasons for resigning are the same as those which recently led Major [Robert] Anderson to evacuate Fort Sumter." Apparently Keiser considered the situation hopeless. Financial stability so eluded St. James that attracting clerical leadership, normally a prerequisite for a flourishing congregation, became difficult.[38]

In short, paying for cupolas, carpets, choirs, chandeliers, curtains, and clergy strained budgets and relations within the fellowships, and debt hung like deadweight around the necks of several congregations. The primary exceptions to the expensive hunger for fashion, style, and improvement were the countercultural

Dunkers, whose largest expense was their Love Feast, and the impoverished AME Zion congregation, which is noticeably absent from this discussion. Poverty inhibited the AME Zion pursuit of refinement. One of their fairs netted only $43.57 profit, a very small sum and little help in the acquisition of gentility. A cash-starved religious society, then, added one more reason for the existence of African Americans on the edge of the community and demonstrates the ability of refinement to define community by leaving some out. Undoubtedly, refinement was costly.[39]

CR

For many, then, beauty and taste were critical to everyday religious life. Facilitated by the new economy, including cash and credit, congregations eagerly pursued gentility by purchasing an abundance of goods. Refinement, however, transcended purchasing power, and with a seminary, a college, new and well-appointed church buildings, a rural cemetery, improved music, one denomination (Methodists) that changed noticeably to accommodate sophistication, and another (Dunkers) visibly opposed to it, at first blush refinement appears pervasive in the spiritual life of this small town. Whether a four-hundred-pound bell shipped by rail or three gaslights rather than two on a chandelier, the quest for sophistication was self-conscious and, in practice, consumed much energy and passion in congregations, including the task of paying for it. While it might be argued that improvement comes naturally and is integral to human nature, the zeal to refine indicates something more. Indeed, the building projects and the trinkets of the market revolution empowered values, including beauty, taste, manners, and comfort. Victorians pursued these concepts in their churches just as they did at home, making refinement deeply ingrained in all of American life, not just in matters of faith. In this regard, Gettysburg religion informs about large American trends.

Divertimento

The Codoris

In 1828 George and Nicholas Cordary, single and brothers, arrived in Gettysburg from Hottviller, France, a town in Lorraine near the border with Germany. In 1850 another brother, Antoine, joined them along with his wife, Magdaleine, their married daughter Catherine (age twenty-six) and her husband, Jean Stab, another daughter, Marie (age twenty), and a son, Jacob (age thirteen). George, Nicholas, and Antoine, French Catholic immigrants, generally moved quickly and comfortably into the American mainstream.

Of the three brothers, Antoine, the most recent arrival, found assimilation the most difficult. He achieved less status than his brothers and lingered somewhat on the margins of the mainstream. True, assimilation worked on Antoine and his family. In 1850 the census called him "Anthony" and the Stabs were "Staub"; in the United States only a few months and already names had been anglicized, whether or not by choice. In 1854 Jean/John became a citizen, and in 1858 Antoine followed. The 1860 census no longer listed Magdaleine as illiterate, as it did in 1850. Perhaps she could now read in English, or maybe the 1850 census taker had simply disliked her foreign characteristics. Yet prosperity was elusive. In 1850 newly arrived Antoine was a "laborer," and by 1860 the enumeration had no occupational designation for him; perhaps the sixty-six-year-old had stopped working. Moreover, after ten years in the United States Anthony and Magdaleine had accumulated very little property ($500 real estate; $100 personal estate). They lived with their son Jacob, an impoverished carpenter, and his wife Barbara, who had very full hands with two children, aged one and four months, and they further shared the residence with a native-born family of three. By 1860 this branch of the family was just getting started in America.[1]

Earlier arrivals George and Nicholas climbed higher. Both married in Pennsylvania and became butchers. George required only one year to take a wife, French-born Regina Wallenberger, but Nicholas, naturalized in 1834, waited longer, perhaps to complete a butcher apprenticeship, and in 1835 he wed Elizabeth Martin, a local woman. It would be interesting to know how Nicholas got his apprenticeship, the gateway into normally a tightly controlled profession. Butchers were well-respected, prosperous tradesmen who avoided the booms and busts of the early nineteenth century because people eat regardless of the economic cycle. Nicholas's son, another George, likewise took up the family business, leaving school at an early age to learn the craft. As testament to their status, the two brothers bought homes; Nicholas's was especially prominent on a centrally located lot that belonged to James Gettys's original town. By 1860 these prosperous lines of the family added servant labor to their households. Second-generation George, son of Nicholas, employed an Irish domestic and a thirteen-year-old Irish boy, who did not attend school and was presumably a child laborer. Also, Nicholas and his brother, George, had adolescent Holland-born boys in their household, Charles Sopan and Detrich Supan, most likely brothers whose surname(s) the census-taker misspelled. Both boys attended school, unusual for apprentices and mere laborers, and perhaps they were part charity cases, part cheap labor. Nicholas's election as a Democratic Party committeeman further documents his success in the community.[2]

Nicholas and Elizabeth particularly flourished. The 1860 census estimated their value at $1,000 in personal estate and $10,000 in real estate, including a farm along the Emmitsburg Road with AME Zion, Dunkers, Lutherans, and Reformed among the neighbors. Their son, George, had $1,200 in personal wealth, also a significant amount.[3]

All of the Codoris participated in the life of St. Francis Xavier parish. They rented pews, and the priest baptized their children. Nicholas, especially active, appears on a membership list as early as 1830, and he served on a building committee for the 1852 building project, keeping plans for the new structure in his home and making them available to the public. Although the Codoris were French, they mixed easily with this German-English congregation. Perhaps growing up in a border region, they spoke German. The 1850 census listed their birthplace as Germany, not France, either yet another census taker's mistake or evidence of German language skills. (The 1860 enumeration got it right and lists them as French-born.)[4]

For the Codoris citizenship indicated official Americanization, but by numerous unofficial markers they were also typically American. Most obviously, their name was Anglicized. Secondly, they enjoyed material stability. Although late-arriving Antoine/Anthony and Magdaleine acquired only a small piece of the American dream by the Civil War, George and Regina did well and Nicholas and Elizabeth did very well. Servant labor eased the burdens of the Codori households. Moreover, the ethnic diversity the Codoris both embodied and encountered was characteristically American. As French Catholics, they embraced a German-English parish, and by 1860 their households included four ethnic groups: Native-born American, French, Dutch, and Irish. Without a doubt, the Codoris exemplified the complexity of Border North society and American diversity.

4 Diversity

Ethnicity and Doctrine

With its first breath the Border North was diverse. Even before William Penn acquired his woods, Swedes and Dutch already inhabited the Delaware Valley, and when Penn arrived, he recruited obscure, oppressed minorities, including non-English, for his self-conscious experiment in tolerance. Native Americans and the involuntary settlement of African Americans further varied the population. By the mid-eighteenth century colonial Pennsylvania boasted of a cultural spectrum broader and brighter than any in the western world. In the next century diversity advanced throughout America, especially with the spread of urbanization and an increase in immigration, but the swath of counties north of the Mason-Dixon Line remained unusually mixed. An uncommonly large variety of religious traditions, including small, nonconformist fellowships, which were legacies of Penn, and ethnic and racial diversity were the critical ingredients in this semimelting pot in which assimilation proceeded sometimes quickly, sometimes slowly, and tolerance reigned mostly but not always.

This chapter draws attention to two particularly strong contributions to diversity in antebellum Gettysburg religion: ethnicity and doctrine. Those unfamiliar with the small town and rural Border North might expect otherwise. After all, the region was overwhelmingly Protestant, and Americanization had approximately a century to work its wonder on minorities. Yet diversity remained powerful, both within the mainstream and on its edges. Germans, the largest ethnic group, pondered how much English to accept, and evangelicalism provoked passionate debate, notably within mainline fellowships. Distinctive doctrines thrived. Dunkers and Catholics were so far from the Protestant center that they occupied outer orbits of Gettysburg religion, although they moved in different, nearly opposite directions. Dunkers, a small, quiet, countercultural fellowship, barely attracted notice, but Catholics, who were countercultural in a different way and often an ethnic minority, drew unwanted attention. Well over a century after William Penn passed from the scene, diversity remained a daily occurrence in the antebellum Border North.

Gettysburg looking east along the Chambersburg Pike, c. 1863. (Courtesy of Adams
County Historical Society.)

CR

Ethnic diversity was obvious to casual observers of Gettysburg. By the antebellum period little remained of Scots-Irish identity, save perhaps for the occasional
reference to the Associate Reformed congregation as "Seceders," but "real, *bona
fide* Pennsylvania Dutchers"[1] were ubiquitous, as a travelling reporter correctly
noted. Dunkers, Lutherans, and Reformed traced denominational lineage to Germany, and St. Francis Xavier Catholic also had many German-born in its pews.
These *bona fide* Pennsylvania Dutchers, or, more accurately, Pennsylvania Germans, had been in North America for several generations and had constructed a
resilient subculture that yielded only gradually to the English mainstream while
more recent German immigrants, especially in St. James Lutheran and St. Francis Xavier, provided fresh impetus for ethnic identity. Like all immigrant minorities to America, Pennsylvania Germans differed, sometimes sharply, over the
absorption of the values and language of the native culture, and they yielded to
Americanization at various paces, which further complicated the community.

Embracing the new nation, its republicanism, and its institutions was the easiest part of assimilation for Pennsylvania Germans. When new German Lutheran immigrants in the Midwest sought merger with the Tennessee Synod, typically American values held by native-born German Americans became insurmountable obstacles. The two groups shared the common theological ground of confessionalism, that is, reliance on catechisms and precise faith statements, but they disagreed on incorporation of their congregations, which the Tennessee Synod, descended from Pennsylvania Germans, considered a dangerous mingling of church and state. Seminaries also blocked merger; the Pennsylvania descendents denounced them as a breeding ground of aristocratic attitudes. Both separation of church and state and fear of aristocratic-minded seminaries stemmed from a populist version of American republicanism, not shared by the newly arrived Lutherans, who were merely confused and insulted over the Tennessee Synod's objections. Another prominent example of German-American acceptance of republicanism was Henry Harbaugh, a German Reformed pastor and Franklin College professor. Harbaugh argued that German Americans embodied republicanism more fully than the English-speaking mainstream. He depicted the Yankee, Puritan-based version of American democracy as intolerant and tinged with crackpots, citing the Salem Witch Trials, Mormons, Universalists, and the spirit-rapping Fox sisters, and, for good measure, he added that victims of New England irrationalism found comfort among tolerant and rational Pennsylvania Germans. Harbaugh suggested that while Pennsylvania Germans remained ethnic Germans, they nonetheless internalized American republicanism more completely than Anglo Americans. Pennsylvania German political values had become thoroughly mainstream.[2]

Language was a more difficult question of assimilation. For some the transition from German to English was gradual and as comfortable as the acceptance of republican ideas. Dunkers, for example, moved steadily and gracefully, if unhurriedly, from German to English. Requests for Yearly Meeting minutes in German continued until 1889, and in the late nineteenth century German language hymnals still came off the press, suggesting a very slow German death, especially in eastern Pennsylvania with its heavy concentration of Dunkers. But many Dunkers sent their children to the new common schools, where they absorbed the dominant English culture, and unlike the Lutherans and Reformed, whose German impulse received heavy reinforcement from recent immigrants, the Brethren, including Marsh Creek, were almost entirely native-born. By mid-century, then, denominational leaders published primarily in English. Dunkers released their first English hymnal in 1791, and the first denominational periodical, *The Gospel Visitor*, begun in 1851, was also English. Likewise, the Marsh Creek congregational church book is all English. Peter Nead, a well-known conservative Dunker, preached and wrote in the mainstream language, which must have made it more palatable to other conservatives. In contrast, German-language publications were short-lived. The *Gospel Visitor's* German counterpart, *Evangelische Besuch*, never acquired more than three hundred subscribers and died in 1861. Another German-language paper surfaced in the late nineteenth century, but it, too, was fleeting. The transition to English evolved with relatively little rancor, and Yearly Meeting ruled on it only twice, both times encouraging bilingualism in order to "preach the Gospel to every nation" (Matthew 28:19). Once it was asked if only a few English speakers were present (an indication of the prevalence of German), should worship still be in both languages, and it replied yes, although adding that English should get minimal attention if most worshippers were non-English. Another inquiry request guidance if some present did not speak German, others did not understand English, and still others opposed bilingual worship in principle? Again, the delegates affirmed bilingualism, this time an implied rebuke to those favoring only German. These are the only times before the Civil War that Yearly Meeting considered language, and the lack of time spent on this topic by the annual gathering, for whom no aspect of faith was too small to ponder, indicates the overall smoothness of the transition.[3]

Among Lutherans and Reformed, language sparked more extensive debate. Some recognized that the linguistic tide was turning, and they were ready to run with it. Advocates of English pointed out that congregations once predominantly German now required more English, which seemed the "natural and inevitable course of events," and they complained that Germans were too "exclusive," assimilating much more slowly than among other groups. English-language advocates observed that in hindsight holding tightly to German for too long had probably damaged the faith. Appealing to the next generation was important. One English proponent lamented that some "labor under the hallucination that children born of German parents in America are also Germans," but, he maintained, in reality those born in America were Americans. Ministers who did not understand this, who preached in German though they were capable in English, sent the next generation elsewhere in search of the language of their birth. One pastor confessed he was "German from the crown of my head to the soles of my feet," and that he "cleave[d] to my mother tongue with my whole soul." He also admitted to having an accent: "Every word I attempt to utter in English betrays the Galilean in me." Even his "external appearance" revealed his German-ness; apparently Germans still looked different, or so he thought. Yet, he continued, he fervently hoped that the current young generation would be converted through English. For many Lutherans and Reformed, English was the language of the moment and of the future.[4]

Those, however, who would pilot their faith towards English were not necessarily ready to cast German overboard. A call for Lutheran ministers in central Pennsylvania specified for preachers in both English and German. Philip Schaff, the German Reformed Mercersburg theologian, urged a blended "Anglo-German" intellectual and religious culture that would "enrich" both traditions. Unwilling to surrender German, Schaff, a Swiss-born immigrant, complained that "Anglicisms and barbarisms" mixed with different dialects had made his native language "almost unintelligible and characterless gibberish." He urged German churches to preserve the "German spirit," which, he said, must be done more earnestly to avoid absorption by English denominations. He protested that preachers who are English-only did not fully understand the church and would "transfer her over into the hands either of Presbyterianism or Arminian Methodism." But while part of Schaff's heart still beat in German, he also believed that Germans needed to accept Americanization. He called for a "living conjunction with American life" in which German Americans contributed to American progress and influenced their English-speaking neighbors. The alternative, he said, was "petrification." As evidence of beneficial Americanization, he noted that English-language congregations gave more generously to support religious institutions than German ones and that German-speakers lagged in education; there were no German colleges in the United States. Moreover, Schaff claimed that Anglo-Germans were the most faithful, generous, and effective leaders of the German Reformed. Schaff predicted that one day Christian unity would prevail, but he hoped that the distinctive qualities of English and German churches would remain. Schaff wanted rich bilingualism, which meant preserving German.[5]

Henry Harbaugh also endorsed the German language, more colorfully than Schaff. Harbaugh created a list of the seven great "learned languages" that not only included German and English but elevated Pennsylvania German, a vernacular dialect sometimes called Pennsylvania Dutch, to this lofty honor, further evidence of his love for his German heritage. (Other languages on Harbaugh's learned list were Greek, Hebrew, Latin, and German Reformed.) Moreover, Harbaugh penned nostalgic poetry in the language of *bona fide* Pennsylvania Dutchers; "Heemweh" (Homesickness) and "Der Alt Schulhaus an der Krick" (The Old Schoolhouse by the Creek) became his two most popular. Harbaugh was hardly a narrow-minded reactionary pining for the old country but, instead, a committed bilinguist, which he considered a higher form of intellectual life. But Harbaugh's ancestors had been in Pennsylvania since 1736—he was born in nearby Franklin County—and his attachment to German and Pennsylvania German testifies to the endurance of the old country language among those with lengthy native-born lineages. In some circles, German had nine lives.[6]

Consequently, many official proceedings of Lutherans and German Reformed were bilingual. They printed meeting minutes in both languages, always more English than German. In Zion's Classis, a south-central Pennsylvania regional organization of German Reformed congregations, fifty-five English-version copies of the synodical report went to congregations and twenty-five in German, a reasonable barometer of the strength of the two languages among fellowships nearest to Gettysburg. Zion's Classis kept its records in both languages but mostly English. Occasionally the book switches to German, though in English-style calligraphy rather than the German *schrift*. Likewise, bilingual public worship was common at annual synodical meetings. In 1859 Lutheran preachers gathered in Hanover held German communion in the morning and English in the evening. The German Reformed Synod generally worshipped in English but included German. An 1857 assembly began its first day with a service that consisted of a German hymn, a German prayer, and a German sermon, then an English hymn, an English prayer, and an English sermon. The Sunday morning communion service, especially important, was in German, but the other preaching was in English. Another annual gathering of the Synod, however, featured all-English worship except for a German prayer. Routine bilingualism hints at peaceful coexistence between English and German.[7]

Other times, however, German and English were more contentious. One observer noticed that some youth spoke German but could not read it and, *vice-versa*, others read English but could not speak it. In these situations, aspiring converts would recite the Catechism in one language, then "try to comprehend it in another." Dunkers, as noted previously, similarly complained of circumstances when the language gap was nearly unbridgeable. Henry Harbaugh opposed public schools because they facilitated assimilation. In 1820 ethnic identity, especially language, figured in a controversy that developed over the new German Reformed seminary. All Reformed agreed that theologically educated preachers would help preserve their German heritage, and all sought to avoid inroads by English-speaking revivalists: evidence of lingering Germanness. But critics of the proposed seminary disliked its exclusive rights over clerical education, ending the practice of preachers educating a few theology students on the side, and issues of ethnicity stirred up a storm. Detractors opposed locating the seminary in Frederick, Maryland, which they claimed was too English, and they distrusted the first professor, a Dutch Reformed pastor from New York City, whose German they charged was insufficient. The anger was deep enough to spawn a rival synod, the Synod of Free and Independent German Reformed Church of Pennsylvania, commonly known as the Free Synod. (Adams County congregations remained with the old synod.) When in the mid-1860s the Reformed reconciled, the Free Synod returned to the German Reformed after deciding not to merge with the Dutch Reformed because they were not German. Ethnicity, then, loomed large for many Lutherans and Reformed.[8]

Occasionally language caused congregational schism. In 1852 German Catholics in York separated, but they kept the priest, James Cotting. Likewise in 1852 in York, Trinity Reformed divided between those who favored English and those who wanted German. Four hundred members stayed with the English language group while 250 formed the new German fellowship, named Zion's. The split was not amicable. The two congregations argued about how to divide the property, and eventually the Classis concluded that efforts to settle the dispute were pointless. Zion's continued all German until 1878 when it allowed English in the Sunday evening service, and then English also quickly entered the Sunday school. Sunday morning services, however, worshipped in German until the 1890s. German could split fellowships.[9]

In Gettysburg recent-arriving, German-speaking Lutheran immigrants also formed a breakaway fellowship. Worship in Gettysburg was seldom in the language in which these newcomers had learned the faith. Christ Church was all English, St. James provided German services only once per month, and the German Reformed preached, prayed, and sung in German once every three months. In 1859, then, frustrated German-language Lutherans withdrew from St. James and organized their own congregation, St. Paul's, and even though the St. James pastor balked at the situation, the synod appointed a minister for them. In 1861 St. Paul's reported the addition of a few members, pastoral visits to Germans in the poorhouse, the beginning of a German Sunday school, and well-attended services, perhaps an embellishment. The congregation donated three dollars and six cents to the synod for missions. The all-German congregation was small, with communicants typically numbering in the forties, but it functioned.[10]

Consensus, therefore, never existed over where to draw the line between the two cultures or how much of each to accept. Among native-born German Americans, such as Henry Harbaugh, the language of their ancestry hung on tenaciously, and recent immigrants contributed to the demand for it. But English steadily gained, and large portions of Gettysburg religion were comfortable with linguistic diversity. German persevered among Dunkers, but they moved comfortably, if slowly, toward English. St. James and the German Reformed still had German worship although not often enough to please recent immigrants. Some still gripped German tightly, but many others had a foot in both linguistic camps, adopting the language of Americanization without abandoning the language of their heritage, and all contributed complexity to the community.

CR

Ethnicity created variety and occasional dispute, but doctrine was genuinely divisive, especially evangelicalism among mainstream Protestants. Like a great fire, from the eighteenth century onward evangelicalism and revivalism, the means to spread evangelicalism, gained strength, singeing Calvinism, catechisms, confessions, and other traditional forms of conversion and consuming an ever-greater portion of the American religious landscape, yet falling far short of consensus. Although the astonishing surge in evangelicalism had peaked by the Civil War, religion of the heart nevertheless retained both a passionate following and a camp of bitter opponents.[11]

Denominationally, evangelicalism was most closely associated with Methodism. Although Methodist revivals and camp meetings declined, as described previously, decorum and respectability were as responsible for the change as theology. Methodists did not doubt the correctness of born-again religion, but they evolved from sudden, dramatic, emotional conversion through revivals and camp meetings to a gradual, nurturing conversion process, heavily dependent on catechisms. They shouted less. Revivalism also generated little controversy among the AME Zion. No record exists of AME Zion awakenings in Gettysburg, but hard evidence could easily have fallen through the cracks of their thin records. Nationally, black Methodists embraced evangelicalism as warmly as white Methodists, maybe more so, and seasons of revival among the Gettysburg AME Zion were quite likely. Wesleyans, then, quibbled little over evangelicalism.

Other fellowships, however, quarreled, often bitterly, over the theology of free will conversion and the use of revivals. From the beginning of North American evangelicalism, Presbyterians, for example, openly clashed over whether revivals were compatible with the Calvinist predestinarian system. Eighteenth-century Old Side Presbyterians, who opposed revivals, maintained the traditional position that humans were so depraved that contribution to their own salvation was impossible, even through revivals, and that God had predetermined the elect. But the New Side movement squeezed free will into predestination by saying that God's decision to save some was based on foreknowledge of human choice. Other disagreements between Old Side and New Side were over assurance received by those saved and the presence of emotion accompanying conversion—both favored by the New Side—and the education of ministers, which the Old Side hoped to control. Additionally, the Old Side–dominated synod assumed the right to approve preachers, a strategy to curb the growth of revivalist sentiments, but this stepped on a traditional right of the presbytery, a more local organization. In the late eighteenth century Upper Marsh Creek leaned toward the New Side, and the synod rejected one of its choices for pastor because he drifted from Old Side orthodoxy.[12]

In the next century this spat persisted among Presbyterians. When one prominent New School (now New School rather than New Side) theologian, George Duffield, published a book, *Spiritual Life, or Regeneration* (1832), the Presbytery of Carlisle, which included Gettysburg, condemned it, and soon Duffield moved to Detroit. Slavery added fuel to Presbyterian internal dissent. Antislavery sentiment ran stronger in the New School, while conservative religion and conservative social policy worked well together for the Old School. In 1837 the Old School gained control of the General Assembly, the national Presbyterian body, and expelled several New School synods. The following year the assembly met again, and in a meeting that included shoving, shouting, and other displays of anger, evangelical Presbyterians departed and created the Presbyterian Church (New School).[13]

Revivalism also provoked doctrinal diversity among Lutherans and the German Reformed. This represented change from colonial Pennsylvania, when the two largest German denominations practiced moderate revivalism based on Continental Pietism, the European version of evangelicalism. Although colonial-era Lutheran and Reformed Pietists taught the doctrine of the new birth, they retained respect for traditional confessions and authority and developed their own catechisms, used vigorously with children and adults alike. Catechisms provided a methodical path to God as participants gradually learned the faith rather than achieved conversion through the quick, emotional, free will choice so often preferred by revivalists. Particularly influential was Henry M. Mühlenberg, the great organizer of North American Lutheranism, who epitomized moderate Pietism. Mühlenberg, who trained at the Lutheran University of Halle, a center of German Pietism, respected the intellect and catechized extensively, but he also emphasized simple, heart-felt faith, unfettered of intellectualism and attractive to common folk, hallmarks of evangelicalism. Eighteenth-century Lutherans and Reformed, then, broadly agreed on born-again religion with restraints.[14]

In the nineteenth century many Lutherans and German Reformed continued to practice evangelicalism. A German Reformed member spoke for many when he listened to the sermon of an Old School Presbyterian and pronounced it doctrinally sound but still flawed because it was "directed almost exclusively to the intellect, and . . . therefore, one-sided." Many Lutherans and German Reformed embraced the waves of revival that swept over American society, praising the anxious bench (designated seating for those especially concerned about their sin and desiring conversion) and protracted meetings, even though these self-styled New Measures called for sinners to come to Jesus in a sequence that upset orderly catechism. Zion's Classis affirmed revivals as "'a set time to Zion' when God pours out his spirit more copiously than in ordinary times" and when the "impenitent are truly awakened." Border North Lutherans often cited specific moments when they believed that God's spirit did indeed pour more copiously. One report celebrated a revival that went on for five weeks, another stressed that the Lutheran Church was a *"revival church,"* and yet another rejoiced over a successful use of protracted meetings. One congregation held a month-long series of services that awakened members who were backbenchers rather than sweeping up nonmembers, but the revival nonetheless left an aftermath of standing-room-only services, a swollen treasury, and a Sunday school that overflowed its basement location. In some measure, Lutherans and German Reformed were indeed revival churches.[15]

Yet Lutheran and Reformed revivalism still stressed moderation. They frowned on uninvited traveling preachers intruding into the territory of settled ministers, even if the local shepherds struggled to stir their flocks. Itinerants were a favored practice of the larger revivalist movement, beginning with George Whitefield in colonial America, but no matter the circumstances, outside preachers with doctrinal innovations were unwelcome among moderate Lutherans and Reformed. Additionally, although the Lutheran and Reformed version of the new birth included emotion, the noise and chaos preferred by unrestrained revivalists was most unwanted by the moderates. John William Runkel, for example, who pastored the Gettysburg German Reformed from 1819 to 1823, approved of the conversion theology of Methodism, but the "crying, shouting, clapping their hands, and stamping" offended him. A Lutheran pastor warned to keep the congregation seated and not allow persons to crowd around the anxious bench, all praying at once. "The brother who leads in prayer," he advised, "should be distinctly heard, and all the rest should keep quiet." Samuel Simon Schmucker embodied moderate revivalism. Schmucker openly embraced Lutheranism's Pietist heritage, and he encouraged catechumens to "find their hearts" and to seek a religious experience in addition to mastery of the catechism. But he also honored the old Lutheran confessions and labored to compile rational arguments that proved miracles and prophecies and to demonstrate the intellectual consistency of the Bible. Many Lutherans and Reformed toned down born-again religion.[16]

As an antebellum edition of moderate Pietism persisted, Old School Lutherans and Reformed gained strength. The conservative response emphasized institutional and traditional means of conversion over the emotional moments of decision at revivals and Americanization. Specifically, conservatives demanded loyalty to the sixteenth-century confessions, which they considered errorless, and members of the Old School movement were often called "confessionalists" for their adherence to these historic faith statements. In defense of confessions, Charles Porterfield Krauth, a Lutheran theologian, exclaimed, "Must Lutheranism be shorn of its glory to adapt it to our times or our land?" He answered his own question: "I am first a Lutheran and then an American." Evangelism came under further criticism for pulling Germans into the American-Protestant mainstream. John Nevin, of the Reformed Seminary in Mercersburg, accused Lutheran and Reformed revivalists of doing their best to have the German denominations absorbed by the Methodists.[17]

Mostly, however, the Old School attacked revivalism for abandoning traditional methods of conversion in favor of emotional techniques and born-again doctrine more common to larger American Protestantism. Charles Philip Krauth, Charles Porterfield's father and President of Pennsylvania College, called for "pure, unadulterated Lutheranism," by which he meant salvation through preaching, catechism, the confessions, and the sacraments of baptism and communion. In particular, the Old School scorned disruptive worship for creating a false sense of conversion and for encouraging converts to "rest their hopes of salvation upon themselves," a criticism of the evangelical emphasis on personal decision and human merit. The New Measures became frequent targets. One critic denounced these innovations as a "convulsing influence," and John Nevin published a book, *The Anxious Bench* (1844), to assail the entire system in which the famous special pew was merely the best-known method. In 149 angry pages Nevin ridiculed revivalism as "mechanical" and "shallow" with a natural inclination toward disorder, noise, commotion, and preaching that was "rude," "coarse," and "vapid." Revivalism led to "the whole wildfire of fanaticism, including the 'holy laugh' and the 'holy grin.'" Nevin was convinced that the excitement associated with popular revivalism inspired irreverence and destroyed the catechetical system. Others agreed. The German Reformed Synod of Eastern Pennsylvania concluded that "extraordinary storms" of revivals produce "extraordinary change" but not an "extraordinary harvest." Rather than the wildfire of fanaticism and storms, Old School German Americans cherished "ordinary means" of conversion. The church and its ordinances—"channels of life," according to Zion's Classis—were superior to "merely human devised means," another slap at the New Measures. Christ had designated methods that relied on the church for implementation, and these means brought conversion through order and stability. "God is not in the whirlwind, the fire, and the storm," said the Classis, "but in the still small voice of the spirit." The "ordinary course of nature," not sudden tempests, "breaks the death-grasp of winter." The most prominent German American opponents of revivalism were Nevin and Philip Schaff, also of the Reformed Seminary, who developed what was called the "Mercersburg Theology" to express their confessionalism. An antebellum version of old time religion made a comeback among Pennsylvania Germans.[18]

Evangelicalism and revivalism created schism for Lutherans, as they did for Presbyterians. Old School Lutherans created their own synods of Tennessee and Ohio, but these connections had congregations scattered throughout Lutheran America, including the Border North. Despite affirming a role for revivals, Zion's Classis (Reformed) was nonetheless heavily Old School, but the Lutheran Seminary, led by Schmucker, leaned toward evangelicism, providing both perspectives with proponents in Gettysburg.

By the 1850s emotional conversion passed its peak in popularity, especially in towns and even among Methodists as refined religion gained favor. But revivals still warmed many Protestant hearts, and emotional conversion still generated heated debate, bringing not only diversity but also division within the mainstream of Border North religion.

℞

Dunkers, thoroughly outside the mainstream, were one of the most uniquely shaped pieces in the mosaic of Gettysburg religion. Especially zealous to restore the primitive New Testament church, they stressed more than most the separation of believers from worldly sin and unity among believers within the fellowship. Dunkers expected members of the faith community to accept the fellowship's collective discernment on how to avoiding corrupting it with worldliness. Consequently, the Brethren, as they preferred to call themselves, were conspicuous outsiders and embraced a particularly unusual doctrine.[19]

As Dunkers pursued their related goals of separation and unity, they did many things differently. Their arms-length approach to the consumer revolution, especially plain dress and untrimmed beards without mustaches, set them apart from the fashionable middle class. A variety of other practices already discussed, including nonviolence, unadorned meetinghouses, and trine immersion baptism, further contributed to unusualness. Additionally, Dunkers' Yearly Meetings kept the Brethren away from camp meeting revivalism and prohibited practices associated with it, such as prayer with uplifted hands or the anxious bench. Dunkers were moderate Pietists, and, like Lutheran and Reformed moderates, they believed in free will conversion and religion of the heart, but equally essential were contemplation of conversion and its consequences, which they could not detect in emotional conversion and the disorder of camp meetings. From consumer spending to the baptism pool to prayer with hands folded rather than uplifted, Dunkers went their own way.[20]

The ministry was another striking contrast between Dunkers and others. Dunkers chose "free ministers," as they called their ordained leadership, from among the congregation, and congregational council, including women, elected them. Bishops and assemblies of clergy, who commonly controlled ordination in other traditions, had no role among the Dunkers. Ministers worked their way up the ranks, beginning with exhorters, who commented on the sermons of others, then ministers, who preached, and elders. Each congregation had several at each stage, except maybe elder, and if more than one elder existed, the senior elder supervised the congregation as elder-in-charge. Free ministers served without pay and kept their secular vocations, in contrast to the other preachers in town, who served fulltime and were compensated accordingly. Even the AME Zion congregation, on the bottom of Gettysburg's economic ladder, dug deep to pay its pastor.[21]

The Dunkers' most cherished ordinance, Love Feast, was also unique. Brethren Love Feast celebrated the Lord's Supper with heavy assistance from intense literalism. Because I Corinthians 11:20 describes the event in the Upper Room as a "supper" rather than a "morning or noon meal," Dunkers insisted that this service only occur in the evening. Similarly, as Jesus washed the feet of the disciples prior to the meal, Dunker commemorations of the Lord's Supper always included feetwashing. Communion concluded the service because Jesus broke the bread and distributed the wine after the meal. Congregations usually held Love Feasts in the spring and the fall. The fall event, the high point of the religious year, attracted visitors, sometimes in large numbers, including Brethren from neighboring congregations, unbaptized children, and non-Dunkers observing from the side. Other groups, particularly Moravians and Methodists, also practiced a Love Feast, but only the Brethren adhered to a rigid, literal recreation of the Lord's Supper, including feetwashing.[22]

Conformity to the fellowship was just as important as nonconformity to the world. Dunkers did outsiderness together, not individually, and those who toyed with their own definitions of nonconformity or who drifted from guidelines laid down by the faith community threatened harmony and risked contaminating the fellowship with worldliness. The Yearly Meeting provided uniform interpretation of God's law across the denomination, but the local society did the heavy lifting and applied the annual gathering's policy through discipline. Excommunication was a last resort, coming at the end of a process that included admonition and visits from ministers, spelled out in Matthew 18, but if that failed, Marsh Creek was willing to withhold certain privileges, such as Love Feast, or expel.[23] Yet, reconciliation came quickly if council deemed repentance heartfelt. Thomas Devers, expelled for "taking money not his own," repented, was restored, and received a certificate enabling him to transfer membership to a congregation near to where he moved. Congregational council suspended two members for intemperance because both furnished alcohol at a barn raising, thereby contributing to public drunkenness, including one of the suspended brothers. Both apologized and were restored to full membership. Discipline, therefore, maintained a unified path to outsiderness, but forgiveness was readily available for those willing to reassume conformity to the fellowship's definition of nonconformity.[24]

Sometimes Dunker discipline made them appear nearly identical to other Protestants. As with other congregations in town, marital discord, sexual transgressions, and public drunkenness resulted in suspensions or expulsion. What made Dunkers different was their broader definition of worldliness. Matilda Beecher dressed in the "Sunday suit" of her recently deceased husband and then attempted to frighten her neighbors after dark. Council considered this and "several other things," unspecified, as "very unbecoming." She told the visiting ministers that they wasted their effort and that her last name had changed; perhaps she now associated with the faith of a new husband. Beecher's sense of humor was an unusual reason for discipline, but the "other things" likely pertained to dress or another aspect of the ancient order, perhaps hair, jewelry, household furnishings, dancing, card playing, or attendance at amusements, and her lack of interest in reconciliation with the fellowship was the final blow. Council concluded that Beecher's disregard for unity damaged the body, and she was excommunicated.[25]

With the Dunkers' emphasis on unity, disharmony between individual members troubled congregational waters, more so than in other meetinghouses. Deacon visits to families prior to Love Feast assured that the brothers and sisters of the fellowship were at peace with each another and with the society in general. When discord surfaced, leaders sought concord, either by mediating personal disputes or by pressuring or persuading an independent-minded soul to yield to the wisdom of the community.

At bottom, the Dunkers maintained sharper and more numerous boundaries with the mainstream than the other fellowships, and they contributed a diversity found in few other regions, especially the South and New England. When they entered the baptismal waters, dressed plainly, shaved their mustaches but left beards untrimmed, shunned camp meetings, sat on benches rather than pews, listened to unpaid preachers whom they had elected, washed feet, voted to expel, and voted to forgive, they knew that they appeared odd to others. That was how they wanted it.

But in another sense Dunkers fit well with the region because small, German-heritage, nonconformist groups like them were common in southern Pennsylvania. Mennonites and Amish, for example, were Anabaptist cousins of the Dunkers with similar concepts of nonconformity to the world and obedience to the faith community. Although Moravians were rapidly moving into the mainstream, their outsiderness, especially through communalism, was still very recent, and they retained distinctive practices, especially music and Love Feasts. Small German evangelical fellowships—the River Brethren, the Church of God, the Evangelical Association, and the United Brethren—were less countercultural, especially the latter three, but they, too, contributed to variety, and the Quakers, an English-heritage, nonconformist society, further added to the regional congregation of minorities. With all due respect to refinement, which created a potent mainstream, from another perspective oddness, exemplified by the Dunkers, was almost ordinary in the Border North.

⌘

Catholics joined Dunkers on the edges of the mainstream. Like Dunkers, Catholics offered doctrinal diversity, but they were much more frightening to guardians of the mainstream. Dunkers in Gettysburg and throughout the Border North were small, Protestant, nonpolitical, and nonthreatening, but Gettysburg Catholics were the local representatives of a strong international organization with a long history of conflict with Protestantism. Catholics tested tolerance in this diverse town.

Like the Lutherans and Reformed, St. Francis Xavier made the town more ethnically diverse. Many of its priests were foreign-born: Michael Dougherty (1829–44) and Miles Gibbons (1845–47) were Irish; George Villiger (1848) and J. B. Cotting (1849–53), Swiss; and Francis Xavier DeNeckere (1853–58), Belgian.

Parishioners, especially young adults, also included immigrants, such as Jean Staub, and preaching was in English and German.[26]

Additionally, Roman Catholic theology clashed with Protestantism on a number of fronts. Catholics, for example, disagreed with the evangelical Protestant assumption that the saved were assured of salvation and could not backslide. Catholics rejected the Protestant tenet saved once, saved forever.

Optimism about human nature further distinguished Catholic doctrine, especially from Old School Presbyterians and confessionalist Lutherans and Reformed. Catholics agreed with evangelicals that humans had the capacity to choose between sin and redemption and that they were capable of works and could improve themselves. Unlike most Protestants, however, Catholics taught that works prepared for salvation. When Protestants charged salvation by works, Catholics responded that the merit derived from works only comes from God's grace and that the works themselves have no inherent value. But, undeniably, Catholics who worried about their eternal life thought about human ability and works more than anxious Protestants.[27]

Francis DeNeckere exemplified the Catholic emphasis on human capacity. In one sermon DeNeckere exhorted Gettysburg Catholics to climb the ladder into heaven rather than descend it into hell, implying that their effort and ability counted. In another sermon, he employed the parable of the 10,000 ducats, which he changed to a story about three sick men who wanted "perfect health." In DeNeckere's version of the parable, the three sick men called a physician. The doctor told the first man to give up wine, but the ailing man replied that he liked wine too much to do that. When the physician suggested watering down the drink, the sick man refused because "water aggravates my stomach." The second sick man would only take powder and plaster but not medicine, including a purgative, or a bleeding. DeNeckere suggested that this man accepted some of the requirements for healing but not all. The third ill man followed instructions completely—"drain blood, apply fire"—and he was healed. The priest concluded that a few good works are insufficient: "To be saved from sickness, other things than powder are necessary." DeNeckere demanded total commitment—take all the medicine, not just some—and implicit in his instruction was that humans had the ability to climb the ladder and to take medicine, that is, to do good works and make an effort.[28]

DeNeckere's medicine was the sacraments, which played a larger role in Catholicism than in most Protestant traditions. The seven Catholic sacraments—baptism, communion, marriage, ordination, penance or confession, and extreme unction (rites for the gravely ill)—stemmed from recognition that human ability notwithstanding, men and women still depended on God's grace, which came through the sacraments. Lutheran and Reformed confessionalists might generally agree on the importance of sacraments, but Protestants typically only had two: baptism and communion. DeNeckere pointed out that God uses many means to make salvation attainable, and he sternly warned St. Francis Xavier worshippers to partake of all the sacraments. Protestants, especially evangelicals, did not similarly emphasize the sacraments as a vital pathway to salvation.[29]

Also, Catholics were more mystical than most Protestants. Catholic emphasis on Mary was especially controversial. A defense of Marianism articulated by the Border North bishops of Philadelphia (Francis Kenrick) and Pittsburgh (Michael O'Connor) fell back on the mystery of the incarnation and the immaculate conception, which, they asserted, made devotion to the Mother of Jesus quite reasonable. Although Protestants charged that Catholics elevated Mary above Christ, the bishops countered that redemption did not require Mary's consent, that the Book of Genesis did not provide textual evidence for Marianism, and that the tradition had not always been clear. For the bishops, at least, Marianism had limits, but it was widespread at the popular level. The Eucharist, or communion, also depended heavily on the supernatural as the bread and cup became Christ's body and blood, and Catholics thought that Protestants were simply too dismissive of the miraculous in this sacrament.[30]

Devotionalism was yet another characteristic particular to Catholicism. Devotions were expressions of piety centering on one aspect of the faith, for example, the passion of Jesus, and they led worshippers to focus their spiritual growth on one person, such as Jesus, Mary, or a saint. DeNeckere was devoted to the Virgin Mary, or B.V.M. (Blessed Virgin Mary), in his notes. Devotionals were most often said privately, but priests also performed them in the church. Promoted by the Papacy, spoken in the vernacular rather than the Latin of the Mass, and fueled by immigration, devotionals became popular by the 1840s. Protestants had no equivalent to this religious exercise for laymen and -women.[31]

Finally, Catholic doctrine did not mix well with American republicanism. In the early nineteenth century Protestants did away with raised pulpits and built sanctuaries that placed the preacher close to the congregation to emphasize his (always male) ability to connect with the congregation. Catholics, on the other hand, gave no ground on clerical authority. As Protestant clergy moved closer to their audience in the quasi-theatrical setting, Catholic priests performed Mass in a low voice in Latin with their backs to the congregation and in a language few in the congregation understood. The only persons who said anything in response were altar boys, who also spoke Latin, though often with a struggle. Missals, which were translations of the Mass, appeared in the 1820s and made the service more intelligible to the congregation, but Sunday morning worship remained undemocratic. Additionally, Catholic governance repudiated republican values. Traditional Catholicism emphasized a chain of command established by God that extended from Rome and the Pope through the cardinals and bishops to the parish priest. This structure guided weak humans toward God. Human merit, while helpful, had strict limits, and improvement, that is, progress toward salvation, was most likely when those in the pews obeyed those in the chancel. Moreover, as many Protestants became more democratic, the Roman Catholic hierarchy enjoyed a revival in authority and respect. Rather than absorbing republicanism, early nineteenth-century American Catholics re-emphasized Papal authority. More monarchical than republican, this system supplanted an eighteenth-century Catholic experiment with a more rational and democratic faith, and local committees of laity now stepped aside in favor of the clergy. The trustee of St. Francis Xavier, for example, was the St. Joseph's College of Philadelphia, a stark contrast to the local lay leaders who served as trustees for Protestant property, and although a building committee of laypersons executed fundraising and construction, they functioned "by order of Rev. Cotting," as a newspaper notice informed, which left no doubt about his authority over the committee. The Catholics' top-down approach made them more European and less American and ran counter to bottom-up republicanism increasingly popular with the American mainstream. With a salvation process neither Calvinist nor evangelical and with greater emphasis on the mystical, the sacraments, private devotional life, and hierarchy than Protestants, Catholicism carved a distinctive niche in Gettysburg and the Border North.[32]

Catholic-style diversity was inflammatory. Some conspicuous contributors to the range of religion in Gettysburg, especially the Associate Reformed and Dunkers, experienced unlimited tolerance, and although the immigrant, German-speaking Lutherans were frustrated at St. James, the synod recognized their upstart congregation. Catholics, however, were less fortunate. Anti-Catholicism had always been deeply embedded in America; the first British North American anti-Catholics lived in Jamestown, Virginia, or perhaps on Roanoke Island. After independence from Britain, nativism emerged as a convenient partner for anti-Catholicism, and the two became nearly synonymous, ebbing and flowing but always present. The latest flood tide of anti-Catholic nativism had been in the 1830s, and during the antebellum period another wave swept over America, including Gettysburg and the Border North.

Several trends and events triggered the antebellum version of anti-Catholic nativism. Immigration surged at a rate five times greater than previously, peaking between 1850 and 1855, and many of the recent immigrants were Irish and German Catholics, who stamped their faith with a foreign identity and were often very visible and robust in urban enclaves. Catholicism was insignificant in 1800 but between 1830 and 1860 its membership increased by almost 900 percent to become the largest denomination in 1860. Other irritants were a conflict over Protestant-dominated public schools, the Catholic custom of having the bishop hold title to church property rather than a board of trustees, and the Catholic threat to recent temperance victories. A lengthy visit in 1853 by a tactless, hard-line Papal Nuncio, and President Franklin Pierce's appointment of James Campbell, a Philadelphia Catholic, to the position of Postmaster General, whose *demesne* included thousands of patronage positions, further rubbed raw Catholic-Protestant tensions.[33]

The political vehicle for antebellum anti-Catholicism and nativism became a third party, the American. Far better known as the Know Nothings, the secret society acquired its popular name from the response of its adherents—"I know nothing"—to inquiries about their membership and party activities. Know Nothingism, like many third-party movements, took America by surprise, and more factors than immigration and Catholicism undoubtedly contributed to its quick rise. For those concerned about unsettling economic change, Know Nothings offered protection from immigrant competition for jobs, and for those in despair over the general health of American politics, the new party promised reform, especially of the sorry state of politics plagued by manipulation, back room dealing, patronage, and sectionalism. Nevertheless, deteriorating politics and dangerous sectionalism notwithstanding, Know Nothings fed primarily on traditional American anti-Catholicism and the promise to protect the Protestant republic. Know Nothings restricted their membership to the native-born of Protestant parentage and pledged to support only native-born Protestants for public office. Although the Know Nothings drew heavily from Whigs, Democrats also contributed to the movement, and the ability to attract support from all major Protestant denominations made Know Nothingism a cross-section of much, but not all, of American society.[34]

Know Nothings scrambled politics in Pennsylvania. In the 1854 statewide elections they controlled approximately one-third of the electorate, emerging from nowhere, swinging elections, and rearranging party fault lines. Democrats won in Whig counties and Whigs in Democratic strongholds. The new governor, a Whig, and the new canal commissioner, a Democrat, both had Know Nothing endorsement, and seventeen of the twenty-five congresspersons elected were Know Nothings. In 1856 Know Nothings were still a force. Contemplating the landscape in southern Pennsylvania, Thaddeus Stevens remarked that "Americanism is the deepest feeling." In the presidential election Republicans wooed the American party and attempted to create fusion tickets, but their presidential candidate, John C. Frémont, refused to deny charges that he was Catholic and this probably cost him the state. Later in the decade Republicans absorbed Know Nothings and sectional issues overwhelmed all else, but not before the American Party had upended electoral politics in the Keystone State.[35]

Anti-Catholicism was rampant in Gettysburg. For example, Lutheran opponents of baptizing children of nonmembers dismissed the practice partly because it was a "Romish superstition." Lutherans believed that unbaptized infants, like all, were redeemed by Christ and, specifically, could not be denied heaven because of the "neglect of their parents," that is, because their parents were nonmembers and did not have them baptized. When the Sentinel, a Gettysburg newspaper, described the new Methodist building in Washington, D.C., as a "cathedral," somebody complained, and the editor ran a correction, reminding readers that the building was a "church," lest anyone think that Methodism resembled Catholicism. A correspondent to the Lutheran Observer, a denominational periodical published in Baltimore, asserted that Protestantism is "another name for the Bible in every man's house, universal education, and free Republican institutions" and by inference suggested that Catholicism opposed these basic concepts of virtue. Nothing in the record of the Evergreen Association indicates that they thought for a minute about including Catholics.[36]

In a sermon delivered at Christ Church, Samuel Simon Schmucker unloaded both barrels of his scholarship on Catholic-style diversity. He repeated standard Protestant disagreements with Catholicism: The Bible says nothing about a pope; the apostles, including Peter, were married and did not maintain a "pretended celibacy," an allusion to alleged immorality among Catholic clergy; only Christ and certainly not Mary can intercede on behalf of humans; and only Jesus—not Mary or the saints—can bring salvation. But most of Schmucker's sermon focused on his chosen text, Daniel 7:23–26, Daniel's visions of four beasts, and he explained why the little horn of one of the beasts was the Roman Catholic Church. According to Schmucker, all of the characteristics of the little horn fit Rome: both were cunning, sagacious, pompous, sacrilegious, and arrogant, and both changed the laws of God while warring against the faithful. Schmucker elaborated. Jesuits were trained spies who reported to their superiors, who then funneled the information to Rome. In this manner, according to the great Lutheran intellectual, "Rome is made acquainted with every thing of importance that transpires in the civilized world." In response, the center of Catholicism dispensed orders for priests and also laypersons, who received instructions on voting. With a "sleepless eye," Schmucker intoned, Rome can "see and resist the movements of the whole Protestant world." This was no less than a secret conspiracy to control the world. Schmucker, the historian, then chronicled Catholic persecution of Protestants, which, he lamented, "stain almost every page of papal history," and he counted sixty-eight million lives taken by Catholic oppression. Finally, Schmucker warned of the present danger posed by this international conspiracy of tyranny. Priests—"selfish, tyrannical," unnaturalized foreigners—interfered in elections as the "enemies of our liberties." Unless Protestants confronted the menace, the next generation, the children in Schmucker's congregation, might lose their freedom, "gradually undermined and eventually destroyed by the foreign priests and Jesuits, the emissaries of papal and imperial despots of Europe." Then "the lamp of liberty" would disappear in the "western world amid the darkness of papal despotism." The sermon on Daniel and the little horn was a routine Sunday morning talk, the topic selected because the great Lutheran theologian considered it edifying for laypersons, but it was so popular that Schmucker published it.[37]

The principle political mouthpiece of anti-Catholic sentiment in Gettysburg was *The Star and Banner*, a newspaper published by attorney and prominent abolitionist David Buehler. Buehler was a member of Christ Church and may have been in his pew when Schmucker preached Catholicism into the darkness. The Whig editor played most of the themes struck by national nativism and the Know Nothings.

Buehler thought that immigrants eroded American society, especially in cities. He dismissed recent arrivals as a "mass of undesirable social material in the shape of restless agrarian agitators, criminals and paupers." Without regular employment and abundant idle time, immigrants filled American urban centers with "low groggeries, lager-beer saloons, and gambling dens." Moreover, "hordes" of them contributed to the increase of crime and swamped penitentiaries and almshouses. Perhaps worse, foreign-born paupers imported "crime and poverty . . . from the hotbeds of European vice and destitution" into small-town and rural communities like Gettysburg. In fact, Buehler visited the Adams County almshouse to learn that the overwhelming majority of "vagrant paupers" were foreign born (German 289, Irish 69, English 9, French 2, Hungarian 1, and native-born American 30). In an article subtitled "Look at This!," the outraged editor charged that the citizens of Adams County paid taxes to support not just their own poor but the "Paupers of Europe" as well. But when immigrants found employment to sustain themselves, Buehler complained that they took jobs from the native-born. Either way immigrants were losers in Buehler's view.[38]

Although most nativist contempt fell upon Catholics, especially Irish, Buehler also disliked recent German arrivals, including non-Catholics, perhaps because they were particularly visible in his community. One article in *The Star and Banner* acknowledged that fifteen years ago Germans were industrious and religious, but within the last five years German immigrants had introduced "political and religious licentiousness," including socialism and so much irreligion that their children were unbaptized. It might be tempting to accuse Buehler of attending Christ Church Lutheran rather than St. James to avoid the immigrants there, but his membership predates their coming. St. James, however, had German preaching much longer than Christ Church, and the outspoken nativist must have been thankful to be spared the presence of diversity in his house of worship.[39]

Whether German infidels or, more typically, Catholic Papists, the impact of immigrants on the political system especially concerned Buehler. He suspected that newcomers corrupted the political system, that political "demagogues" of both parties targeted them, and that Catholics sold their votes to the highest bidder. In one close statewide race, Buehler requested the numbers of naturalized foreigners by county because he was convinced that the narrow majority for Democrats, less than 3,000, came from foreigners naturalized within the year.[40]

The Star and Banner also sounded a loud alarm over foreign influence and Jesuit conspiracy. Under the heading, "True Americanism," Buehler recounted the admonitions of American heroes about foreign power. He quoted George Washington's sage advice that "it does not accord with the policy of this government to bestow offices, civil or military, upon foreigners, to the exclusion of our own citizens." The Marquis de Lafayette predicted that "if ever the Liberty of your Republic is destroyed, it will be by the Roman Catholic Priests," and the "Last Prayer of General [Andrew] Jackson" beseeched the almighty to "preserve our country from all foreign influence." Apparently Buehler considered these words persuasive because he ran them often.[41] Buehler also warned that Jesuit conspirators had infiltrated Adams County. He described an undercover Jesuit attempt to remove the local postmaster when a special agent of the Postal Department, an Irish Catholic, visited Adams County incognito. Although the local postmaster remained in office and this effort to have the postal system "prostitute to Jesuit purposes" failed, Buehler accused the opposing press of "servile truckling to Jesuitism" for not rebuking the alleged ploy. According to Buehler, Jesuits had rival presses under their influence and "muzzled" them.[42] True, Buehler affirmed the right of Catholics to worship as they chose, and he also pointed to contributions made by Catholics, especially Charles Carroll of Carollton, during the American Revolution. But, overall the editor painted the conflict in simple terms: opponents were the "Foreign party" or the "Anti-American Ticket," and his candidates were "true-blue American candidates." Americans, he said, simply would not tolerate allegiance to a foreign power, especially one that granted a foreign ruler—the Pope—the power to determine whether the American Constitution was consistent with God's laws. This judgment, Buhler maintained, was reserved for the American people, including Catholics, to which he claimed founder Charles Carroll would have agreed. At bottom, according to Buehler, the question was "whether 'Americans shall rule America' or whether we shall give the control of government into the hands of the Foreign party and their Papal satellites."[43]

Despite the power and popularity of nativism, recent immigrants also had friends among the native-born. Devoted Methodist Sallie Myers often attended Catholic services, where she was especially "fond of the music." Once she stayed up all night for Christmas Eve, then went to St. Francis Xavier at 5:00 A.M., listening to "splendid music." Eventually, however, she pronounced the sounds "silly," and her attendance ceased. Myers decided that she disagreed with Catholic theology and worship style, but no more than that and her matter-of-fact attendance suggests her broad tolerance.[44]

Others who were more political than Myers considered the nativist party itself antithetical to republican values. Objections arose because Know Nothings appeared to contradict America's tradition as a refuge for oppressed foreigners or its mission as a divinely designed melting pot. Many evangelicals, who operated missions in cities, were more optimistic than nativists about urban immigrants. Still others remembered their tradition's struggle with political power in Europe and retained suspicion of any combination of religion and politics, especially for purposes of suppression. And, the frequency of urban riots concerned many in the middle, created a backlash of sympathy for immigrant Catholics, and cast Know Nothings as the scapegoats for the mob action. After an election riot in Washington, Henry Stahle in the *Republican Compiler* editorialized that responsibility for the violence lay with trouble-seeking Know Nothings from Baltimore who had come to the nation's capital. Additionally, the stealth of the movement disturbed some. While the charm of ceremonies, grips, passwords, signs, handshakes, and pledges of a secret society contributed to recruitment, it reminded others of Freemasons, against whom many evangelicals, especially smaller fellowships like the Associate Reformed, had long feuded. Dunkers barred Know

St. Francis Xavier Church, a robust parish coexisting with nativists. (Courtesy of Gettysburg National Military Park.)

Nothings from membership, more so for their secrecy than for sympathy with immigrants. Know Nothings knew that their stealth damaged the movement—it made them look a little like Jesuits—and they abandoned their secret oath in 1855. Political opponents of Know Nothings, usually Democrats, turned around the argument about the decrepit political system and drew attention to Know Nothing secrecy and bargaining. Stahle, for example, bristled at an accusation that a subscription of fifty dollars by a Democratic politician to a Catholic building fund in nearby Littlestown was a poorly concealed bribe for Catholic votes. The editor replied that the candidate's gift was only two dollars and fifty cents (some bribe), but the opposition candidate had given fifty dollars to the same campaign and wanted it kept confidential. During another campaign Stahle protested that Know Nothings desired their candidates to remain secret until the election, but, he reported, their identity had nevertheless leaked and they were "maneuvering and plotting" with Whigs for a fusion ticket. Those in this "midnight plot," he charged, "are the loudest in the exclamation that the Democracy 'is tampering with the foreign and Catholic vote.'" Antinativists portrayed themselves as the defenders of civil and religious freedom and enemies of fanaticism, intolerance, and political corruption.[45]

In some ways Catholics were no more countercultural than Dunkers. Unlike the Dunkers, they did not dress differently; even the special day-to-day garb for priests did not come until later, and Catholics did not look unusual in public. Unlike the Dunkers, Catholics were not pacifists, and if their ceremonies struck Protestants as odd, the Dunkers with their austere meetinghouse, trine immersion baptism, Love Feast, and feetwashing were likewise strange. If Catholics were unusually hierarchical, Dunkers were unusually congregational. The free ministers of the Brethren, untrained by anybody save mentors and ordained but unpaid by the congregation, may have been further removed from mainline Protestant clergy than Catholic priests, who were paid, educated by the priesthood, and ordained by the bishop. In Gettysburg both Dunkers and Catholics had German heritage. Both were far distant from Gettysburg's Protestant center.

Yet Dunkers enjoyed more acceptance than Catholics. Dunkers were small and native-born, and although nobody made the point, their simplicity and bottom-up governance was consistent with American republicanism. Unlike Catholics, they avoided politics and voting, but nobody questioned their loyalty.

Still, viewed broadly, antebellum Catholics, though remote from Gettysburg's Protestant mainstream in doctrine and polity, enjoyed general acceptance. Although some in the Border North public square detested Catholics and while never asking them to leave, denounced them for an unholy combination of political and religious sins, Pennsylvania's famed tolerance endured as a future saint laid a cornerstone and priests turned their backs on the congregation to pray in a language almost nobody else understood. At least one teenaged Protestant drifted in and out of worship without notice. More than any other group, Catholics tested tolerance but without breaking it.

CR

Thus, evangelicals, semievangelicals, and antievangelicals, disputing within and across denominational lines, created a varied theological population among mainline Protestants, while language and immigration provided ethnic variety and more points along the religious continuum. Dunkers and Catholics contributed genuine outsiderness to Gettysburg's faith community, and their nonconformist practices—usually but not always understood—added particularly thick diversity to Gettysburg religion, more complicated than the rest of America, and foretold of a nation that would be ethnically and doctrinally complex and as a rule, with some big exceptions, tolerant.

Divertimento

Abraham and Elizabeth Brien

Abraham and Elizabeth Brien lived on a small farm just south of Gettysburg along the Emmitsburg Road. Abraham was born a slave in Maryland in 1804, but in 1840 he lived in Gettysburg with his first wife, Harriet, and three children. Most likely he was a runaway, but maybe he was emancipated. Prior to purchasing the farm in 1857, Abraham lived in town and worked as a handyman and hostler, that is, someone who tends horses at an inn.

Elizabeth, Pennsylvania-born, was Abraham's third wife; he was a two-time widower. The 1860 census lists them with two children: William, fourteen, and Francis, eleven. Daughters by Abraham's previous marriages were grown and gone.

The four Briens lived in a small, frame weatherboard house, twenty and one-half feet by fifteen feet, with one and one-half floors. It had two rooms downstairs and a garret. Their farm was a similarly austere twelve acres divided into two parcels along the Emmitsburg and Taneytown Roads with a barn, wagon shed, corncrib, orchard, and tenant house. The Briens always had a horse and a cow, often two of each, and wheat, barley, hay, and grass for a meadow grew in their fields. Their last name was spelled a variety of ways (Brien, Bryan, Brian, O'Brien), and Abraham sometimes was "Abram," evidence of their illiteracy and low standing in the community.

Alfred Palm, his common-law wife, Margaret "Mag" Divit, and their one-year-old son Joseph occupied the tenant house. Palm was a bridle-maker, and the census taker listed Margaret as "mistress-harlot." Perhaps this mother of a small child practiced the world's oldest profession, but more likely her listing reflects the enumerator's thoughts about her race and common-law circumstances. Once kidnappers attempted to kidnap Divit and carry her into slavery, but she was large and with the help of a white man who heard the scuffle she protected her freedom. According to legend, Mag wore a blue 1812-vintage officer's military coat, bought a musket, and assisted runaways.[1]

The Briens were members of the AME Zion congregation. Elizabeth belonged to a class supervised by Eden Devan, also a hostler, and she contributed towards the pastor's salary. For much of his life, Abraham was less interested in religion.

Once authorities arrested him for fathering a child out of wedlock, and another time he lost favor with his class for something unspecified. Had he been active in the congregation, Elizabeth's donation would have come under his name instead. But as Abraham entered his most mature years, his faith grew, he became more involved, and eventually the Zion made him chair of the board of trustees.[2]

It could have been worse. Abraham was born into slavery, and from his farm the South's institution loomed almost literally just over the horizon. But the Border North was just a little better for African Americans. The Briens were free, and, moreover, they owned land. Their humble farm yielded a small income and little influence in the larger community, but real estate, no matter how unassuming, bequeaths the self-esteem of property holding. Their children attended school. Life was a struggle for Abraham and Elizabeth, but they nevertheless advanced.

Likewise, the religious home of the Briens, the AME Zion congregation, subsisted on the periphery of Gettysburg's social structure. Small, financially strapped, and excluded from community events like Evergreen Cemetery and union prayer meetings, it persisted, providing dignity and independence for its members. This was the future of American race relations: freedom without equality.

5   Diversity

Race

The racial climate of the Border North was fickle. Blacks were borderline social outcasts, frozen out of the mainstream by poverty and racism. But the local racial environment also contained conflicting winds that blew from all directions, and some currents tempered the racist environment. White progressives, in particular, offered support, including assistance with the Underground Railroad and outspoken abolitionism, and interracial worship was gracefully accepted, if not widely practiced. On race the Border North was a zone of contrasts, but unlike nearby Maryland, blacks controlled their own religious life.

ᘓ

On Sunday mornings *de facto* segregation was the norm in Gettysburg. Two African Americans participated in the Catholic parish and Dunkers probably had a black member or two, but the membership rolls of the Associate Reformed, the German Reformed, and the three Lutheran congregations were all white. Lingering German-language worship must have discouraged African Americans from associating with the Dunkers, Lutherans, or Reformed, but worship style may also have been a factor. As a group blacks never warmed to the formal liturgical practices of Lutherans, Reformed, or Catholics or the simple, sober worship of the Dunkers. Presbyterians employed more blacks than they admitted to membership. A married couple, Hannah and James Johnston, transferred membership from Wellsville, Ohio, and received the dignity of "Mr." and "Mrs." in the session minutes, and one list of communicants includes four "colored women."[1] But at least six identifiable African-American men worked as day laborers on the construction of the new Presbyterian building in the early 1840s, laboring at tasks such as digging the foundation or the well for seventy-five cents per day, and Owen Robinson, the confectioner, served Presbyterians as their sexton. With but a few rare exceptions, African Americans were absent from the membership rolls of congregations except for the AME Zion.[2]

Even local Methodists struggled to attract black worshippers, a small surprise given that evangelicals won many African-American hearts across the nation. As a rule, blacks frequented camp meetings and revivals, and by 1815 over 40,000 had joined the ranks of Methodism. (Baptists were the other evangelical tradition with a significant black membership.) That Elias and Hester Patrick, who were members of neither the Methodist nor AME Zion congregation in Gettysburg, named their child "Francis Asbury," after the great organizer of American Methodism, testifies to the popularity of evangelicalism and Methodism among African Americans.[3]

But few African Americans affiliated with the white Wesleyans in Gettysburg. In 1854, for example, Gettysburg Methodists counted only nine black members. They included Jerome and Jane Warfield, no occupation listed; Maria Cowens, aged forty-five, who lived on a farm with John and Hannah Welty and their five children, apparently assisting with the chores; and Sarah Brown, aged seventy-one, single, propertyless, and with no obvious source of income. The Church Book listed them separately from whites under the heading "colored members."[4] While the nine black Methodists outnumbered black Catholics, Lutherans, Reformed, and Presbyterians combined, perhaps signaling some Methodist advantage with blacks after all, they still represented a very minimal portion of the town's African-American community.

Instead, most black churchgoers in Gettysburg belonged to the AME Zion congregation. Although this was the smallest congregation in town with approximately forty-five members, it was still several times larger than the number of black Methodists. With approximately two hundred blacks in Gettysburg, including children, the ability of the Zion fellowship to attract over 20 percent of them is notable.

These church membership patterns in Gettysburg were typical for the Border North. Lutheran synodical and Reformed classis annual reports did not list black members, probably because they had none, and Methodist counts for nine congregations near Gettysburg had only zeroes in their column for African Americans. In this context, the handful of black Methodists in Gettysburg becomes exceptional.[5]

White households with the employment of live-in black domestics and laborers were more integrated than churches. Marie Cowens, as mentioned, lived with a white farm family. Samuel Simon and Mary Steenbergen Schmucker always had a black woman to help with their large brood. Clara Diggs (aged thirty-two) lived with Robert and Eliza Smith, middle-aged Presbyterian farmers who had no children at home. Twenty-two-year-old Lucy E. Butler served as a domestic for Moses and Hannah McClean and their five children, ages ten through twenty-three; McClean was a lawyer and a member of the Presbyterian session board. Thirteen-year-old Mary Smallwood belonged to the household of Valentin and Rosa Risling, shoe-making German immigrants and members of St. Paul's German-immigrant Lutheran. The Rislings had four children, ages six through fifteen; the three oldest went to school but not Mary, apparently a very young and inexpensive domestic. John Biggs was an eighty-four-year-old illiterate day laborer for John and Rachel Pfoutz, Dunkers and farmers. As an octogenarian, Biggs must have had limits in the fields and barn, but in the previous census he was absent from the Pfoutz farm so the family apparently took Biggs on late in life rather than keep him as he aged. Perhaps Biggs's employer, who was a preacher, accepted him as a charity case, but maybe Biggs was just cheap labor. This is not to say that most whites hired black live-ins, but the presence of African-American workers in the homes of a Lutheran academic, an immigrant Lutheran shoemaker, a Presbyterian lawyer, a Dunker preacher, and a Methodist farmer demonstrate the general acceptance of this labor practice among whites.[6]

Nevertheless, this close interracial contact in small, mid-Victorian homes usually did not transfer to church. Gettysburg's Protestant fellowships were nearly all white and reinforced the image of persistent racism in the Border North.

❧

Membership patterns, however, do not reveal the entire story, and beneath the apparent simplicity of segregated membership figures lay more complex race relations. Opinion on race and the related issue of slavery was as varied and complex as the region's ethnic and doctrinal diversity. In predictable borderland fashion, some viewpoints fell on opposing ends of the spectrum while others reflected various hues of the middle.

One option was to say little. American Roman Catholics, for example, were very cautious about slavery. The European branch of Catholicism, more outspoken, focused on the crisis of slavery politics rather than the morality of bondage and blamed the sorry state of American politics on unchecked Protestant individualism, materialism, and democracy. When the American Catholic leadership joined in the slavery debate, moderation prevailed, and, in particular, they kept their distance from antislavery Protestantism. Several factors accounted for this. One, American Protestant liberals, including antislavery advocates, prominently assumed the cause of the Italian antipapal movement, thereby creating a huge gulf between American Catholics and Protestant reformers. Also, Protestants lambasted Roman Catholics for their hierarchy, sometimes likening Catholic structure to slavery, hardly a strategy designed to build an interfaith antislavery coalition. Finally, nineteenth-century Catholic devotionalism recognized suffering as part of the journey to salvation, which made Catholics less sympathetic to the affliction of slaves.

Thus, Catholic commentators on slavery were thoroughly mainstream. They thought that slavery escaped biblical censure, that emancipation was irrational and dangerous utopianism, and that abolitionists were religious rationalists and humanists, thus anti-Catholic. Francis Patrick Kenrick, bishop of Philadelphia and then archbishop of Baltimore, typified the middle, both non-Catholic and Catholic. He asserted the humanity of slaves, complained about their mistreatment, and urged masters to treat their human property kindly, but he also instructed slaves to be obedient. Archbishop John Hughes of New York condemned the slave trade saying that enslavement of other persons was wrong, but he added that the Church did not require current slave owners to return servants to worse circumstances in Africa. Southern Catholics echoed the Southern mainstream. Bishop Augustine Verot of St. Augustine, Florida, for example, asserted that slavery was biblical and abolition was not. Mostly, however, Catholics knew that they had Northern and Southern parishes, and as Catholicism flourished, it nevertheless felt pressured by growing nativism. Faced with this threat, Catholics sought unity and approached America's most divisive issue carefully. As testament to Catholic caution on slavery, no prominent Catholics became abolitionists prior to 1862.[7]

Lutherans and Reformed were similarly guarded. The Lutheran *Evangelical Review* waited until after Fort Sumter to publish a scholarly discussion of Hebrew slavery that said nothing about the American institution. But the article had a different tone from the robust biblical defense popular with proslavery promoters, and the Lutheran publication held it back, lest it anger Southerners. Annual gatherings of Lutheran and German Reformed ministers in the 1850s did not mention slavery or race as Sunday schools, revivals, other forms of membership growth, recruitment for the ministry, and general matters of faith dominated the discussion.[8] Of course, church records tend toward internal affairs and often reflect the commonplace business of sustaining an organization, but other fellowships were vocal on racial matters, which suggests that for Lutherans and Reformed these topics were either low priorities or too divisive to discuss.

In fact, many other individuals and religious organizations were quite outspoken about race and slavery. The most conservative public voice on race in Gettysburg was Henry Stahle, publisher of *The Republican Compiler*, a Democrat, and an active member of the German Reformed congregation. Antebellum northern

Democrats were often race-baiters, and Stahle was no exception. He printed racist humor (described in Chapter 1) and routinely referred to the opposition party as "Black Republican" (e.g., "the nominations made by the Black Republicans in Lancaster County"),[9] an ugly, racist usage. The *Compiler* also approved of slavery. An article entitled "The Dignity of bein' Niggers" pointed out the "superiority of slavery to freedom" by quoting a Virginia slave whose high price on the auction block gave him self-esteem, unlike whites and free blacks who had no cash value. Free blacks, noted the "philosophical darkey," were clueless about their dignity. Another account in the *Compiler*, by a northern traveler in Georgia, depicted warm bonds of friendship between master and slave and fervent African-American Christianity in the slave quarters. According to this sentimental representation, a plantation owner sunk into depression when his servant died with last words of "Master, meet me in heaven," evidence of devotion to the white owner and to white religion. The funeral, a nighttime service, included a long, somber torchlight procession, a lined hymn—"the most solemn, and yet the sweetest music that had ever fallen upon my ear"—and a black preacher of "gigantic frame and stentorian lungs." The description concluded that "the negroes of the South are the happiest and most contented people on the face of the earth."[10] Stahle offered little nuance on race as he sustained slavery and white supremacy.

At the other end of Gettysburg's spectrum were the opponents of slavery. As a rule, blacks kept public silence about their situation, perhaps from fear of white retaliation or because poverty and undereducation deprived them of the basic tools of public discourse. Once, however, in 1847 almost all black residents of Gettysburg petitioned the Pennsylvania legislature about pending legislation. They asked the lawmakers to repeal statutes allowing slaves to reside within the state; the petitioners wanted to prevent slave-owning travelers or temporary residents from bringing their bondpersons with them. The petition also opposed laws that authorized the legal system, including courts, sheriffs, and jailors, to capture and return fugitives. Finally, the appeal requested the state legislature to urge Congress to abolish slavery. Signatories numbered 111 of both genders, a significant portion of the adult African-American population and a bold assertion of citizenship by persons, including females, whose right to that status was ambiguous. This rare public statement made the African-American position on slavery crystal clear, and their participation in civic affairs signified desire for equality.[11]

Blacks had white allies, the most public of whom was David Buehler and his newspaper, *The Star and Banner*. Buehler, of Christ Lutheran Church, abstained from racist humor and instead lampooned slaveholders. One anecdote told of an old planter who asked his slave, Cudjo, if he had followed instructions to attend church that day. Cudjo had but added "an' what two might big stories dat preacher did tell." The planter admonished Cudjo to "hush" but inquired about the "stories." "Why," the slave replied, the minister "tell de people no man can sarve two masses—now dis is de fuss story, 'cause you see old Cudjo sarves you, my old massa, and also young massa John. Den de preacher says 'he will lub de one and hate de other'—while de Lord knows, *I hate you boff*."[12]

The Star and Banner candidly reported racial conflict in the region and openly sympathized with African Americans. When authorities mistook a free black man for a runaway, arrested him in Philadelphia, and carried him to Elkton, Maryland, editor Buehler wanted the victim compensated for his lost time, and he complained that the Commissioner who sent the victim to Maryland received a ten dollar fee. (Commissioners received five dollars if they ruled that the accused was free.)[13] *The Star and Banner* noted that authorities in Hagerstown had arrested a "colored Preacher" on a Sunday for violating a state law against "convening and addressing" meetings of slaves. Another item recounted that a slaveholder from Maryland had tried to recover runaways near Coatesville, Pennsylvania, but a gunfight broke out, injuring several blacks. When several slaves in Carroll County, Maryland, fled their masters, Buehler sarcastically commented that they were "not exactly comprehending the force of the philosophy that a negro is better off in a state of servitude than in one of freedom." Someone spotted one of the Carroll County fugitives in the Gettysburg area, and a slave-catcher arrived in town. Again, in Buehler's sardonic words, the slave-catcher sought "the fugitive and his restoration to the delightful servitude which, in his ignorance and simplicity, the poor fellow had foolishly sought to throw aside." But, according to the account, "a gentleman of color" quickly sized up the situation, grabbed a horse from a nearby livery stable, and out-raced the slave-catcher's buggy, saving the runaway. Another time, Buehler reported that two whites from the county had captured four runaways: a husband, his wife, their child, and another man. The single man soon escaped, so the slave-catchers bound the husband/father. After one of the whites went ahead to Gettysburg to arrange for the coming prisoners, the wife untied her husband, who quickly jumped off the wagon and was gone. Arriving in town, now with two prisoners, the wagon driver sought a magistrate, leaving the woman and child unguarded. Then, according to Buehler, who claimed to have witnessed the event, "a kind word from a gentleman passing by [Buehler himself?] induced the weeping mother to leap from the wagon." The wagon was empty. That night the fugitives were reunited and sent off on the Underground Railroad. Buehler published the names of the two local whites who captured the fugitives, perhaps to embarrass them, and as a matter of general principle informed readers about the efforts of borderland African Americans to resist bondage.[14]

Those who held an idyllic image of slavery, like Stahle, must have flinched at Buehler's attitudes about race. His detailed and realistic coverage distinguished *The Star and Banner* from other newspapers and publicized the difficult life for African Americans. Moreover, Buehler publically flaunted black resistance to white men, and he usually referred to African Americans with respect, using "colored," "negroes," or even "gentleman of color" instead of "dusky" or "darkey."[15] Rather than hurl the epithet "Black Republican," Buehler was one.

African Americans also had a friend in the local ivory tower. Samuel Simon Schmucker spoke for black rights in the academic venue, and, as might be expected, Schmucker, the scholar, saw more nuance than Buehler, the editor. Schmucker evolved into his antislavery position. When he moved to Gettysburg with his Southern wife, Schmucker was close to being a slaveholder, and at one point, he so feared unemployed African Americans that he urged the state to bind black children into apprenticeships to ensure occupational training. But Schmucker apparently dropped this draconian proposal in favor of black rights. He conceded northern complicity in slavery and the practical difficulties of immediate abolition. He also acknowledged that many Christian masters treated their lifetime servants humanely and that some slaves enjoyed better conditions than free blacks in the North. Nevertheless, he claimed, this was exceptional, and he believed that most slaves experienced "severity" and "degradation." Furthermore, bondage destroyed marriages and parenting, promoted promiscuity, denied basic economic rights, discouraged work, encouraged laziness, and impeded the spread of the Gospel among its victims. Intellectually, Schmucker attacked slavery with the basic argument of natural rights. Although an 1846 Thanksgiving Day sermon denounced the institution as "offensive" to God, this great preacher and religious scholar relied primarily on secular concepts rather than biblical or other religious arguments. He considered all discriminatory laws, whether bondage or laws in free states that denied equal rights to blacks, as "wrong in principle," and his textbook, *Popular Theology*, denounced slavery as a "reproach to our political system and a violation of the natural rights of 'equal' man." Schmucker was convinced that many Southerners were reasonable on slavery and would respond more readily if approached "in the spirit of Christian kindness," and he refused to join an antislavery society because he thought they were too confrontational. Schmucker, the pragmatic abolitionist, advocated gradual emancipation that prepared slaves for freedom, chiefly through education, but Schmucker, the active abolitionist, participated in the Underground Railroad. From the young academic's first days in Gettysburg, when he advised Mary on how to bring her slaves into the community, he changed considerably to become an unmistakable antislavery, evangelical scholar.[16]

Schmucker also befriended Daniel Payne, the African American who came to Gettysburg and helped blacks take their spiritual matters into their own hands (described in Chapter 1). Payne was a free black from Charlestown, South Carolina, and in 1836 he left home to seek a career as a minister to his people. Arriving in New York, Payne called on several white preachers, who treated him kindly and pointed him toward Liberia, not at all what the young idealist had in mind. The city's Lutheran cleric, however, suggested the denominational seminary in Gettysburg, where a Society of Inquiry on Missions wished to educate a talented black person to pastor free blacks. Lutherans were scarce in South Carolina, and Payne spent a few days researching their doctrines by reading Schmucker's *Popular Theology*, perhaps noticing the volume's condemnation of slavery. After receiving assurances that the mission society did not require conversion to Lutheranism or endorsement of colonization, Payne enrolled, and Schmucker soon clarified that the mission society was abolitionist and not seeking deportation of blacks cloaked in high-mindedness. To support himself, Payne performed menial tasks—cutting wood, cleaning boots and shoes, and giving shaves—but he found "many kind friends" at Gettysburg and singled out Schmucker for showing the "kindness of a father." Payne enjoyed his years among the Lutheran seminarians, especially Schmucker.[17]

Dunkers added another identifiable antislavery and egalitarian voice to Gettysburg's racial dialogue. Unlike the reticent Lutherans and Reformed, their annual gatherings confronted race and slavery. From the late eighteenth century, the Dunkers' denominational position had opposed slavery, and the instructions of its Yearly Meeting on broad questions of race relations were similarly egalitarian. In 1782 one of the first recorded Dunker annual meetings denied membership to slave owners and participants in the slave trade, and in 1812 Yearly Meeting insisted that slavery "be abolished as soon as possible," using a variant of the charged word, *abolition*. The annual gathering criticized bondage seven more times before the Civil War, adding in 1845 that hiring slaves was the equivalent of ownership, and, therefore, unchristian and unacceptable for members. Hiring bondpersons, that is, renting them for a year of service, was especially popular in Virginia's Shenandoah Valley, where Dunkers had a concentration of members, and the ruling excluded Dunkers there from an available source of labor. Dunkers went against the grain on slavery, as they did on almost everything.[18]

The denomination's antislavery position apparently met with approval from the membership at Marsh Creek and certainly from their elder, David Bosserman. In 1853 Yearly Meeting named Bosserman to a small committee of elders to study the dilemma caused by slaveholding states, particularly Virginia, that expelled emancipated slaves and free states that barred their immigration. How could Yearly Meeting require slaveholding converts to emancipate if the liberated persons had no place to go? The study committee, comprised of borderland elders from Maryland, Virginia, and southern Pennsylvania, affirmed the denominational position that "under no circumstances can slavery be admitted into the church" and suggested that congregational councils, not the former masters, set wages for emancipated but stranded adult slaves until their labor could purchase travel to a "land of liberty." Regardless of whether this report solved the problem, border-state elders, including the one from Marsh Creek, still firmly opposed bondage.[19]

Yearly Meeting's egalitarian recommendations on race relations were a harder sell to its membership. Yearly Meeting counseled local congregations to treat African Americans with equality and to "make no difference on account of color." It specifically banned discriminatory seating, a countercultural rebuke to the widespread practice of consigning blacks to the rear or the gallery. Difficulties, however, arose when some white Brethren withheld the Holy Kiss from members of color. Converts received the Holy Kiss, another example of Brethren unusualness, from members of the same gender as they rose out of the baptismal water, and members also exchanged the Kiss after feet washing at Love Feast. But some whites refused to kiss blacks. Yearly Meeting criticized this white resistance as a "weakness" but refused to press the point, advising blacks to be patient. Later Yearly Meeting retreated further by granting local fellowships the right to decide about the Holy Kiss, although it reiterated that blacks should receive the distinctive greeting and that full racial equality was the "more perfect way," still an extraordinarily liberal position. Nevertheless, enough congregations resisted exchanging the intimate greeting with blacks that Yearly Meeting could not insist on it.[20]

Marsh Creek, in particular, resisted. In 1851 its congregational council agreed to greet blacks only "by the right hand of fellowship," still an egalitarian gesture in the context of mainstream racism. The next council meeting, however, decided to vote on this again at the following council, a delay indicating unusual magnitude because the only other deferred decisions were elections for ministers. The revote also suggests significant progressive opposition to the council's decision, but ultimately the original verdict prevailed.[21]

Despite the decision of the majority twice, Marsh Creek continued to struggle with race and the Holy Kiss. In 1855 the congregation sent a question to Yearly Meeting asking, "How is a church to proceed where their Bishop cannot conscientiously teach or practice the salutation of the Kiss at Baptisms, Ordinations, and at the communions?" The church book does not indicate why the Holy Kiss troubled Bosserman, but odds are high that it related to race, which during this period was the only aspect of the Holy Kiss seriously disputed across the denomination. Maybe the elder simply disliked doing the Holy Kiss, but it was unlikely that the congregation selected to leadership someone opposed to a core practice. Conveniently, Bosserman was a delegate to the annual gathering, and Standing Committee, a committee of elders that prepared the agenda, persuaded him to concede his position to preserve unity: "Finding him willing to yield, and to try for love's sake, as a rule and order, to serve the Church, and to try to die in himself, or in other words, to keep his opinions to himself." Standing Committee then urged the congregation to receive Bosserman "in love" and to "rejoice with us at the happy prospect" that he was once again useful to it and to the "whole Church." Disagreement, however, quickly returned. In 1859 Marsh Creek skipped its small Love Feast "owing to the want of union between the Bishop and the other members." Again, Marsh Creek kept further details out of its records, but the suspicion is that once more race and the Holy Kiss divided the body of believers.[22]

The controversy at Marsh Creek over the Holy Kiss reveals several characteristics of the Dunkers on race. In the first place, it suggests that Marsh Creek probably had black members. Because Dunkers did not keep membership lists, believing that counting members was prideful and worldly (even the Marsh Creek Church Book is rare by antebellum Dunker standards), locating black Dunkers is almost impossible unless they were elected to leadership, extremely improbable, or disciplined, neither of which happened at Marsh Creek. But this congregation developed a policy regarding black members, and barring the unlikely event that it engaged in a hypothetical or preemptive exercise, at least one African American must have been a Dunker. Secondly, the Holy Kiss flap reveals the willingness of many Dunkers to exchange the greeting with African Americans. At the minimum, the vote in congregational council was difficult and apparently included a significant minority favoring the denomination's progressive position. Reluctant Holy Kissers overcame racial egalitarians, but it was a struggle. Also, black Dunkers presumably participated in feet washing during Love Feast, a ritual that celebrated stark equality in a very physical and humbling manner. If the Dunkers had a black member, a white must have washed his or her feet with no qualms, save for the Kiss.

On race, then, Dunkers were different from the other white congregations in Gettysburg, and though short of modern standards of equality, were distinctly more egalitarian than other white fellowships. The only argument was over what to do after feet washing and baptism, kiss or shake hands. Not surprisingly, Dunkers, the determined nonconformists, were preoccupied by something nobody else was, and they were so far outside Gettysburg's mainstream that their influence over other fellowships was minimal. But Dunkers were the only white congregation in Gettysburg to ponder race, and the question was whether racial equality should be unlimited. Their long-held belief in freedom over slavery was not up for debate.

African Americans, Buehler, Schmucker, and the Dunkers each had slightly different perspectives. Blacks spoke clearly and simply for freedom, Buehler was an attacking editor, Schmucker pondered natural rights and complexity, and the Dunkers applied race to their distinctive practices. Yet in opposition to slavery and willingness to consider some dignity for African Americans, they were much more similar than different as they proclaimed progressive race relations only a few miles from slave territory.

◌

Other views on race and slavery fell somewhere between proslavery racism and antislavery progressivism. The *Adams Sentinel*, for example, published by Robert Harper, sent conflicting signals on race. This journal, like Stahle's *Compiler*, included racist humor and harbored many traditional assumptions about slavery and race. In one account, when a slave-master from Mississippi visited relatives in Erie, Pennsylvania, and brought along a female slave, locals took her case to court and won her freedom, but the *Sentinel* reported that the servant refused liberty: "Well, bos, I jus tell what it am—I jis warnt to go back to Mississippy, and dat's all I's got to say." Misspelling "bos" and "Mississippy" did not change pronunciation but only further mocked the woman's lack of education and accent. Harper also printed the same proslavery article, "The 'Dignity of Bein' Niggers,'" used by the *Compiler* to extol pride emanating from a high price won on the auction block. Additionally, Harper's readers learned that "a giant negro" had died near Charlestown, South Carolina, when a pistol pointed at him in play by his drunken master accidently went off, an image that insulted blacks with a dehumanized description ("giant negro") and also disparaged the master class by portraying irresponsible behavior. More than anything, Harper deeply feared the impact of slavery on the common weal. He reprinted the *Baltimore Clipper*'s suspicion that slavery-motivated territorial expansion would cause the United States to disintegrate into smaller, regional republics. The piece predicted that those eager to "extend the limits of freedom," a sarcastic reference to slavery expansion, would start with Cuba and then would take Mexico and Pacific islands, all for slavery. Moreover, according to Harper, slavery jeopardized law and order. He reported the lynching in Culpeper, Virginia, of a free black, twice convicted of murdering a white but each time acquitted on appeal due to lack of evidence. Participants in the extra-legal act included justices of the peace and church members. Harper also believed that the Fugitive Slave Act endangered public peace. In 1850 the *Sentinel* complained that the new law, enacted as part of the Compromise of 1850, returned to slavery runaways who had married and become economically productive, a policy the journal predicted would inevitably result in violence.[23] Sometimes editor Harper made fun of blacks and brushed off the pain of bondage and other times he showed sympathy, but mostly he was concerned about irresponsible, immoral slaveholders and precarious national civic health.

Methodists also belonged in the muddled middle. Race plagued American Methodists from their beginning. In 1784, when American Methodists organized themselves at what became known as the Christmas Conference, they barred slaveholders from membership. Too many, however, had already slipped into the fellowship, and under pressure from Methodist slaveholders in Virginia and North Carolina, the General Conference retreated and instead expressed "deepest abhorrence" of bondage and proclaimed determination to destroy slavery "by all wise and prudent means." Although Methodists still claimed that the concept of human property disgusted them, they dropped slaveholding as a test of membership, and their manifesto to liberate the captives was carefully worded and cautious. By 1808 the General Conference gave more ground by allowing regional conferences to make their own decisions about bondage.[24] Yet Methodists could not shake the issue any more than the rest of the nation, and in 1844 they suffered schism when a bishop from Georgia, James O. Andrew, married a slaveholding woman. Four years prior the Methodist General Conference had ruled that slave ownership did not bar ordination or office holding, but antislavery northern Methodists sought to cleanse the episcopacy of bondage and in 1844 they won the next vote. Andrew had to choose between his slaves and his office. Angry Southerners left the denomination, forming the Methodist Episcopal Church, South (ME South), and Methodists, the largest institution in the nation other than the federal government, had secession over slavery sixteen years before South Carolina walked out on the Union. David Buehler considered the schism "lamentable" and reported that northern Methodist preachers were threatened with lynching, a reference to embarrassing Southern methods of race control, unless they departed Methodist Episcopal, South border regions. Horace Holland, who rode the Gettysburg Methodist circuit just a few years later in 1848 and 1849, worried more about the damage to the faith than the merits of either side in the slavery debate. He grieved that "bishop Andrew and the negroes" had caused Methodist preachers to say bad things about each other, and that Methodists, "not satisfied with the opposition from the world, the flesh, and the devil," now arrayed "themselves one against the other." He appealed for "peace and quiet once more to prevail in our Zion." But slavery dogged Methodism, and Holland would have to wait a long time for peace to prevail in his Zion.[25]

Holland's moderation was typical of borderland Methodists as they searched for the middle. Holland and Gettysburg belonged to the Baltimore Conference, a quarterly gathering of preachers that encompassed south central Pennsylvania, Maryland, Northern Virginia, and Virginia's Shenandoah Valley. After the exit of the ME, South, this amalgamation of Border North and Border South became the southern boundary of northern Methodism. With preachers and congregations on both sides of the slavery line, the Baltimore Conference was self-consciously moderate on the great issue of the day.

In pursuit of the middle, the conference consistently rebuffed abolition. In the late 1850s it routinely and unanimously rejected antislavery petitions circulated by northern Methodist conferences. In 1857 Gettysburg and the Carlisle Circuit moved into the newly created East Baltimore Conference, which contained western Maryland and central Pennsylvania. Having shed the more heavily enslaved southern Maryland and portions of Virginia, the new jurisdiction might have tilted toward a tougher position on human chattel, but northern Maryland was still slave territory and in 1860 East Baltimore unanimously rejected three calls to make slave ownership a test of membership by votes of 156–0, 156–0, and 148–0. Moderate borderland Methodist preachers wanted nothing to do with abolition.[26]

But if Baltimore, and later East Baltimore, took a hands-off policy toward abolition, this unique Conference, a divided house, half slave and half free, nevertheless desired its clergy unsoiled by the South's institution. Methodist policy allowed members to own slaves, but the Baltimore Conference assumed that nonslaveholding congregations would reject slaveholding preachers. Consequently, the Conference was on guard, lest bondage seep into its ranks chiefly through marriage and inheritance, and between 1813 and 1845 it considered twenty-seven cases of slave ownership by traveling or local preachers or their wives, typically from the slaveholding portion of its bounds. The most prominent case occurred in 1844 when Francis Harding, filling a Maryland pulpit, married into five slaves. The Conference suspended Harding until he freed them, but he appealed to the General Conference. This was the same General Conference that heard Bishop Andrew's case, and it upheld Baltimore's suspension of Harding by a two-to-one margin (117–56). Thus, the Baltimore Conference ironically detested both abolition and slaveholding clergy.[27]

Further complicating spiritual life for borderland Methodists were the African Americans in their midst. Several majority black congregations existed in Baltimore city and Alexandria, and other stations in Virginia and Maryland had sizeable African-American minorities. The Baltimore Conference considered them trouble: "sheep without a shepherd." According to the Baltimore ministers, their black membership was incapable of functioning without assistance. African Americans were financially unable to construct their own buildings or support pastors and Sunday schools, and, worse, they were "insensible to the importance of the subject." Consequently, the white ministers assumed that black Methodists naturally looked to them for leadership, and they were determined to shepherd their black flocks carefully. To "keep our coloured societies as closely united as possible" to the whites, the Conference advised that blacks worship in the same building as whites and receive maximum attention from the circuit's preacher. The white minister should discipline, conduct Love Feasts, supervise classes, and catechize children and adults, while other white officers and teachers should lead Sunday school. Clergy were also to remind masters and employers of their duty to encourage religion among African Americans under their authority. The Baltimore parsons assumed that blacks would always be a "source of ungovernable and angry excitement both in the church and in the state," which necessitated the benevolent presence of white shepherds.[28]

In sum, race was on the borderland Methodist agenda. Denominational schism was traumatic, "ungovernable" blacks in their midst were a problem, and supervision was the answer. Baltimore Conference preachers wanted themselves free of slaveholding, but they tolerated it in others. Ill-defined moderation was the Methodist doctrine on race and bondage.

The only viewpoint approaching common ground in the Border North was colonization, which, while hardly a consensus, enjoyed support across ideological lines. Even Samuel Simon Schmucker and David Buehler, staunch opponents of slavery, respected the effort to Liberia. Initially attracted to colonization, Schmucker never abandoned it, but he doubted that colonization was a way out of the slavery quandary. If blacks needed to return to Africa, then, Schmucker suggested that logic "would send us [whites] back to Europe." Buehler praised the effort of missionaries departing from Gettysburg to Liberia. A service in the Presbyterian church building to send off David Wilson "and Lady," that is, Wilson's unnamed wife, featured addresses by Robert Johnston, the host preacher, and Henry L. Baugher, a Lutheran and president of Pennsylvania College. Buehler lavished praised on Wilson and Lady, Lutherans, for their "self-sacrificing spirit," and he wished them success. *The Star and Banner* editor conspicuously withheld endorsement of colonization, but it was certainly possible to wish individual missionaries Godspeed without proclaiming removal of blacks as the solution to America's slavery problem.[29]

Buehler and Schmucker were marginal allies of colonization, but many others were enthusiastic about the ambitious project. Every time it met, the Baltimore Conference extolled the virtues of colonization, and Harper's *Sentinal* also sang the praises of mass migration to Africa. To expedite colonization, Harper suggested three or four steamers operating continually between the United States and Africa, transporting "energetic, brave, industrious men," words of respect for African Americans. In March 1861, as war over slavery became increasingly likely, 43 mostly weighty members of the Gettysburg community still believed in the cause and petitioned the Pennsylvania legislature to pay for it. The petitioners informed their elected representatives that in 1859 and 1860 the Pennsylvania Colonization Society had funded transportation for 108 migrants to Liberia, but now the organization was broke and 90 African Americans were currently "impatiently awaiting . . . the like boon" of migration. Included among the signatories were businessmen, farmers, attorneys, two professors from Pennsylvania College, a former U.S. Congressman, and the current Presbyterian preacher, evidence of broad support among the town's leadership.[30]

Borderland arguments for colonization usually emphasized idealism, benevolence, and practical gains. To begin, removal was good for African Americans. The Baltimore Methodist preachers assumed that the "natural prejudices" of whites would never tolerate black equality and that race relations in America had a bleak future. Racist whites would oppose "to the last any encroachment on their 'reserved rights'" that might even hint at racial equality, but colonization would provide "peaceable separation" of the two incompatible races. As an added benefit, resettling African Americans in Liberia would spread the repub-

lican form of government and Christianity. According to the Baltimore Conference, the population shift would evangelize a "whole continent of savage and
barbarous men" by populating Africa with Christianized African Americans.
Additionally, "civilization" (Harper's word) of the African Slave Coast would finally end the "infernal" slave trade, a task for which naval patrols had proved
inadequate. Another practical benefit was that Liberia would become an overseas
trading partner for the United States. Finally, colonization offered hope for the
beleaguered Union. Blacks had become pawns in sectionalism, but taking those
pieces off the board would remove the basis for the argument. Indeed, colonization advocates summoned many reasons to justify their astonishing proposal for
population movement.[31]

Colonization enthusiasts often used overblown language to praise their project. Baltimore Methodists claimed that the Liberian effort was "the most glorious enterprise of private benevolence of modern times" and "ranks among the
grandest conceptions that adorn the pages of history." Harper trumpeted the removal of blacks to Africa as "the most important enterprize [sic] commenced in
any part of the world since we began life."[32] Recent scholars deride colonization
as "one of the most grandiose schemes for social engineering" in American history or "so farfetched as to be unworthy of serious consideration," but many in
antebellum Gettysburg's mainstream, including Lutherans, Methodists, Presbyterians, college and seminary professors, and influential businessmen, thought it
made sense.[33]

White opinion, then, was jumbled. Colonization appealed to many but not
all. A few white organizations were silent on race and slavery (Lutherans and
Reformed), and blacks spoke rarely but clearly for freedom. Beyond that, whites
in Gettysburg included a race-baiting editor (Stahle) who praised slavery, a racist
editor (Harper) who distrusted slavery and Southerners, an antislavery editor
(Buehler), an antislavery intellectual (Schmucker), an abolitionist and mostly
egalitarian fellowship that was far outside the mainstream (Dunkers), and a
middle-of-the-nation and middle-of-the-road conference (Methodists) with
slave-less clergy who feared abolition and distrusted blacks in their congregations. Judgment about the relative popularity of rival opinions is risky, but it
seems safe to say that the poles, that is, unabashed opposition to and support for
slavery, were a minority and that the broad spectrum created by signatures on
the 1861 colonization petition indicates substantial support for the middle. Most
whites in Gettysburg found something distasteful about slavery but not enough
to support immediate emancipation or full racial equality. Also, Democrats pro-

vide another general barometer on racial attitudes. As a rule, they were openly racist, and they were very competitive in Gettysburg and Adams County. More clear, however, is the wide range of opinion in Gettysburg and the Border North from raw racism to abolition, not a surprise in a widely diverse community.

ℭ

Mixed signals notwithstanding, the little town gave black Christians the freedom to conduct their own affairs. The diminutive AME Zion congregation hardly matched the Lutherans, Methodists, and Presbyterians, or even the Associate Reformed and Catholics in grandeur or institutional maturity, but it always kept its head above water, surviving despite obstacles. Ironically, one reason for the whiteness of most Gettysburg Protestant congregations was the success of the AME Zion fellowship and the attractive alternative it offered African-American Christians.

But this undersized congregation persisted without prospering. The fellowship was small with membership typically numbering in the mid-forties, and impediments to growth were numerous.[34]

The poverty of Gettysburg's African-American community infected the congregation's financial health. Congregational minutes commonly recorded small balances, $1.92 and $2.19, for example.[35] A fair netted $43.57 profit, far under what similar white events earned. In 1854 the Zion were so broke that they asked whites for help. The appeal in a newspaper advertisement expressed desire for "a comfortable house" of worship and announced the appointment of a representative (Eden Devan) "to go through the county" soliciting donations on behalf of a "needy people." The Black Protestants may have been institutionally independent, but they still needed to go hat in hand to big whites.[36]

The small, impoverished fellowship also struggled with undereducation and high levels of illiteracy. Elizabeth and Abraham Brien placed their two sons in school, but only 46 percent of Gettysburg's black children had this experience. Education was free but not compulsory, and many families, especially the poor, sent their children to the work place rather than the schoolhouse. This was particularly true for blacks. Mary Smallwood, the thirteen-year-old domestic for Valentin and Rosa Risling, did not go to school. Neither did the four school-aged children of Harry and Statia Butler (the census lists Harry as a "laborer") or the children of Thomas and Rachel Rideout, recently arrived illiterates from Maryland. John Hopkins, the Pennsylvania College janitor, sent his seventeen-year-old son Edward to school but not the sixteen-year-old brother Wilson. Eleander (aged eight) and Wilson Gibson (aged seven) comprised a Maryland-born household with their grandmother, Hester Gibson, aged sixty-five, an illiterate with no apparent source of income and two uneducated boys.[37]

With schooling in short supply among the black population, the Zion had a higher rate of illiteracy than white fellowships. The nonconformist Dunkers, for example, who considered higher education useless except to inflate the ego, nonetheless had an 87 percent literacy rate, while the Zion fellowship's rate was 64 percent, still a majority but with one out of three illiterate.[38] Poor spelling in the AME Zion Church Book further documents an undereducated membership. One entry, for example, recorded the creation of "a comitee of a piece [peace] meeting." Another stated that "it was move and seconed [sic] that Sara Tomson" be disfellowshipped.[39] Many of the black day laborers who worked on the Presbyterian church building signed their pay receipts with an "X." Undoubtedly, poverty fed undereducation—illiterates owned only 10 percent of black realty—and low levels of education plagued the Zion.[40]

A shallow pool of talented lay leaders further hindered congregational life. The leaders committee complained about a shortage of males qualified to perform committee work: "For want of a competent male member in full standing to sit on the case." Consequently, they appointed David Biggess, a sixty-three-year-old day laborer who just had moved to town from Frederick, Maryland. The committee considered Biggess a "well-known" Methodist, but he had arrived without a certificate from his previous congregation. Normally, in these "peculiar circumstances" his membership would have been deferred until a letter verifying good standing arrived from his previous congregation, but the impatient leaders could not wait and appointed Biggess to their committee.[41] Furthermore, committees sometimes met irregularly, another indicator of thin leadership timber. Between February 1858 and April 1859, for example, the leadership committee, which usually assembled monthly, went without meeting.[42] Undersized membership, economic hardship, undereducation, and a leadership shortage—all interrelated—provided complications unique to Gettysburg's black religious society.

But despite an unstable foundation, the AME Zion society built a functioning congregational structure. True, this "colored Wesleyan society" drew inspiration from whites, namely John Wesley and the white Methodists. But it examined candidates for membership, baptized children, celebrated Love Feasts, organized fairs, maintained two classes, and collected money for church repairs and for the pastor's salary—all basic functions of congregational life—without instruction, assistance, or supervision from whites.[43]

Like many Christian fellowships, the AME Zion faith community was more than the minutia of congregational life with baptisms and fundraisers but an alternative society with its own rules and relationships. Consequently, discipline was important. Class leaders and the leadership committee handled individual cases and typically censured nonattendance at worship, alcohol abuse, and "imprudent conduct." Eliza O'Brien's class leader spoke to her about excessive needlework, which some Protestants considered frivolous, and O'Brien "partially promised compliance."[44] More seriously, Rebecca Lewis, pregnant, charged Amaur (?) Hammond, a preacher, with "criminal sexual intercourse." The leaders committee suspended him, and so did the quarterly conference until the annual conference could deal with the case.[45] Worldly entertainment received attention. After the pastor and class leaders warned about the circus, two female members went under the big top. When questioned, the women "justified themselves in their conduct," according to the church book, and asserted that they would return to this traveling spectacle "again if they felt like it." By talking back to those entrusted with care of the congregation's spiritual health, the women demonstrated that their spines were strong but their souls weak. The leaders committee expelled them. On another occasion a member attended a party or ball but claimed that she did not dance. The committee postponed judgment but resolved to investigate. Standards of conduct were important to the set-apart community of the AME Zion church.[46]

Reconciliation of disputes between members, including married couples, further fostered distinctive community life. When Eden Devan, a class leader, learned of "disgraceful conflict" between a husband and wife, he informed the elder, who desired the couple to meet with a committee on a Saturday evening. After each spouse spoke, the committee concluded that the wife was largely at fault, but both husband and wife confessed to error and promised to change. The pastor "rebuked them sharply," but the couple was apologetic and the committee, exerting strong lay authority, decided that they "be borne with longer."[47] A few disputes became fierce. In one case, a woman called another a "yellow bitch, a bald-face bitch, and a runaway bitch," indicating tensions over race and status within the faith community. On another occasion two women fought after church when Sara Tomson allegedly had Sister Harris by the throat, for which she was expelled. The members of the Zion fellowship expected to live in harmony with one another, and when that did not happen, the leaders committee restored unity.[48]

Thus, despite the handicaps of poverty, poor education, and few leaders, the AME Zion congregation baptized, organized classes, admitted new members, and expelled others. As an institution, it was modest, but surely the congregation provided meaning and support for its membership.

ℭℛ

Segregated membership rolls and the internal weaknesses of the Zion suggest a sizeable gap between black and white religion, but the two racial communities had enough in common to connect occasionally. Although falling far short of full interracial understanding, the interaction between black and white Christians added complexity to the image of a simple, small-town social structure.

To be sure, other than the reference to "runaway bitch," much of black religious life in Gettysburg seems routinely Protestant. Mediation of conflict between members and censure of dancing, the circus, and, especially, public drunkenness and sexual misconduct were widespread among Protestants, though more intense in some than others. Additionally, the disciplinary mechanism of the Zion fellowship, that is, its committee of elders and other leaders, easily fell within the broad spectrum of Protestant authority, and the Methodist template of circuit riders, local preachers, elders, and class leaders created a wider organizational structure for the Zion denomination. This resemblance of the Zion polity and practices to white customs fits the larger antebellum pattern of northern blacks seeking their place in mainstream America. It comes as no surprise, then, that northern African-American faith was in many ways simply American.[49]

A shared evangelical salvation process prepared much of the common ground between the races. Evangelicalism provided new life for anyone who would give themselves to Jesus, rendering wealth, class, gender, and race irrelevant. Although this egalitarian theology emerged from European Protestants, it made deep inroads into African-American religion. The opportunity for choice and to control eternal fate especially interested slaves, who as prisoners had few options in earthly life, while the predestination of Calvin, who left salvation to a mysterious, distant, and judgmental God, repelled those who felt overwhelmed by social forces. Free will evangelicalism also offered hope for sin in contrast to Calvinism, which preached total human depravity. Hope was another scarce commodity in African-American lives, and depravity had little appeal to those degraded daily by social forces. Furthermore, free will conversion placed African Americans on an equal plain with whites because every person could have a relationship with Christ in this life and in the next. Sometimes evangelicalism even offered the prospect of superiority for blacks if they were born-again and whites were not, and this outlook further promised eventual judgment for all, including slave masters and other white elites. As a democratic belief system that offered choice, hope, and justice, free will evangelicalism became pervasive within African-American Christianity.

Additionally, the worship style of early evangelicals overlapped with African customs and eased the transition of blacks to Christianity. Evangelical emotionalism that included shouting, jumping, and other movements connected with traditional African religious behaviors. Movement during singing and verbal participation, including calling out encouragement or affirmation during the service, was reminiscent of African communal worship. Lining hymns resembled African call and response. The personal relationship with Christ—"I'm gonna walk with Jesus"—blurred earthly and spiritual boundaries similar to African religions in which spirits were part of daily life. When Zilpha Elaw, a young African-American woman from Burlington, New Jersey, experienced sanctification[50] during a camp meeting, she also nudged temporal and spiritual limits in a typically African way. Elaw recounted that God's spirit so overwhelmed her that she fell down. Then, with her body on the ground, her spirit "seemed to ascend up into the clear circle of the sun's disc" where she heard God's voice and saw "bodies of resplendent light." She believed that she momentarily left the earthly world and was "immensely far above those spreading trees." Whether moving the body, speaking freely, or comingling the temporal and spiritual, African Americans discovered the familiar within evangelical Christianity.[51]

Despite the common ground shared by black and white evangelicals, by the antebellum period the distance between African Americans and increasingly refined town evangelicals had widened. On at least one documented Sunday evening the Methodists sent a preacher to the AME Zion meeting, and perhaps they did more often. But whites had never warmed to organized, autonomous black religion, and generally the AME Zion inhabited the fringes of Gettysburg religion, practically invisible to most whites. No whites, for example, suggested for a moment that the Zion be included in Evergreen Cemetery.

As whites reached for gentility, the greatest difference between black and white religion became music and worship style, which, unfortunately, is the biggest gap in the record of the Gettysburg AME Zion congregation. Yet the few brief descriptions of worship at the Zion meetinghouse—all from Sallie Myers—suggest that commonality had not evaporated completely. When Myers, the young Methodist schoolteacher, and her evangelical friends visited the Zion services, they apparently fit in and felt comfortable.[52]

In the first place, the hymns were probably recognizable to whites. The AME Zion denomination had a hymnal, a step towards refinement, that contained the standard Protestant repertoire, including "Am I a soldier of the cross," "Blest be the tie that binds," "Come thou fount," "From all that dwell below the skies," "Hark! The herald angels sing," and "On Jordan's stormy banks." From Charles Wesley, the great Methodist hymnist, came "A charge to keep I have," "Christ the Lord is risen today," "Love divine, all loves excelling," and "O, for a thousand tongues." This common hymnody was a source of shared religion between the two traditions.[53]

The singing style of blacks also might have appealed to white evangelicals. The hymns were likely lined because small African-American congregational budgets could not handle expensive hymn books useless to illiterate worshippers. If the AME Zion meeting had a copy of the denominational hymnal, a leader probably used it to give the hymn to the congregation. Visiting white Protestants, especially evangelicals, whose own congregations had elevated their music, would still have recognized lining. But perhaps the singing was livelier than lining. African-American singers often embellished on the melodies with falsetto, harmonization, sliding, and other ornamentations. After Daniel Payne left Gettysburg, he mocked popular African-American religious music and complained about singing led by the loudest, who beat time with a handkerchief and pounded the floor with his feet like a bass drum, and he dismissed the tunes as "corn-field ditties." This suggests a melodic and upbeat style. Other northern African-American religious elites often agreed with Payne—they were just as committed to refinement as whites—and the preface to the AME Zion hymnal urged "avoiding the irregularity in singing which destroys the harmony." But ministers who stressed regularity and harmony, including choirs, often faced rebuke from the membership, and refined African-American religious music fought a losing campaign. Whether the congregational response was lined and improvised, a raucous cornfield ditty, or choir-led, chances are that it was a little different from what Sallie Myers listened to her Methodist congregation. Once Myers remarked that she went to the AME Zion "to listen to them singing," and whatever she heard, she liked.[54]

In all likelihood, the worship style of the AME Zion fellowship was also more than a little different. Ring shouts, singing, or alternating long dances and short prayers consumed large portions of the black worship experience, sometimes beginning after the sermon or other times starting after the regular service ended and lasting until midnight. (Perhaps Myers and her young white friends attended a more formal service and then left before the dancing and shouting began. Once she noted that she "stayed about an hour," inferring that she and her friends left before the service concluded.) Some black leaders, especially Payne, abhorred common African-American worship. Payne protested that prayer was directed by the most thunderous, like the singing, and was "secondary" to the music. The well-educated Payne tried to change those around him by urging dignity, but he admitted that he made little headway with the rank-and-file in his quest for less "heathenish" and "disgraceful" worship. Many blacks, he confessed, considered the traditional practices with traces of Africa customs as essential to their conversion and faith, and they would leave the church rather than curb their worship style. Perhaps Payne's legacy was strong enough that restraint characterized AME Zion worship in Gettysburg, but more likely the membership of the AME Zion congregation shouted, danced, and sang with energy as they praised their Lord. Whites who favored the earlier style of evangelical worship and swallowed growing refinement in their congregation may have warmed to the unrestrained emotion of black evangelicalism.[55]

Whether many whites held special affinity for emotional worship or not, a small circle of young evangelicals, including Myers, found something pleasing at the AME Zion fellowship. One late November Sunday evening Myers went to what she called the "Colored People's Church." It had already been a full day of religion for her, starting in the morning with Sunday School, then lay-led prayer meeting, then class meeting, and at 5:15 P.M. back to church for more preaching. Walking home in the dark after the last service, two friends overtook her and invited her to join them in visiting the Zion meeting. She accepted the offer and loved the sermon, which she related as follows:

> The preacher was describing the damnation of a sinner from the land of Bible and Christian privileges, described him as going down, down, down, into the "Bottomless Pit" until he came to the Sodomites, and telling them to get out of the way & let him down, farther; then going on down until he came to the Antediluvians & telling them to get out of the road further & let him down, further, & going down, down, forever down.[56]

Myers and her friends had a "hearty laugh" about this, and she pronounced the sentiments "original and very good."[57]

Perhaps the energy of black worship appealed to youth. Perhaps the swaying and other bodily movements were welcome outlets for young Christians whose own fellowship had mixed feelings about dance. Old-time Methodists condemned dancing, a norm that Myers accepted but many of her friends ignored. Perhaps participation in black worship was youthful rebellion, especially for Myers, whose romantic life led to intense conflict with her mother. Perhaps interest in black worship was youthful exploration, curiosity about forbidden fruit, or simply entertainment for young singles. Perhaps Myers tired of refinement and sought spiritual renewal through less sophisticated worship. Regardless of the motivation, the African-American fellowship was strong enough to contribute to the spiritual walk of Myers and her friends, to their social life, or, most likely, to both. Myers never complained about the size or efficacy of the Zion congregation. Instead, the interracial interaction provides evidence of a functional African-American society.

We might argue about how blurry Myers, her friends, and the AME Zion fellowship made the lines that separated the races. Does the thin evidence she provides exemplify deeper, on-going interracial interaction or were these few fragments the entire story? At the least, the contact illustrates the variety of relationships possible within the diverse community.

○ℛ

This small-town African-American congregation contrasted noticeably with black religion in the nearby Border South, particularly for its independence of white influence. Admittedly, the Gettysburg Zion required occasional financial assistance and whites may have assisted with Sunday school teaching,[58] but otherwise the congregation ran its own affairs. Nothing in the church book hints at control or influence from outside.

Just a few miles south in Maryland, African Americans were much less autonomous. True, the borderland was a transition zone, and predictably the Border South had independent black congregations. When the Frederick AME congregation announced a dedication service and invited "our white friends to attend and aid us in paying" for the new building, it sounded remarkably similar to the notice published by the Gettysburg Zion congregation for its project. Maryland AME fellowships existed in Darlington (just south of Pennsylvania near the Susquehanna River), Suitland (between Baltimore and Washington, D.C.), Oella (near Baltimore), Frederick, Funktown (south of Hagerstown), and Hagerstown in addition to congregations on the Eastern Shore and urban societies in Baltimore and Washington, D.C. Pennsylvania, however, had marginally more AME and AME Zion congregations, including Carlisle, Chambersburg, Columbia, Greencastle, Lancaster, Marietta, Peach Bottom, Shippensburg, Wrightsville, and York plus Gettysburg and urban connections in Harrisburg and Philadelphia. While a few more African-American congregations organized north of the Mason-Dixon Line, many more blacks lived south of it, making black churches in southern Pennsylvania noteworthy on a per capita basis.[59]

More importantly, black religious societies in Maryland endured a more restrictive environment. After Nat Turner's rebellion in 1831 unsupervised black religion, especially late-night services and shouts, struck Southern whites as a security threat, and all over the South the anxious master class responded. In Virginia, especially in cities, quasi-independent fellowships replaced autonomous black congregations. Under the new arrangement, blacks generally managed congregational affairs, including discipline, and were only nominally supervised by whites. Also, blacks continued to preach, even if not formally ordained. The biggest trade-off for blacks—and the white gain—was the decrease in the traditional night services; surreptitious black religion was now in the open where whites could observe and, if necessary, control. Black religion was out of the nighttime shadows, and whites were pleased.[60]

In Maryland, however, semiautonomous black religion was less prevalent, and more traditional supervision prevailed, especially under the auspices of the Baltimore Conference Methodists, as described earlier. On the outer ring of slavery, Maryland whites were just as nervous as anybody. But the smaller black populations in the Baltimore Conference were less likely than those in Virginia to maintain an underground religious network, and concession of semiautonomy to bring African Americans under scrutiny was unnecessary. Instead, Baltimore Methodists operated from a position of strength, and they insisted on more direct control. Other whites in the area likewise opted for close supervision of black associations. In Frederick the editor of the local newspaper, *The Examiner*, thought that black-run affairs endangered public safety, and police monitored secular black celebrations and public events. When whites complained about night services north of town, *The Examiner* surmised that a newly erected African-American church "must produce very unpleasant feelings to the slaveholders generally for miles around." The editor elaborated that the services at this new building risked the health of "overheated" slaves, kept them up late, made them unfit for work the next day, and provided an opportunity for young men to plot drinking, gambling, and theft. Laws banned black religious meetings without white oversight in Baltimore, Annapolis, and Frederick, and *The Examiner* endorsed similar legislation for the entire state. A black minister in Hagerstown faced arrest for preaching on a Sunday to a group of slaves. When the Frederick AME congregation had a successful series of protracted meetings, white preachers from other congregations threatened to expel their black members who attended. Blacks in the Border South had little religious independence.[61]

Methodist membership statistics document the lack of autonomy for blacks in Maryland and the appeal of it in the Border North. Like Gettysburg, all of the Methodist congregations in southern Pennsylvania (Carlisle, Chambersburg, Hanover, Shippensburg, Waynesboro, Wrightsville, York, and York Springs) were

Table 1.   Blacks in Methodist Congregations and Circuits in Southern Pennsylvania (1860)

	Whites	Blacks	Percentage Black
Carlisle	145	0	0%
Carlisle circuit	290	0	0
Mechanicsburg	169	0	0
Shippensburg	132	0	0
Chambersburg	356	0	0
Mercersburg	440	0	0
McConnellsburg	330	1	>1
York	320	0	0
York Springs	281	0	0
Hanover	47	0	0
Gettysburg	372	6	1.5
Shrewsbury	480	65	13
Wrightsville	120	0	0
Waynesboro	105	0	0

Table 2.   Blacks in Methodist Congregations and Circuits in Western Maryland (1860)

	Whites	Blacks	Percentage Black
Boonesboro	284	89	25%
Emmitsburg	118	47	28
Frederick Circuit	206	163	44
Hagerstown	186	0	0
Hereford	541	100	16
Westminster	444	100	18

almost completely white, except for Shrewsbury, near the line with Maryland, with 65 African-American members. Gettysburg, in fact, was the only other congregation with any blacks on the rolls (see Table 1). Yet in western Maryland, African Americans occupied many Methodist pews. Boonsboro had 89 black members; Hereford, 100; Frederick circuit, 163; Westminster, 100; and Emmitsburg, 47. Only Hagerstown had no black congregants (186 whites). Especially striking is Emmitsburg, the nearest congregation to Gettysburg, eleven miles away and one mile across the state lane, where 47 African Americans worshiped with 118 whites, a much different racial composition than any congregation in Gettysburg (see Table 2).

The numbers demonstrate that Border North blacks gave their loyalty to independent fellowships. Black Methodists on both sides of the Mason-Dixon Line faced the untrusting Baltimore Conference, but in Maryland the difference between the AME/AME Zion congregations and the Methodists was smaller because both remained under the white thumb. Hostile white public opinion and legal controls plagued black Methodists and independent black denominations alike. North of the slavery line, however, the black denominations were truly independent, and African Americans deserted Methodism almost completely for the AME and AME Zion rather than remain sheep to the Baltimore Conference shepherds. All over the Border North, African Americans replicated the experience of the Gettysburg AME Zion by making their own choices in religion.[62]

∝

Border North outlooks on race defy simple categorization. Some whites espoused pure racism and endorsed proslavery arguments that bondage was a positive good. Others ridiculed slavery and approached racial tolerance. Some caught fugitive slaves while others assisted them. White Methodists discouraged independent African-American religion and community ecumenism ignored the AME Zion, but a few whites sought spiritual nourishment from black faith.

In this complex environment, black religion was alive. Problems continually threatened its health; black congregants were poor, undereducated, and weighed down by racism. But the AME Zion congregation functioned, evidence of an active, up-and-running fellowship. African Americans controlled their congregation with minimal assistance and no oversight from whites, and the little congregation in Gettysburg survived, no small victory. Black religion, independent but barely, was especially characteristic of the Border North and would soon be the national pattern for a long time.

Divertimento

Mary and Joseph Sherfy

Mary and Joseph Sherfy lived on a fifty-acre peach farm one mile south of Gettysburg along the Emmittsburg Road. They had six children—three sons (Raphael, John, and Ernest) and three daughters (Otelia, Mary, and Anna)—and Mary's mother, Catherine Heagan, also belonged to the household, placing a family of nine in this two-story brick farmhouse. The size of the farm was average and the soil not especially fertile. The peach specialty, therefore, demonstrates an entrepreneurial impulse to squeeze as much as possible out of the modest acreage.[1]

The Sherfys were Dunkers. They dressed differently, wore their hair differently, furnished their homes differently, and carefully regulated their relationship with the larger community. Their photographs, taken after the Civil War, show acceptance of Yearly Meeting's guidance regarding appearance and dress. Joseph wears an unstylish haircut and the untrimmed beard without mustache. Mary has no jewelry, a simple hairstyle, a bonnet instead of a fashionable hat, and a plain dress with a form-hiding cape over her shoulders and front. Counterculturalism, however, did equate with complete isolation. The Sherfys exchanged labor with neighbors and advertised their peaches, and the children attended school. According to tradition, James Warfield, an African-American blacksmith in the neighborhood, was a friend.[2]

Joseph Sherfy was also a preacher. His path to ordination was typical for the Dunkers. In 1851 congregational council selected him as one of two new deacons, that is, an unordained associate of the leadership team who assisted ministers, directed support for the poor, and visited membership. Two years later Marsh Creek elevated Sherfy to exhorter, the first degree of the ministry, and as a young, entry-level preacher Sherfy commented on the sermons of others. Peach-grower Sherfy, like all of the free ministers in his tradition, served for life without pay, and his seat on the preachers bench exemplified Dunker nonconformity.[3]

Just months after Joseph Sherfy became a minister, a "private council" of the other preachers "advised" him not to speak during the service unless urged by elder Brethren. The records do not reveal the cause of this young minister's rebuke. Perhaps he was more articulate than the older ministers. Or, perhaps he spoke poorly, too often, or too long, especially for a novice. But the congregational council's first meeting after the private council "now unanimously agreed" to remove the restrictions so that Sherfy was "at perfect liberty" to talk. Perhaps the council overrode the ministers, but more likely Sherfy confessed to error. At any rate, Sherfy's silencing was brief, the council's authority prevailed, and vital unity and harmony returned to Marsh Creek quickly.[4]

Sherfy did more than offer thoughts on the sermons of older ministers. He was often a "visitor," one of four or five ministers and deacons elected at the beginning of every year to call on members and take measure of congregational peace prior to Love Feast.[5] Once council asked Sherfy to "reconcile a difficulty" he had with another member. Sherfy's alienated brother in Christ suffered bad economic luck so perhaps the dispute was over an unpaid debt.[6] Sherfy also represented Marsh Creek at Yearly Meeting. In 1857 along with Elder David Bosserman he attended the great gathering when it convened in nearby Washington County, Maryland.[7]

The numerous walls against the world built by Yearly Meeting often created conflict for individual Dunkers, even for those like the Sherfys who were generally committed to the Brethren's ancient order. Politics, for example, interested Mary and Joseph even though Yearly Meeting placed this in the worldly kingdom. In 1835 Mary, a silkworm buff, sent a ball of silk and a letter of political support to President Andrew Jackson. He replied with the gift of a copper bowl and a handle for making silk, which became treasured family objects shown to special guests. But Mary's overture to Old Hickory was before Joseph's election to the ministry, and apparently Joseph and Mary withdrew from politics after he became a preacher.[8]

The photographs of Mary and Joseph Sherfy also fell outside the Dunker order. In 1849 Yearly Meeting advised against "likenesses," an admonition it repeated in 1857 and 1858, when it cited Romans 1:23 ("changed the glory of the incorruptible God into an image made like corruptible man") and Deuteronomy 27:15 ("Cursed be the man who maketh any carved or melted image, an abomination unto the Lord"). Yearly Meeting was adjusting, drawing new lines as technology made available new temptations from popular culture. After the Civil War when Mary and Joseph had their photos taken, the annual meeting still considered likenesses worldly, not repealing its ban until 1904. The photographs confirm that although the separate community at Marsh Creek resisted change, it nevertheless included discretion and flexibility. In this case the Sherfys were out of step with the fellowship but still remained in good standing, suggesting flexibility in the Dunker system.[9]

Joseph and Mary Sherfy in late middle-age, undated photographs. (Courtesy of Adams County Historical Society.)

On balance, Mary and Joseph Sherfy seem like misfits compared to the rest of society, their thriving peach farm notwithstanding. The Sherfys knew that their Dunker ways made them appear odd to others. But in another sense the Sherfys fit well with the region because small, German-heritage, nonconformist groups like the Dunkers were common in southern Pennsylvania. Mennonites and Amish were Anabaptist cousins of the Dunkers with similar concepts of congregational unity and nonconformity to the world. Although Moravians were rapidly moving into the mainstream, their outsiderness, especially through communalism, was very recent, and they still had distinctive practices, especially music and Love Feasts. Small German evangelical fellowships—the River Brethren, the Church of God, the Evangelical Association, and the United Brethren—were less countercultural, especially the latter three, but they, too, contributed to variety, and the Quakers, an English-heritage, nonconformist society, further added to the regional congregation of minorities. With all due respect to refinement, which from one vantage point created a potent mainstream, from another perspective oddness, as expressed by the Sherfys, was almost normal in the Border North.

6   War

"W ar Commenced," announced *The Compiler*, and "Commencement of Civil War!" exclaimed *The Adams Sentinel.* The longtime journalistic foes found something on which they agreed.[1]

Historians trumpet the power of this great conflict to alter America. They note large national changes, including emancipation, physical destruction of the South, the triumph of federalism, the emergence of a modern nation-state, and constitutional amendments that laid a foundation for future social revolutions. Thus, Gettysburg, a typical wartime community, save for its battle experience, is a logical place to find evidence of a remade America. Yet change in local religion was measured. Once the shooting started, the religious community settled into a pattern in which matters of faith remained much as they were before Sumter. Eventually the war came directly to Gettysburg and briefly shredded order, but recognizable religion, not a new version, reconstructed stability. As in the antebellum period, when congregational affairs frequently concentrated on mundane matters, during the Civil War worshippers in the pews often fixed on the familiar. Religion nevertheless could not completely avoid the great conflict, and most notably the relationship between faith and the nation-state grew much closer. Religion, then, felt change, but modestly rather than fundamentally.[2]

◌੭

With the surrender of Fort Sumter, secession, and President Lincoln's call to suppress the insurrection, Gettysburg became a home front. Undoubtedly, wartime differed from peacetime and the community encountered new experiences, but the first years of conflict left core religious practices basically unaltered.

The prologue to war had divided Gettysburg, as it had the rest of the nation. During the critical and bitterly fought election of 1860, local editors Robert Harper and William Stahle argued about everything except that the outcome might threaten the Union and lead to war. Harper praised Republican nominee Abraham Lincoln as a conservative opposed to racial equality and denied that his election would produce secession. Stahle underscored the dangers of electing a "Black Republican President," which he predicted would cause secession. "Black Republican" became common usage in the *Compiler*. Stahle also pointed with alarm at the Wide Awakes, a Republican club for young men. Wide Awakes marched in torchlight processions, and with their oilcloth or glazed capes and military-style hats with an eagle in front they resembled a paramilitary organization. Gettysburg had a chapter; it marched, which required practice, and Stahle wondered why they needed to drill in a peaceful community. Abraham Lincoln won Gettysburg and Adams County by slender margins in a record turnout, indicative of the grave circumstances. That Lincoln carried a community so near to Maryland slavery was remarkable, but the closeness of the victory signified the polarization of popular opinion.[3]

After Lincoln's election the Deep South threatened secession. Local citizens gathered in the German Reformed church to hear D. M. Smyser, a former resident and current judge in eastern Pennsylvania, lecture on "The Cardinal Duties of the American Citizen in the Present Crisis." Others turned to prayer. Gettysburg observed President James Buchanan's proclamation of a national day of "Fasting, Humiliation, and Prayer" for Friday, January 4, with a morning service in the United Presbyterian Church and evening worship in the German Reformed building. A few days later a daily "Union Concert of Prayer" began with pulpit exchanges moving through the Presbyterian Church, Christ Church, the German Reformed, and the Methodists and concluding on a Sunday afternoon with the United Presbyterians and in the evening at St. James Lutheran. A day or two after these services, news arrived that South Carolina had fired on the *Star of the West* as it attempted to reinforce Fort Sumter.[4]

The exchange of fire in South Carolina brought perceptible change in Gettysburg. *The Compiler*, which had recently denounced "anti-slavery radicals" and "Black Republicans" for bringing the nation to the brink, now pledged to "stand by the old flag" and support the Union. The rest of the community responded similarly. The day after Fort Sumter surrendered, Captain Charles H. Buehler issued a call for a defunct militia unit, the Independent Blues, to reorganize. The following day, a Tuesday, the mayor called a town meeting. On Wednesday the Blues met. Two days later, on Friday, April 18, the community ceremoniously ran a flag up a 120-foot pole on the square, or "Diamond," as it was called. On Saturday the Blues, numbering sixty, paraded in civvies, then formed around the flag on the Diamond and took an oath to the state and the nation. The "fever of military spirit [was] at high pitch," according to *The Compiler*. On Sunday, a union prayer meeting gathered in St. James Lutheran with ecumenical leadership representing St. James and Christ Church Lutherans, Methodists, Presbyterians, and United Presbyterians. On Monday, just eight days after Sumter, the Blues, now swelled to 130, "left in the cars," that is, by rail, for war via Harrisburg. A Relief Committee organized to provide for the families of departed volunteers, and a Home Guard formed the first line of local defense. On Tuesday, April 23, two men interrupted a large rally in the courthouse by carrying a flag to the front, which "called forth deafening and long continued applause." In a matter of days, the town felt the conflict conspicuously.[5]

A now unified community began immediate transition to home front status. *The Compiler*, beckoned "Men of Adams County, your country calls." Soon young men enlisted not only in the Independent Blues but the Adams Rifles and the Gettysburg Zouaves, clad in gaudy French uniforms. Sallie Myers thought the Zouaves "made a very fine appearance," and they often escorted new recruits to the train station. Every evening cavalry drilled in the square. On May 6 women gathered at the Methodist Church to form a Union Relief Society that made flannel shirts, havelocks (cloth coverings for hats that protect the back of the neck), and other military garments. By summer, Gettysburg fell into a new routine. Women sent food, clothing, and blankets to the troops and money to the U.S. Sanitary Commission, a national organization that coordinated volunteers, especially females, and provided nurses, camp kitchens, and soldiers' homes. Local authorities recruited men for uniform and raised funds for bounties while soldiers came and went, drilled, and paraded. Gettysburg mobilized.[6]

Among those who rallied to the colors was Charles L. K. Sumwalt, assistant preacher for the Gettysburg Methodists, who joined the Zouaves and eventually became colonel of the 138th Pennsylvania Infantry. Fellow Adams County officers pushed Sumwalt's candidacy for the colonelcy by stressing his pastoral vocation, but they also pointed to his superior intellect and striking appearance. Sumwalt dazzled with his ability to quote Shakespeare, and he also entertained friends by imitating Ajax, a mythical horse, defying lightning. (In 1863 Reverend Sumwalt's military career ended with a court-martial trial for alcoholism and Southern sympathies.)[7]

Mobilization created new relationships and experiences. In December 1861, the 10th New York Cavalry (Porter's Guards) arrived in Gettysburg for the winter, and the town adopted them. Locals enjoyed the bugle calls and band music, often on the Diamond, and townswomen presented the New Yorkers with a banner. When the troops moved to barracks just east of town, many residents made the trip to watch them drill, no small effort in the horse-drawn age. Sallie Myers commonly attended social gatherings at which enlisted men of the 10th were present, and several courted her, one with some success. When the dancing began at Myers's aunt's party, Private Ed Casey walked out with her, and after the 10th left for the front, she corresponded regularly with "Mr. Casey," as she called him, while her on-again, off-again affair continued with Snyder. The experience with the New Yorkers coupled with donations to the Sanitary Commission re-flected a growing national perspective, but, on a simpler level, a grand cause, bugle calls, new friends, and new beaus enlivened Gettysburg.[8]

The close proximity of Gettysburg to the military front provided more signals that life had changed. Home-guard scouts patrolling roads leading into Mary-land periodically encountered hostile forces, sparking a mad dash into town with the warning, "the rebels are coming." A female resident recalled these episodes as "comical." Much more dangerous was the 1862 Confederate invasion of Mary-land, culminating in the Battle of Antietam. Several hundred Unionist refugees, mostly from the nearby towns of Frederick and Emmitsburg, flooded into town, sometimes with livestock and other property, and filled the hotels. Authorities arrested six of the new arrivals as spies, some of whom posted bail and others swore an oath of allegiance. *The Star and Banner*, certain that more agents hid among the refugees, hoped for a Provost Marshall, who would have military au-thority over civilians. With real danger nearby, the town raised three companies of militia, and businesses closed at 4 P.M. so that the newest citizen-soldiers could drill. The Adams Dragoons with just-arrived sabres and pistols paraded in the streets and, according to *The Star and Banner*, were now "partly prepared" to fight. The nearby enemy reminded all of the gravity of war.[9]

A few weeks after the scare from the Maryland campaign, the enemy again appeared on Gettysburg's doorstep. Confederate cavalry under General J. E. B. "Jeb" Stuart road through southern Pennsylvania, including Chambersburg, where the raiders burned supplies and machinery, destroyed railroad equip-ment, and looted a shoe store. The Confederates also carried off eight young African-American men and boys, presumably for the auction block, as their par-ents begged for them. Returning to Virginia from Chambersburg, Stuart's men crossed South Mountain at Cashtown, Adams County, then road south along the ridge, taking horses, supplies, alcoholic beverages, and a few hostages. Stuart's ride came within four miles of Gettysburg, another close call.[10]

Despite the nearness of the enemy, many residents believed that the peril would pass them by. Why, they asked, would Confederates bother with a town so small? Streets crowded with refugees and enemy troops almost within earshot were tangible evidence of war, but the alarm was momentary and the home front remained calm.[11]

Like civic life, wartime religion was a little different. In March 1861, before Fort Sumter, Zion's Classis (German Reformed) noted "the excited state of the public mind, with rumors of civil war filling the air from one end of our land to the other." In September 1861, several months after Bull Run (July 21), West Pennsylvania Synod Lutherans reported that attendance and benevolent contributions had declined and that Sunday schools suffered from military parades on the Lord's Day. Still, overall Sunday attendance remained at prewar levels, and the Lutheran divines considered the war a poor excuse for lower giving because it had not significantly impacted their territory. But, the assembly observed, "war is always the enemy of the Sanctuary," and it cited the conventional wisdom that war has no Sabbath, a complaint with a ring of truth. Armies marched, fortified, and fought seven days a week, and camp services, when held, struggled to recreate the atmosphere of religion at home, where well-dressed worshippers gathered in well-furnished surroundings. Other religious districts and congregations also experienced the war a little. The Carlisle Presbytery admitted into its membership a minister from Confederate territory, John O. Proctor from Winchester, Virginia, perhaps a Unionist and almost certainly fleeing a war-torn town on shifting front lines. Quartermaster Sergeant J. B. King, a Congregationalist in Porter's Guards, preached to the Methodists several times. After the battle of Antietam, the Gettysburg German Reformed postponed communion because their pastor had gone to tend the wounded. Among the town congregations, this fellowship initially felt the war more than the others. The Reformed planned to enlarge their building and had impressively raised $1,500 pledges of the total estimate of $1,800, but they nevertheless scrapped plans "in view of the increasing stringency of monetary affairs" and the war. Perhaps they lost faith in the pledges. Admittedly, the Civil War occasionally intruded into the meetinghouse.[12]

In 1862 the most pointed comments about the conflict came from the Lutheran Synod of West Pennsylvania, which met perilously close to the fighting. On September 11–13, just before the Battle of Antietam, the synod assembled in Shippensburg while Confederates occupied Frederick and Hagerstown, Maryland, the latter only thirty-five miles distant. In sharp departure from their previously mixed but generally positive outlook—in 1861 giving declined but attendance held steady—the gathered Lutherans now considered the past year as "one of peculiar trial, both to Church and State." Membership growth had stopped, and men who contributed to congregational life were gone. Although participation in Sunday services held stable, weekday lectures and prayer meetings suffered. Perhaps worse, the war exposed men away from home and church to new vices, a common fear, but even at home intemperance rose, especially among young men, and Sabbath-breaking and profanity also increased. Finally, the preachers prayed that public opinion would soon cast aside its "gloom." Earlier in the summer Union troops had suffered a deflating defeat in the Peninsula Campaign, and now Lee's army was in nearby Maryland; no wonder optimism was in short supply. With the Army of Northern Virginia only a day or two's march away, the Lutheran Synod felt the war's hot breath on its neck.[13]

Yet, many religious organizations operated as if there was no war. After two years of fighting, Carlisle district Methodists reported their condition "good," though not nearly as effusive as the Juniata District in the central Pennsylvania highlands, which boasted of camp meetings, numerous conversions, and a "gracious revival of religion." Likewise, Zion's Classis had no complaints about the war, observing a "more charitable and denominational spirit" in their territory. Congregations stuck to routine business. Just prior to the 1862 invasion the local German Reformed celebrated communion, and on the eve of the 1863 incursion, the women of the congregation organized a Strawberry Festival. Christ Church Lutherans tuned their organ, and St. James Lutherans worried about unpaid pew rents and took the dubious step of borrowing money to pay a debt obligation. St. Paul's Lutheran started a German Sunday School. Presbyterians, a little behind, added gas-lighting. As the fighting raged elsewhere, Marsh Creek Dunkers held Love Feasts, attended to discipline, and elected preachers as they always had. In May 1863, council advanced Joseph Sherfy to the second level of ministry and installed him on the evening of May 30, following the spring Love Feast.[14]

As further evidence that peacetime resembled wartime, the two financially struggling Lutheran fellowships labored to find leadership. At Christ Lutheran pastor Charles P. Krauth resigned, citing failing health and picking Christmas Eve to inform his congregation. In truth, Krauth's vigor had waned, and the congregation hired a carriage for him. Krauth's replacement, Henry L. Baugher, who wore another hat as Pennsylvania College president, received relief from preaching chores from other members of the congregation; as a college and seminary congregation, Christ Church was well-stocked with ordinations. Baugher nonetheless served reluctantly, and he, too, soon attempted to take leave. At St. James Lutheran the pastor, James R. Keiser, left because of the congregation's financial difficulties. In December 1860 the "Ladies of the Congregation" had organized a successful fair to pay for gas installation even as the fellowship lacked funds to compensate Keiser. Perhaps gathering in a gas-lit sanctuary was a higher priority than paying the preacher, and in early May 1861 Keiser resigned with his timely paraphrase of Major Anderson.[15]

The early years of the war, then, modified without transforming Gettysburg religion. Like the civic community, the religious community changed a little but not much. The German Reformed called off a building project, some detected declining attendance, and a Lutheran synod with Confederate drumbeats just over the horizon sounded like preachers at war. But most regional religious assemblies registered only modest concern about the conflict, and most congregations focused on gaslights, debts, or empty pulpits. The mundane prevailed inside the wartime meetinghouse.

 beta

Relative tranquility ended in the summer of 1863 when Robert E. Lee's army unexpectedly spilled into southern Pennsylvania. Lee assumed that crossing the Potomac would pull Northern troops out of Virginia, including the beleaguered Shenandoah Valley, and force the Federals to change their strategy for the summer campaign season. Additionally, he hoped to loot Pennsylvania of badly needed food, horses, and supplies and decisively defeat a Union army, which might demoralize northern public opinion and produce a negotiated peace and Southern independence. Accordingly, beginning on June 3 elements of the Army of Northern Virginia headed north, hidden behind cavalry screens and passing through gaps in the Blue Ridge and into the Shenandoah Valley. On June 15 advance units crossed the Potomac River at Williamsport, Maryland, and others soon followed, moving along a broad front while wagon trains followed the Valley Pike through Chambersburg, Shippensburg, and Carlisle. The route included side roads, and some units detoured west to McConnellsburg while others reached the outskirts of Harrisburg. Another line of march resulted in the capture of York and threatened to cross the Susquehanna River at Wrightsville before defenders burned the magnificent wooden span there. The Union Army of the Potomac followed, unsure of Lee's intentions.[16]

For an invading army, the Confederates were well-behaved, but the prosperous towns and farms of southern Pennsylvania nevertheless suffered heavily. Lee's men sometimes paid for what they took, albeit in worthless Confederate paper. One of the wagons rumbling north contained a printing press to crank out scrip, and the invaders left receipts with those who would not accept another government's worthless paper. Jedediah Hotchkiss, a mapmaker and member of the general staff, wrote to his wife, Sara, in Staunton, Virginia, that in Chambersburg he "bought" one hundred dollars worth of fabric, hoops, thread, and pins, all scarce consumer goods back home. Enforcement of rules against looting also created an impression of limited warfare. When an enlisted man walked out of a store with unpaid-for ladies' dress goods, an officer—a general no less—ran him by the collar back into the shop to return the items. Of course, property with military value, such as bridges and railroad equipment, was a target, but Confederates on occasion helped civilians extinguish fires that spread to nonmilitary property and in York Jubal Early decided not to burn lest the fire spread to civilian property. The war still had a few limits.[17]

More typically, Confederates confiscated food, thousands of horses and live cattle, and other supplies, including socks, hats, and drugs, and officers demanded large amounts of cash from municipal officials. As a Dunker congregation met, five Confederate foragers arrived and capitalizing on a bonanza of horses all in one place took the animals. However, while the lieutenant distributed receipts, Union cavalry appeared, captured the Southerners, and returned the horses to their owners. In Mercersburg one resident recalled that store shelves were "almost stripped" bare. After the Confederates left that town, few country people attended church—their transportation was gone—and those who did walked. In Chambersburg soldiers forced storekeepers to open under threat of force, and in Shippensburg a merchant claimed that Confederates looted for four days. If Jedediah Hotchkiss paid for his hoops and pins, he used Confederate money, and he purchased from storekeepers forced to sell and who surely considered his "bought" items stolen. In the countryside, where officers were scattered, circumstances could be particularly difficult. At one Mennonite farmhouse three soldiers lined the wife and children against the wall at gunpoint and took the father into a bedroom, demanding money. The farmer had stashes around the house and revealed them. After the soldiers had the cash, one pointed a gun at the farmer and prepared to fire, but another interceded and saved the man's life. In a Maryland household, plunderers destroyed the garden, placed their lice-ridden clothing in women's dresser drawers, and stole numerous household items, including dress patterns and letters from the daughters of the house, all while an officer looked on. Depredations notwithstanding, generally residents were thankful that the Confederates were no worse, that private property other than war material often received respect, and that most civilians were not physically harmed. But although scrip-paying Confederate officers who remained within the rules of war could satisfy themselves that they were gentlemen, they nevertheless plundered, and civilians lost considerable property.[18]

Nonwhite civilians suffered worse treatment. Confederates considered black Americans—whether born free, manumitted, or runaways—as contraband, that is, property legitimately confiscated during a military operation. One eyewitness in Chambersburg described Confederates hunting for blacks and "driving them off by droves." The dragnet yielded mostly women and children because men had left, thinking that women and children would be unharmed. Another observer saw Confederates riding off with captives, including children, doubled up on their horses, either in front or behind them. In Greencastle Southern soldiers searched homes and surrounding wheat fields for African Americans. Many were caught, sometimes after a chase and shots fired. In Mercersburg, the behavior of one unit that "came to town on a regular slave hunt" appalled Philip Schaff, the Reformed theologian. First, Confederates demanded the surrender of all fugitive slaves within twenty minutes and threatened to burn houses that hid them. Then, Southern soldiers searched suspicious homes and found several African Americans, including a woman with two little children. The next day the unit returned and drove their spoils of war through town, including horses, cattle, five hundred sheep, two wagons of store goods, and twenty-one blacks. As with other witnesses, Schaff was certain that some of the prisoners, including his long-time wood-splitter, were free-born and raised in the neighborhood. The Reformed scholar's contribution to the secession crisis had been a thirty-two-page biblical defense of slavery, but now he pronounced the round-up as "a most pitiful sight, sufficient to settle the slavery question for every humane mind." Usually, sympathetic whites could do little, but in Greencastle as wagons from Chambersburg rolled into town with human contraband, citizens overwhelmed the five guards, including a chaplain, placed them in the town's jail, and freed the captives. When General Albert Gallatin Jenkins, commander of the cavalry that took Chambersburg, heard of this, he demanded $50,000 and threatened to burn Greencastle in two hours if not paid. Fourteen blacks then offered their surrender to spare the town, but white leadership refused to back down. Jenkins never returned, and Greencastle escaped the torch. Blacks in Greencastle had a close brush with slavery, and for African Americans, in general, the turn taken by the war into the Border North jeopardized freedom.[19]

As the plundering, slave-catching Southerners advanced, some residents of Gettysburg thought that the campaign might bypass them for larger, more strategic targets, but others—black and white alike—were alarmed as never before. For several weeks businessmen had closed stores and banks while sending goods and cash to Philadelphia for safekeeping, and by this point in the war many horse owners, who had concealed their steeds several times previously, had the routine down. A June 20 fire in Emmitsburg cast a glow in southern sky and led some to wonder whether Rebel hordes approached, but the fire was unrelated to the invasion. According to Sallie Myers, at this point anxiety was "worse than ever" and "about as bad as it can be"; for the first time she was "alarmed and excited." Myers heard no preaching on Sunday, June 21, because the preacher had left. Blacks in Gettysburg had more to fear. The town's newspapers reported the kidnappings of blacks in Hagerstown and McConnelsburg, and as the Confederates neared, many African Americans in Gettysburg fled for their lives. Harrisburg, York, and other towns east of the Susquehanna were favorite destinations. This invasion scare was different.[20]

Whites had mixed sympathies about the plight of their African-American neighbors. One white resident, Tillie Pierce Alleman, recalled that during the numerous false alarms, many blacks had hid outside of town in woods around Culp's Hill. "They believed that if they fell into [Confederate] hands, annihilation was sure." Alleman remembered refugees "with bundles as large as old-fashion feather ticks slung across their backs, almost bearing them to the ground" and the children also carrying improvised baggage, "striving in vain" to maintain the pace. She described disorganized panic. "The greatest consternation was depicted on all their countenances as they hurried along; crowding, and running against each other in their confusion; children stumbling, falling and crying. Mothers, anxious for their offspring, would stop for a moment to hurry them up, saying: 'For' de lod's sake, you chillen cum right long quick! If dem rebs dun katch you dey tear you all up.'" This struck Alleman as "amusing."[21]

Other whites were more sensitive about the dangers African Americans faced. Catherine May White Foster, for example, a thirty-seven-year-old living with elderly parents, recalled that one Sunday the AME Zion bishop, "a large, fine looking and able speaker," arrived in town for quarterly meeting, and Foster, a United Presbyterian, was invited. (As a Presbyterian dissenter, Foster presumably disapproved of musical innovations, making the African American worship a large leap for her.) Attendance was low, and during a hymn word arrived that "the rebels are coming," whereupon the bishop and the congregation vanished "in a moment." Sallie Myers also noted the departure of blacks, adding her "pity for the poor creatures."[22]

As Lee's men roamed the region unmolested, seizing property and African Americans, a hastily organized regiment of the Emergency Volunteer Infantry arose to stand between Gettysburg and the gray horde. Companies from around the state comprised the regiment, but its first company formed in Gettysburg on June 19 with ranks filled primarily by seminarians and college students. One historian has described the Emergency Volunteers as "well uniformed in blue but greener than grass" and the product of a Minuteman myth that untrained, hastily recruited civilians could withstand veteran troops.[23]

On June 26 Confederates led by Jubal Early quickly brushed aside the green-as-grass, modern-day minutemen, and later that day Southern cavalry galloped into town chasing stray horses, yelling, pointing pistols, and waving swords. Columns of infantry soon followed. Sallie Myers began her diary entry for that day with "In Rebeldom," and she described the enemy as a "mean looking lot of men" and dirty. Early demanded large quantities of food, shoes, hats, and cash, but the president of the town council, David Kendlehart, persuaded him that the mandate was beyond the town's means. Many of the defending Emergency Volunteers were captured, marched back into Gettysburg, and then paroled, quite an experience for seven days of soldiering. Early's troops burned railroad property and played "Dixie" in the town square, and one brigade got drunk, but they found only modest amounts of contraband. Merchants, after all, had sent away much of their stock. *The Star and Banner* editor conceded that the Confederates "did no considerable damage" to civilian property, and he confessed that the invaders' "hated presence and their calls for something to eat" were the primary aggravations. Still, he added that they broke into locked stores and warehouses "with the cool assurance that they would respect private property" and "took what they pleased." Myers and her father had a two-hour "interesting" conversation with two "very reasonable" soldiers on their doorstep about the issues underlying the war. Father and daughter felt sufficiently safe to express unconditional Unionism bluntly. Nicholas Codori lost his horse. He sent his seventeen-year-old Dutch immigrant-employee, Charlie Supann, toward the Susquehanna with the animal for safekeeping but instructed him "not to drive fast." The young man did as he was told, and Confederate troops caught up with him and took the valuable horse. The wife and daughter of Abraham Cole, the AME Zion circuit rider, were alone and, according to one sympathetic white, "did not know what to do." Presumably Cole was off riding circuit or had simply left, and the daughter's husband was in the army. Kindly white neighbors hid the Cole women in the loft above the kitchen, where they stayed the night, listening to Confederate soldiers below them. The daughter was certain that soldiers knew who was upstairs. Gettysburg was in rebeldom for two days, then Early left for York.[24]

Gettysburg's fate changed when Lee learned that three corps of the Army of the Potomac had crossed the Potomac and were near Frederick, Maryland. The Southern commander needed to keep the Union army away from his lines of communication in the Cumberland Valley, the Chambersburg-Shippensburg-Carlisle-Harrisburg corridor, and, therefore, he quickly ordered his forces to concentrate east of the South Mountain near Cashtown and Gettysburg. Early's men in York would have to retrace their steps. Meanwhile, the new commander of the northern army, General George Gordon Meade, moved further north to protect Washington. Meade was prepared to fight if Lee turned toward Baltimore or perhaps strike Lee's rear if he advanced on Harrisburg. Meade sought a battle.[25]

Many in Gettysburg concluded, perhaps wrongly, that Lee had set his sights on Baltimore, and noticing the convergence of roads in their hamlet, they more correctly feared that the impending battle might be fought in their town. On June 29 Sallie Myers saw "very ominous" Confederate campfires on South Mountain, but the following day, June 30, protection in the form of a cavalry division under the command of General John Buford entered Gettysburg and took positions near the seminary. Myers and her friends sang for them as they passed. Union scouts and pickets made contact with a Confederate brigade sent by General Henry Heth toward Gettysburg in search of supplies. Perhaps Heth did not know about Early's raid just four days previously, which should have cleaned out the town.[26]

On the morning of July 1 two Confederate divisions headed toward Gettysburg, seeking to determine what Union forces lay before them. As the Confederate column approached town, it encountered Buford's cavalry, set up near the seminary, fighting dismounted, and yielding ground gradually until infantry support arrived. Indeed, relief soon appeared as General John F. Reynolds's First Corps rushed north along the Emmitsburg Road to join the fight. As they marched past the Sherfy farm, Joseph drew water from his well, and Mary baked bread for the passing soldiers. The children were with friends, also Marsh Creek Dunkers, on the eastern side of the Round Tops and behind Union lines. When the first brigade in the line of march along Emmitsburg Road reached the Codori farm, it halted and began to dismantle the fence for a short cut across fields, avoiding the town, to the fighting near the Seminary. An officer recalled that an "old gentleman," perhaps Anthony Codori, ran out, opened the gate, and asked that the soldiers move around his wheat field, a request denied.[27]

Although commanders on both sides only slowly realized the magnitude of the escalating fight, Confederates generally arrived in force earlier and gradually overwhelmed Union defenders, who retreated from ridge to ridge north and west of town. By 4 P.M. Union lines were backed up to Seminary Ridge, where troops had erected a two-foot high semi-circular breastworks of fence rails and debris in front of the seminary building that connected to a stone wall west of the Krauth house. The defenders withstood one assault but were soon overpowered

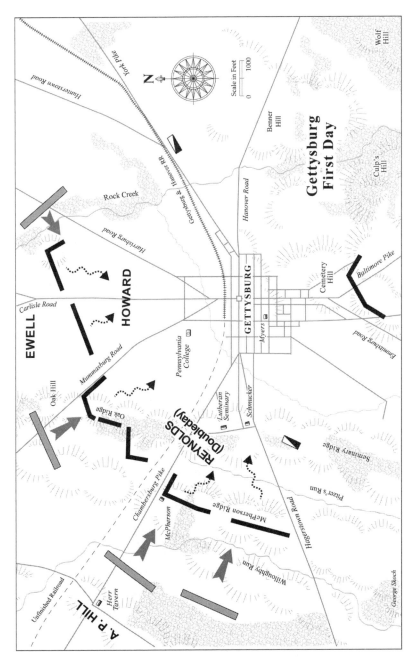

Gettysburg Day 1. Confederate forces drive back Union defenders, swarm around the seminary, and occupy the Schmucker home.

and retreated, sometimes in panic, to new positions on Culp's Hill, Cemetery Hill, and Cemetery Ridge just to the south of town.[28]

As the battle began, lingering African Americans escaped. Somehow they had survived Early's brief occupation, but the unmistakable signs of a large engagement provided new impetus to leave. Basil Biggs, an influential member of the AME Zion fellowship, had sent his family away earlier, and as Confederates entered Gettysburg from the north and west, Biggs rode out of town, heading east, on a borrowed horse. He spent the battle in York. On July 1 Elizabeth and Abraham Brien left town with their children as the battle began. Perhaps their status as property owners caused them to linger longer than most.[29]

Sallie Myers heard a cannon shot at approximately 9 A.M. as she was ironing. The first evidence of fighting she glimpsed was a bloodstained horse led along the street and then came a soldier with a bandaged head and supported by comrades on either side. She thought it "sickening." Myers spent the afternoon standing in a driving rain giving water to troops as they marched past. Abraham Essick, pastor of St. James Lutheran, watched the developing battle from his church's steeple before retreating to the parsonage basement, where he saw nothing but heard much. Nicholas and Elizabeth Codori in the center of town also sought refuge in their cellar. Myers, too, eventually took to her basement with neighbors, forming "a huddle of women and children, some crying and some praying." She remembered this as the "awfullest time" when she saw little but heard the shells, the retreat of Union troops, and the "unearthly yelling of the pursuing Rebels." A few retreating soldiers ran through her house—in the back door and out the front—but afterwards the only item missing was a linen apron she had been ironing. As Myers and the others peered out the basement windows, they saw Union soldiers now prisoners, and the new captives stood close enough to talk with the women. The men expected to be sent South and requested Myers and the others to contact their relatives. "One after the other," she recalled, "they gave us their names and the addresses of the persons to whom we were to write." When Myers emerged from her basement shelter, she observed many Confederates in the street and a decapitated Union soldier lying there, whom she surmised had been overtaken by cavalry.[30]

Other civilians had similar experiences on the first day of the battle. One family watched enemy soldiers loot the house across the street from top to bottom and carry off household goods in a large wagon. They expected a similar fate but were spared. Michael Jacobs, the math and science professor at Pennsylvania College, had Confederate troops spend the night on the sidewalks in front of his house. They demanded entrance to his home in search of Union soldiers and quickly found three Yankees in the cellar. Jacobs thought the rank-and-file Southerners were taunting, but he considered the officers as "intelligent and polite gentlemen" who welcomed conversation with civilians. Toward the end of the day Confederates took possession of Samuel Simon and Esther Schmucker's house. (Esther was Samuel's third wife, whom he married in 1849.) Heeding a warning from a Lutheran pastor in Frederick, Maryland, that Confederates might arrest him, Samuel spent the battle with friends in York, but Esther and a single twenty-two-year-old daughter, Alice, remained in the house by the Seminary as the first day of fighting closed in around them. Confederates evicted the two Schmucker women without time to gather possessions, and Esther and Alice waited out the rest of the battle in town with another daughter, Catherine, and her husband, William Duncan.[31]

The few African Americans who remained often depended on white assistance to stay concealed. A black farmhand hid in a wagon for three days while his employer's son periodically checked on him and provided food. The farmhand's wife was captured but released when the farmer's wife had her assist with the care of a wounded Confederate officer. Outside of town two others crawled under their employers' porch with stones and sacks hung over the wall to camouflage their spot. One woman was among a group of blacks captured by the Confederates on the first day. As her captors marched her and others out of town, she managed to escape in the confusion and slipped into Christ Church, where she spent the rest of the battle hiding in the belfry without food or water.[32]

On the next day fighting shifted south of town. Union troops remained on Cemetery Ridge, east of the Emmitsburg Road, and Confederates held the town and a long, low continuation of Seminary Ridge to west of the road. The Emmitsburg Road ran parallel to these two positions in a shallow valley with the Sherfys, the Staubs, and the Codori farm between the two armies. The Brien farm was part of the Union lines and hosted a battery of artillery with a regiment of artillery in support.[33]

Early on the morning of the second day a doctor came to Sallie Myers's house with instructions for her and her sisters to help, and he led them to the nearby Catholic Church. The scene appalled Myers; "everywhere was blood." The young teacher knelt by the first wounded man inside the door and asked what she could do for him. He replied, "Nothing. I am going to die." That sent her flying out the door, and she sat on the church steps crying. Then, composing herself, she went back inside and got to work. Soon, as the battle raged, she was "too busy to be afraid." Myers brought one soldier, shot through the lungs, home and watched him through the night except for two hours when she slept. While she fanned the wounded soldier, a bullet pierced two walls and hit the floor where she sat just moments previously. Had Myers remained there, she thought she would have been hit in the neck.[34]

The adult Sherfys remained on their farm through the morning of July 2. Even as skirmishers fought in the woods approximately one-third of a mile to the west, they stayed. When Mary's mother, Catherine Heagan, walked across the farmyard, a stray Minié ball passed through a fence and struck the folds of her skirts, thankfully spent. Heagen picked up the ball and kept it as a souvenir. Around mid-day, Union troops prepared a major advance from Cemetery Ridge to the Emmitsburg Road, and an officer ordered the Sherfys away "on account of danger," in Joseph's words. The family reunited near Littlestown.[35]

Catherine Staub, daughter of Anthony and Magdaleine Codori, was in her ninth month of pregnancy, and she probably hung close to home. Catherine's husband Jean was in the army, and she most likely spent the battle with her parents, perhaps on the small farm between the Sherfys and Confederate lines along Seminary Ridge or in the basement of the Codori farm along the Emmitsburg Road. Both were precarious positions.[36]

Most churches became hospitals. Union wounded arrived in the German Reformed building by 11:00 A.M. on the first day of fighting and within thirty minutes filled the building. Ten or twelve amputation tables were busy as blood-covered doctors rolled up their sleeves and cut. Observers reported blood on pews, walls, floors, and windowsills. Because pews were too narrow to serve as beds, attendants placed boards across them, covering the boards with blankets and straw. At St. Francis Xavier a soldier wounded in the elbow had a pew door torn off its hinges and placed across the pew, where he rested his swollen arm until the surgeon cut it off. After the amputation he swung his feet off the operating table, walked to the back of the church, and climbed the steps to the gallery, which was empty. At Christ Lutheran amputated arms and legs, tossed out of windows, littered the churchyard. Albertus McCreary, a young boy, lived behind the United Presbyterian church and watched surgeons working on an outdoor table so long that he got "pretty well hardened to such sights."[37]

At 1:30 P.M. on July 2 Union troops commanded by General Daniel E. Sickles advanced to the Emmitsburg Road. His troops in Sherfy's peach orchard occupied a particularly strategic point, one of the highest elevations on the battlefield other than the Round Tops and the closest point to Southern lines, but they also formed a salient, vulnerable to attack from the south and west. Late in the afternoon Confederates attacked. Southerners moved through the peach orchard and flanked northern troops along the Emmitsburg Road, driving them back toward

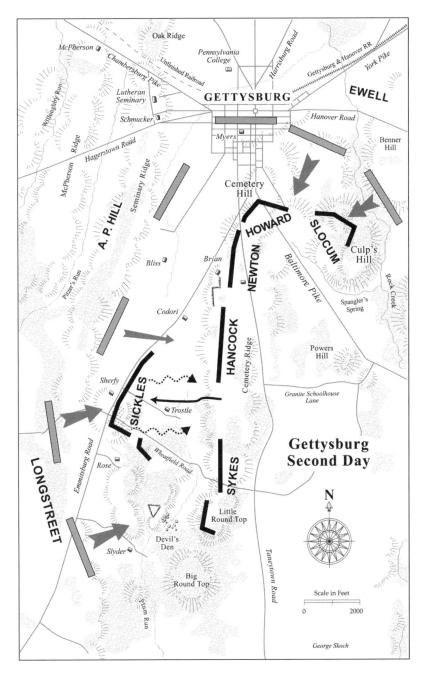

Gettysburg Day 2. Confederates attack, sweep through the Peach Orchard, and past the Sherfy farm. (Map by George Skoch.)

German Reformed Church, the first hospital, filled by 11:30 A.M. on July 1. (Courtesy of Gettysburg National Military Park.)

Cemetery Ridge. Fierce fighting occurred in the Sherfy farmyard. Northern sharpshooters fired from the house's windows and from the cellar, and Confederates captured fifty enlisted men and four officers on the property, including some still in upstairs rooms as Southerners came up the steps. When the fighting moved away, dead and wounded animals and humans lay in the yard, around the property, and in the road. Other wounded horses remained on their feet, adding

United Presbyterian Church, where fourteen-year-old Albertus McCreary observed surgeons at work in the yard. (Courtesy of Gettysburg National Military Park.)

to the gruesome scene. A Confederate artillery unit stopped when it encountered
dead and wounded Northern soldiers in the road and carried the wounded into
the Sherfy cellar. Other injured soldiers sought shelter in the barn, which one
officer described as "riddled with shot and shell like a sieve from its base to the
roof." Later it caught fire. One of the Sherfy girls thought that Union artillery
shells set it afire on July 3, but others understood that Confederates deliberately
torched it. Regardless, approximately one dozen were too injured to escape and
burned to death inside the structure.[38]

On July 3 Confederate batteries on the Sherfy property and Union guns on the
Brien farm contributed to a great artillery duel that preceded a large Confederate frontal assault, commonly called "Pickett's Charge," on the Union center. As
advancing Confederate lines crossed the Emmitsburg Road on their way to Cemetery Ridge, they passed around the Codori buildings, and General George E.

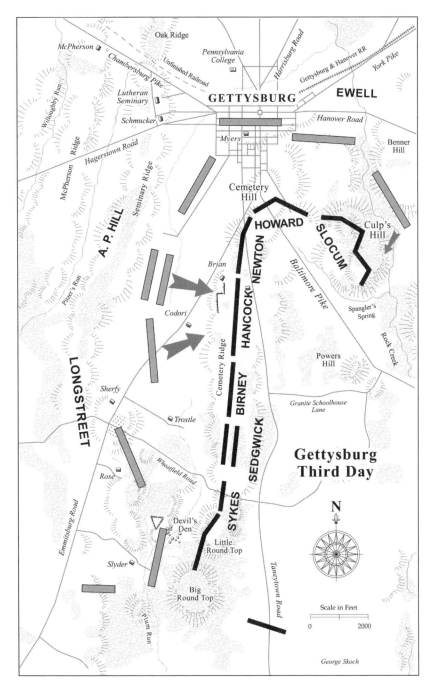

Gettysburg Day 3. Confederates attack the Union center.

Pickett probably watched the decimation of his division from the Codori farm. A few Mississippians took temporary shelter in the Brien barn, got cut off from their brigade, and surrendered. The attack on Cemetery Ridge failed horribly.[39]

Between 1 and 3 A.M. of July 4 Confederates evacuated the town and took positions on Seminary Ridge. Myers remembered that "everything was quiet the night following the battle, except for the squawking of chickens" taken by the departing army, and most civilians first learned that the town changed hands when Union troops led by bands marched down their streets. Southerners, however, still held Seminary Ridge on the edge of town, where they hoped to draw a Federal attack, and bullets from their skirmishers and sharpshooters made venturing outdoors hazardous. Moreover, the newly arrived, friendly troops were just as hungry as the departing enemy, and a food shortage added to the hardships of isolated, beleaguered civilians. One young woman claimed, perhaps with some embellishment, that after the Southerners left, she was so hungry that she ate an entire orange, "skin, seeds, and all." Nevertheless, the three-day ordeal had ended.[40]

George Codori, in his late fifties, was a prisoner of war as were approximately nine other civilians from the area. Family tradition tells several versions of Codori's capture; one is that cavalry arrested him on return from Baltimore, and another is that Confederates detained him on July 4 as he returned home and found a wounded Confederate in his basement. Both stories have him seized when control was in flux. He may have worn a Union jacket or cap. Codori's captors marched him into Virginia, then transported him to Salisbury, North Carolina, where he remained a prisoner until the war was almost over. He returned home in early March 1865, but died tragically three days later of pneumonia.[41]

Gettysburg religion had seen the elephant, the phrase soldiers used to describe experiencing combat for the first time. The terrible casualties, the horrors of hospitals, and the bizarre existence in a dark basement surrounded by battle sounds would linger long. For a child captivated by the gore of military surgeons, for a young woman who saw a decapitated corpse, for a family whose home was searched by armed strangers looking for other, concealed strangers, or for another family in whose home fighting took place, the elephant was surreal. For three days in July life was as chaotic as possible.

⚭

The battle, then, turned life in Gettysburg upside down. Damage was extensive, and it took approximately four to six weeks before congregations could function close to normal. By 1864, however, congregational life showed little impact from the battle. Although two small congregations—St. Paul's Lutheran and the AME Zion—never fully recovered and paying for the clean-up burdened several others, nevertheless one year after the armies came to Gettysburg, religion very much resembled its prebattle state.

The fight left a landscape that staggered observers. Sightseers—the first tourists—appeared just after the shooting stopped, and they reported devastation. Bodies and debris littered the streets. Michael Jacobs went out "immediately" after the battle and saw "shattered trees, perforated houses, fences swept away, trodden-down corn and wheat fields, scattered blankets, coats, knap-sacks, scabbards, canteens, muskets, rifles, and hundreds of thousands of Minié balls, shot, and shell." Thick swarms of green and blue flies coated fences and bushes. They fed off the dead flesh of humans and animals and multiplied at an astonishing rate. Scavengers already had begun the task of recovery by scouring through the rubbish for whatever had value: blankets, guns, or harnesses cut away from dead horses. Bodies of horses and swollen, discolored human corpses were everywhere. John Walker Jackson, a black Methodist minister from Harrisburg who arrived six days after the battle in a carriage full of white politicians, including the governor of the state, reported guns gleaned from the battlefield lying on the sidewalks and rusting while red hospital flags flew from churches, public buildings, and almost every home. The stench was overwhelming. The odor subsided somewhat in the center of town, but in the countryside the smell was unbearable. The stink hit Jackson before he could see the town's spires. On the Sunday after the battle Henry Baugher conducted a service in Christ Lutheran, and though brief five died before it ended.[42]

Property holders suffered extensively. The farm of Abraham and Elizabeth Brien sat on the edge of the great, third-day Confederate attack on the Union center, and soldiers tore down the fencing for firewood and fortifications, destroyed the garden, and took one and one-half tons of hay from the barn. They used the wheat field for food, trampled what they did not consume, and flattened the barley. All of the Briens' buildings had major damage from artillery fire, perhaps from the barrage on the third day, and an outdoor bake oven and the orchard were destroyed. A second rental house on the property was, according to Brien's damage claim, "torn and riddled and almost destroyed by the artillery fire of both sides." Farm animals had disappeared.[43]

The Schmuckers' house had been occupied by Confederates. The piano, bureaus, and some beds remained, but every room required repairs. Bayonets had slashed oil paintings of Schmucker and his father, and the home's temporary occupants destroyed the furniture, ruined window frames and sashes, and broke most of the glass. Garden and yard fencing were gone. Soldiers also ransacked Schmucker's library and scattered books and papers about the floor. Confederate artillery positioned around the Schmucker home and seminary had drawn fire from Federal batteries, and Schmucker counted thirteen holes, several two to three feet high, in the brick walls of his house. Only Schmucker's Bible rested undisturbed, picked up out the mess and restored to its spot on the bookcase by a Rebel soldier, who recorded his good deed in the Good Book. ("J. G. Beardon of the rebel army. This is the Holy Bible. I picked it up out of the . . . and have placed it back in the bookcase.") One scholar believes that Confederates knew of Schmucker's abolitionism and deliberately vandalized his house; in contrast Charles Philip Krauth's nearby home experienced much less damage and a Confederate officer ordered the return of a purloined silver set when Mrs. Krauth complained. But perhaps the Krauths were just lucky. The seminary, much like the Schmuckers, suffered with its archives and papers flung about, fencing removed, and holes and a two-story crack in the wall.[44]

The Sherfys probably endured as much destruction anybody. Joseph and his eldest son, Raphael, returned on July 6, and the rest of the family came the next day. The barn and hog stable were in ashes, and the fencing was down. The brick walls on the south and west sides of the house were bullet-scarred, and the roof had several holes made by shell fragments. A cannon ball damaged a corner of the home, and another lodged in an old cherry tree in the yard. The house's interior had bloodstains and bullet holes, which indicated that fire had come from all directions. One cow, three calves, and two hogs were dead. Combatants had pulled up or knocked down most of the trees in a new peach orchard, and the mature orchard suffered severe damage. Dead soldiers had already been buried in very shallow graves, but the bodies of horses rotted where they fell, moistened by heavy rain that fell on July 4 and cooked by the summer heat. Battle trash— guns, haversacks, blankets, bits of clothing, harnesses, broken caissons, canteens, paper, cartridge shells, and stolen civilian property—littered the property. Artillery maneuvers left deep ruts in the ground. Confederates had emptied the dresser drawers, and one witness reported "clothes, bonnets, towels, linen, etc., trampled in indistinguishable piles from the house out to the barnyard." Kitchen and household items, bedding, and clothing were gone. Mary's silk worms had starved to death, and the gifts from Andrew Jackson had disappeared. The Sherfy farm was a wreck.[45]

Not just physical damage but life's routine was another battle casualty that required time to heal. The Schmuckers remained with their daughter, Catherine Schmucker Duncan, and her husband in town, but every day Samuel, who had returned, walked out to his house to organize his scattered books and papers. Visitors swarmed into town, either to see the battlefield, to work in the hospitals, or to search for dead or wounded friends or family members. Guests overwhelmed the local hotels and often stayed in private homes. Two weeks after the battle Catherine Duncan complained that every day several appeared at her door to request lodging, and Sallie Myers's family also accepted out-of-towners while still nursing wounded officers. Schmucker's daughter grumbled about the burden of providing hospitality to a steady stream of houseguests, and Myers slept in her day clothes on the floor in an upstairs hallway with a carpet roll for a pillow. When members of her family ate, they helped themselves, and, Myers recalled, "it was a long time before we all sat down together." Lives remained disrupted weeks after the armies departed.[46]

Congregations, therefore, faced a steep climb to normalcy. The thousands of wounded gradually left town by rail, but the process was slow and many, especially the severely wounded, lingered in church buildings. For those who could not be transported away, the army built a general hospital, Camp Letterman, on the eastern edge of Gettysburg. Named for Dr. Jonathan Letterman, the medical director of the Army of the Potomac, this was a tent city on a scenic tract with woods, a strong spring, and good drainage located conveniently near the railroad and the York Pike. Prior to the war it had been a popular picnic spot. Camp Letterman officially opened on July 22 and closed on November 20, serving approximately 4,000. Despite the relative success of Camp Letterman, the public school did not open until October 1 because it was a hospital, and several churches, including the Methodists, Christ Lutherans, and Catholics, hosted wounded until mid-August, which effectively shut down their buildings for worship. Taken together with the period of disruption prior to July 1, it would be several months before Gettysburg could have a "Sunday."[47]

Unsurprisingly, the smallest and weakest congregations, St. Paul's Lutheran and the AME Zion, felt the battle most severely. In 1864 St. Paul's, the German immigrant fellowship, made no contributions to the Synod, pleading its general poverty and the added hardships caused by the battle. After conducting marriage ceremonies for six couples in 1861, nearly all German-born immigrants, St. Paul's only witnessed one wedding in 1862 and 1863 each, a sign of declining vigor. In April 1865 the congregation closed. To be sure, the limited appeal of all-German worship and the correspondingly powerful draw of the American mainstream probably factored into the demise of St. Paul's, but the disruption caused by the fighting added to the burden of this small society.[48]

The AME Zion survived but in reduced numbers. The AME Zion building may have escaped severe damage because it probably was not a hospital. Maybe it was too small, accounts of others do not mention it as hosting wounded, and its own records are silent about battle damage. The AME Zion trustees met six weeks after the battle for normal items and reconvened approximately one week later to take stock of the church's finances. Twenty dollars remained from a fair they had sponsored. By December congregational life appeared customary. On the day after Christmas 1863, class leaders were appointed and classes met. A woman who had married "contrary to Discipline" was dropped. In some ways, then, this fellowship showed postbattle signs of life quickly. But many of the black residents of Gettysburg who fled the Confederate army never returned, and by the fall of 1863 only sixty-four African Americans were on the town's tax roll. Sixty of the sixty-four who remained owned real estate or lived with a close relative or spouse who did, whereas refugees without realty had little incentive to return and simply planted new roots where they had escaped. The elevation of Reuben Robinson, an illiterate, to chair the board of trustees indicated the new African-American demographic, and the diminished number of blacks in town hurt the AME Zion. Small in the best of times, now it was smaller.[49]

Catholics also struggled particularly hard to recover from the battle. On July 5 two Sisters of Charity arrived from Emmitsburg and testified to the disorder they encountered. (Other Sisters came later, worked in other hospitals besides St. Francis, and won widespread acclaim for their service.) The odor of gangrene filled the church, and lockjaw was widespread. So many wounded lay on the pews, under them, and in the aisles that walking about was difficult. On July 10 William F. Norris, a doctor from a government hospital in Washington, D.C., took control at St. Francis Xavier, and the chaos similarly appalled him. Norris was dismayed that two hundred patients, including men with serious wounds, received little attention or food and that general confusion prevailed. He immediately set in motion changes to improve the diet, cleanliness, and general order. St. Francis Xavier hosted two baptismal ceremonies in July: one on July 12 and another on July 30 for June and Josephine Staub—twins (!) born five days after the battle to Catherine Codori Staub—although these rituals may have occurred outside the building. On July 26 the hospital closed with all remaining wounded transferred to Camp Letterman, but by January 1864 the Catholic building was still in disrepair and had not been cleaned.[50]

Other fellowships began their institutional recovery in late summer and more quickly than St. Francis Xavier. Dunkers, for example, had a congregational meeting five weeks after the battle. Like the AME Zion, their church book does not mention property damage, and apparently none of their buildings became hospitals. Moreover, had Dunker facilities been utilized, their minimalist décor without carpets, cushions, pews, railings, and other fancy woodwork required less effort to restore. At the Dunkers' first council meeting, in mid-August, the first item of business scheduled a large Love Feast for Saturday and Sunday, October 3 and 4, an indication of the high priority this ritual enjoyed in the Brethren universe and that the congregation could undertake an event requiring significant resources and preparation. Additional familiar practices, such as the election of deacons and visitors to prepare the congregation for Love Feast, quickly reappeared in the months after the battle.[51]

Recovery included financial assistance. The Dunkers' council distributed sixty-six dollars to thirteen persons, including Joseph Sherfy, who received six dollars. The money came from a congregation in York County, but non-Brethren also donated and they wanted to assist persons of all faiths. Consequently, recipients included the Staubs (Catholics), three Lutherans, a German Reformed, and Abraham Brien, a new step in ecumenicity for the nonmainstream Dunkers. Surely the beneficiaries of these funds appreciated the help, but it was pocket change and losses were many times greater. Joseph and Mary Sherfy's estimated damage of $2,466, perhaps understated, was the greatest of any within the congregation.[52]

In late October Sherfy had enough stability in his life to travel to Westminster, Maryland, to attend another congregation's Love Feast. He returned with an itinerating Brethren minister, hosted by the Sherfy family for the night. The guest looked around the property and concluded that the battle damage "considering all together beggars description." Nevertheless, the Sherfys, now welcomed overnight guests, and the Dunkers were on the road to recovery.[53]

Healing came to other congregations at a similar pace, working through late summer and the fall to restore worship. Although the Presbyterian session did not meet until January 1864, its trustees gathered much more quickly, assembling on July 27 to appoint a committee to clean the building, hire a lawyer to obtain damage payment from the government, and gather estimates for painting and covering the backs of the pews with damask, an upgrade. By September the church had been cleansed except for the basement, and the trustees decided to paint a fence behind the building. In November, when Abraham Lincoln attended a ceremony after the dedication of the national cemetery, the sanctuary must have been suitable for a presidential visit. Likewise, religious activity resumed elsewhere. In early October Marsh Creek Presbyterian, just off the battlefield, scheduled communion. St. James Lutherans had a congregational meeting on August 29 when they appointed a delegate to the upcoming synodical meeting, but they also created a committee to assess battle damages. Apparently, almost two months after the battle, the recovery process for their facility had just begun, but in October they expressed interest in replacing stoves with furnaces; perhaps their building was repaired and ready for refinement. In December Methodists hosted the quarterly meeting, and the minister, George Berkstresser, planned a protracted meeting in a county congregation. By the end of the year routine patterns were back.[54]

In 1864 the impact of the battle on local religion was barely discernible. Available attendance figures provide few clues about trends. Methodists showed a sharp decline from 248 members in 1863 to only 129 the following year. But Christ Church Lutheran began the period in 1860 with 127 communicants, dropped to 99 in 1863, probably owing to departed seminarians and collegians, yet rebounded to 131 communicants in 1865, after the war ended and when students had returned. (Christ Church did not report attendance figures in 1862 and 1864.) In 1860 St. James Lutheran reported 300 communicants, the number increased to 333 in 1863, and then to 357 in 1864 before falling to 300 in 1865. St. Paul's Lutheran, the German-immigrant congregation, held steady at between 46 and 50 throughout before closing. Apparently the comings and goings of war little influenced the number of persons walking through the doors of Gettysburg churches.[55]

In the year following the battle two fellowships—Christ Church and Gettysburg Presbyterian—had not quite completed recovery and needed the help of women to pay for it. Previously female contributions to congregational budgets had come through fairs, but maybe they could do more. Christ Church, desiring paint, carpet, and a railing in front of the pulpit, appointed three women—all with husbands or a father among the trustees—to raise the money in Philadelphia. The "Committee of Ladies" was successful beyond imagination and within approximately six weeks had obtained $1,251 in cash plus another $200 or $300 promised. With money burning a hole in their pockets, Christ Church went on a spree, remodeling the pews, improving the heating, painting the exterior woodwork, including the cupola and fence, staining or painting the brick front, and buying a reading desk. While some of this likely removed battle damage, other items, especially the reading desk and the pulpit with sofa, represented an improvement. For the women's contribution to the treasury, male leadership granted them input into the color of the pews and authority to furnish the church, including the carpet, pulpit, and cushions. Perhaps asking women for thoughts on color and

furnishings merely cast them in a traditional domestic role, but this was more
influence in congregational matters than they had previously and fundraising in
a distant urban center lay far outside women's traditional sphere.[56]

The perennially indebted Presbyterians also authorized a "Committee of Ladies" to obtain subscriptions for repairs, dispatching them to Washington and
Philadelphia. They, too, were successful, and soon trustees laid plans for "refit-
ting" the church and adding a new lecture room.[57]

The role of the Christ Church and Presbyterian "Ladies" mirrored that of
women in the larger society. Antebellum women had always raised money to
support benevolences through fairs, and during the war they turned their efforts toward charities such as the Ladies Relief Association, the U.S. Christian
Commission, and the U.S. Sanitary Commission. Public presentations of hand-
sewn flags to military units also became commonplace, another new public role
for women. (Porter's Guards had benefitted from the stitching ability of Gettysburg women.) Entreaties of women from the now famous battle town must have
pulled on heartstrings connected to wallets, and traveling to cities in search of
cash was something new for females. Although scholars disagree on the overall
impact of the war on gender, local women inched a little higher in status.[58]

Extraordinary fundraising stemmed from lingering problems for a few congregations, but resumption of routine business reveals recovery more generally.
AME Zion church leaders, for example, convened infrequently until the end of
the war, perhaps a consequence of wartime hardships, but sporadic meetings
were also part of antebellum congregational life. The December 23, 1864, meeting reported that the classes were "in order" and that the congregation was out
of debt with a surplus of ninety-three cents. For this poverty-stricken congregation the ordinary had returned. St. James Lutherans confirmed new members,
accepted a pastoral resignation, called another preacher, and decided to continue
German preaching once per month. Presbyterians also lost their minister, who
was not fully paid—hardly a first for this fellowship—and reported "some dis-
satisfaction" with his performance. Perhaps departing Lutheran and Presbyterian
pastors indicate continuing difficulties from the battle—perhaps the ministers
left for less challenging parishes—but pulpit turnover was routine before the war.
Christ Church Lutherans told students to stop sitting in pews not designated
for their use. Early in 1864 Joseph Sherfy and the elder of Marsh Creek, David Bosserman, "amicably settled," according to the church book, a difference as
each promised to "drop what had previously passed," whatever it was. Harmony
within the faith community was a long-standing concept for Dunkers, and reconciliation between two squabbling preachers, role models no less, must have

made a warm moment within the fellowship. Council also appointed Bosserman and Michael Bushman, another preacher, to admonish sisters who wore hoops. Classes in order, debts, empty pulpits, and discipline testified to the restoration of traditional practices.[59]

In sum, viewed from the perspective of fresh paint and remodeled pews, the great armed clash changed Gettysburg religion little. Admittedly, the high human cost of the war rattled the faith of some, especially New England intellectuals, and spiritualism—the ability of the living and dead to communicate with each other—gained popularity in North and South. Additionally, the great carnage of the war caused a fundamental revision in popular concepts about death. Bodily resurrection—possession of bodies in heaven—once popular lost support given the butchery of battle. Orderly, Victorian death became nearly impossible on battlefields and in campgrounds, but the federal government filled the void by creating national cemeteries, cataloguing casualties, and generally restoring some structure to the process of death. To be sure, popular religion felt the impact of the war.[60]

But on the local level the religious *status quo* often held sway. Picking up the pieces of religious life and restoring them to their proper place replaced chaos with order on the community level and within the individual psyche. The Confederate intruder who returned Schmucker's Bible to the bookcase was the first to do this, probably unintentionally, and after four to six weeks of disruption the rest of the community turned to the reconstruction of religion. Congregations slowly healed as the wounded gradually departed, and by Fall everybody but the Catholics had made significant progress. The most conspicuous change to local habits came in gender as women in two congregations assisted in fundraising in large urban areas. Moreover, one fragile fellowship, St. Paul's Lutheran, weakened by the battle, failed to survive the war while another, the AME Zion, suffered permanent injury. But after other congregations swept, scrubbed, and painted, they returned to worship and routine business, such as discipline, pastoral placement, and finances, that concerned them prior to the battle. The quest for improvement (i.e., refinement) endured, a signal that the war had not revolutionized faith. The traumatic battle, then, brought some change to local religion, especially female fundraising, but much appeared the same.

◌੨

If three days of battle had little long-term impact on daily religion, four years of war had more lasting influence on broader religious patterns, most noticeably in the relationship between church and state. Protestantism had always embraced American republican values, religious reform advocates had entered politics by calling for temperance laws, proslavery advocates like Philip Schaff had thumped the Bible in defense of slavery, and antislavery Christians had lobbied for freedom. Politicians knew that many voters were religious and they responded accordingly. Yet many preachers, particularly Democrats and Southerners, had often avoided mixing affairs of state too closely with religion, especially partisan politics and particularly from the pulpit. During the war, however, a new, cozier relationship emerged between religion and the now more powerful, more intrusive state. Scholars call this arrangement "civil religion" and define it as the intermingling of church and state so much that loyalty and service to one becomes loyalty and service to the other. The nation-state acquires sacred characteristics and borrows the rhetoric of religion while religious organizations become sounding boards for patriotism. The American version of civil religion often adds that God has special designs for its nation, that is, a mission for the "city on a hill" to spread liberty to the rest of the world. Or, as Henry Baugher, president of Pennsylvania College and St. James preacher, affirmed, the "hand of God" was clearly visible in the American story. The Civil War version of national religion adapted to the enormous sacrifice of life by linking it to a revival or rebirth that would eventually create a more unified America. "There is no doubt," asserted the Gettysburg-published *Evangelical Review* after Lincoln's assassination, that America would emerge from its "trials, from the terrible ordeal through which [it] has passed, a purer, stronger, and a better people than we were before the war." Another piece in the *Evangelical Review* assured that no matter how high the cost, the "final results will be God's glory . . . and the good of his creatures promoted." Civil War–era national religion began when many preachers responded eagerly to President James Buchanan's call for a national day of fasting with their thoughts about slavery and national sin in a last-ditch attempt to avoid war, and as the conflict evolved, the statehouse and the meetinghouse came together like never before.[61]

One big step toward civil religion was demolition of the wall between religion and politics in the pulpit. Now, instead of maintaining separation between faith and politics, many argued that God had joined the two and that they belonged together naturally. Often preachers of civil religion still paid homage to separation of church and state but in practice violated it clearly. East Baltimore Conference Methodists, for example, specifically absolved themselves of mixing religion and politics—"we are not justly liable to the charges of political teaching"—as they did it. "Patriotism is a Christian virtue, taught in the Word of God," the Conference proclaimed, which they could say because promoting national loy-

alty from the pulpit no longer violated the traditional ban on political preaching. At one annual gathering the East Baltimore Methodists placed "with great
enthusiasm" a U.S. flag in front of the church. Henry Ziegler went a step further
and asserted that mixing religion and politics was a higher form of faith. In the
Evangelical Review, Ziegler pointed out that government commonly regulated a
long list of issues vital to religion, such as judicial oaths, care for the poor, duel-
ing, brothels, the Sabbath, murder, theft, fornication, and adultery. Additionally,
the Bible freely discusses government and public leaders, charging them to be
just (Deut. 1:13), asserting that their authority is from God (Rom. 13:3–6), and
urging obedience upon magistrates (Tit. 3:1). In fact, Ziegler, a former resident
of Gettysburg and now a professor at a new Lutheran seminary in Selinsgrove,
Pennsylvania, argued that religion and politics were so close that weakening the
relationship, much less ignoring it, was very wrong. According to Ziegler, when
preachers yielded to the mantra not to "meddle with politics" and, therefore,
did not hold public policies accountable to the gospel, the state controlled them,
making an informal but "practical" union of church and state. Ziegler wanted
open discussion of political matters in church similar to traditional questions of
faith, such as repentance and regeneration, and he thereby laid a vital stepping-
stone along the path to civil religion.[62]

At the core of the new relationship between church and state was outspoken
support for the Union's cause, the conviction that God approved this effort, and
the related assumption that the Confederacy embodied evil. (Southern civil religion reversed positions.) Admittedly, not all embraced the effort to suppress
the insurrection. Border North Germans acquired a reputation for Copper-
head sympathies though lukewarm might more accurately describe their attitude about the war. In Gettysburg some considered the German Reformed as
the "Rebel Church" for their alleged Southern inclination. But the assumption
that God backed the war was widespread. John Walker Jackson, for example, the
black Methodist from Harrisburg who visited Gettysburg after the battle, got into
a disagreement with a Confederate chaplain tending wounded, told the white
man that rebellion was a sin and departed. It must have been a brief but vivid
scene. White preachers often instructed slaves that rebellion violated God's will,
and one wonders if Jackson or the Confederate chaplain caught the irony when
Jackson turned these tables on his foe by lecturing him about rebellion. Regardless, Jackson was certain that God wanted Northern victory.[63]

Others likewise expressed certainty that God smiled on the war. *The Evangelical Review* likened the war to a second crusade that would finish the task of the
medieval Crusades by buckling on the "armor" and not taking it off until "vic-

tory in this great battle for liberty and right." Another article in the same journal identified the war as the "holiest cause for which men have ever fought." Henry Baugher told the graduating class at Pennsylvania College that it was the "will of God" to suppress rebellion, and the Lutheran Synod of West Pennsylvania considered it a "Christian duty" to suppress the "wicked insurrection" and "unholy rebellion."[64] East Baltimore Methodists concluded that if Lincoln "had not done all that he had to sustain the Union, he would have been a traitor himself" and emphasized that they "supported their country in the time of need." The South, in contrast, was "treasonable" and injurious to liberty around the world, while the Union's cause was "wise" and "patriotic." This represented a significant shift in position and tone for these self-described borderland moderate Methodists, who through the 1850s and the secession crisis remained passionately committed to colonization and rejected with large unanimous votes proposals from other conferences to bar slaveholders from membership. But now East Baltimore Methodists took sides—indeed, neutrality was virtually impossible—and only a small minority, including Gettysburg's pastor, George Stevenson, dissented. By 1864 East Baltimore condemned the rebellion as a "crime against God" and "against humanity," and it praised those who punished Confederate "enemies of society" as "minister[s] of God" who "beareth not the sword in vain." Although this does not declare that soldiers fought and died for their faith, it comes close.[65]

If God was a Yankee, it seemed only natural to credit the Divine for Northern victories. A statement from a Methodist Conference meeting in York, written in part by former Gettysburg pastor J. H. C. Dosh, thought that the "baptism of fire and blood" would only end when God's "purposes were accomplished." After the war, Philip Schaff, certain that God's purposes had been accomplished, told European audiences that God had given the North its recent success, and John Nevin, in a July 4, 1865, address, similarly declared that the war was "God's work," which made possible the triumph of the "better powers." The East Baltimore Methodists felt "profound gratitude" for military triumph given by the "hand of God,"[66] and the Lutheran Synod of West Pennsylvania thanked "Divine Providence" for "so speedily delivering our territory from the invading foe" and for preserving from greater injury the college, the seminary, and the churches in its territory.[67] F. W. Conrad, publishing in the *Evangelical Review*, demonstrated how specifically God's hand could bring victory by listing numerous turning points in the Gettysburg campaign. Conrad, a Chambersburg clergyman, reminded Lutherans that the Army of the Potomac changed commanding generals (Meade for Joseph Hooker) on the eve of battle, a very risky step; Cemetery Hill effectively anchored the Union position even though the less desirable Seminary Ridge was the first choice of commanders; the compact, horse-shoe shape of the Union lines facilitated defense; the "hollow of God's hand" protected Meade personally from artillery fire; mistakes or poor performance that had too often plagued the Northern effort in other battles were absent this time; and the army fought on its own soil with special inspiration. According to Conrad, all showed God's influence.[68] When in 1865 news arrived of General Jubal Early's defeat and the capture of most of his army between Staunton and Charlottesville, Virginia, the East Baltimore assemblage rose and sang the Doxology. Early was responsible for the burning of Chambersburg the previous year, and his demise, therefore, must have had special meaning for this Methodist conference. Praising God for the flow of all military blessings bound church and state together more tightly than ever.[69]

God-given victories might even lead to a new millennial age of liberty and justice. John Nevin thought that the Northern triumph was a "national deliverance" and a "world-historical act" of God. F. W. Conrad predicted that once slavery was eliminated, under God's guidance the United States would become the most powerful nation in the world and "usher in the day of Jubilee, when the Angel of Freedom shall ascend the political heavens, and taking the trumpet of God, shall proclaim liberty to the earth, and to all the inhabitants thereof." Like Julia Ward Howe's "Battle Hymn of the Republic," which foresaw "the coming of the Lord," a "terrible swift sword," and "his day . . . marching on," Conrad envisioned Divine-led entrance into a period of freedom. Reliance on America's destiny for a millennial era created an especially overt form of civil religion.[70]

But the millennium was in the future, and the suffering was now, which jeremiads explained. Jeremiads, or self-critical appraisals of society, helped to understand God's mystery and drew attention to America's exceptional status, thereby bringing faith and nation together. Jeremiads assumed that God blessed the chosen people but also held them accountable and punished them when they strayed, which was probably inevitable. The purpose of the punishment, however, was corrective rather than destructive because God intended to restore the erring children to a closer relationship. Jeremiads were an old American custom. Puritans used them to build an alternative to Anglicanism in the New England wilderness, and the American Revolutionary generation employed this sermonic device in their quest for independence and republicanism. In the 1830s abolitionists created antislavery jeremiads, but this was a fringe movement and their jeremiads fell on few ears. But during the Civil War this time-tested and familiar genre was at hand and employed with frequency.[71]

As the losses piled up, jeremiads became a logical explanation for the apparent irrationalism. Northerners gradually concluded that the war was more than punishment for the South but chastisement for all, that is, punishment for all national transgressions. The atonement-like sacrifice of life—the "martyrdom" and "baptism of blood"—would purge the nation, including the North, of its sins, and if the North genuinely repented, it would achieve victory. Daniel Payne thundered that noncombatants could influence the war by invoking the "right arm of God," which "lifts up and casts down nations according as they obey or disregard" God's principles. When Lutheran preachers of the West Pennsylvania Synod noted the "sobs and sighs of widows and orphans, the wail which raises unsuppressed from desolate households, and the blackened remains of burnt houses and villages," they reasoned that God demanded such a terrible sacrifice not just because of slavery but because of other sins, as well. Then they produced a traditional laundry list of misbehavior—greed of gain, intemperance, profanity, Sabbath-breaking, neglect of family religion, amusements, dancing, cards, horse-racing, the circus, and so on—all of which led to God's punishment and the current afflictions. Abraham Lincoln became increasingly comfortable with this motif. His 1861 proclamation for a national day of fasting incorporated the traditional jeremiad, suggesting "in sorrowful remembrance of our own faults and crimes as a nation and as individuals, to humble ourselves before him." Perhaps this was a bit formulaic, but Lincoln's later calls for fasting and repentance were more heart-felt. In March 1863 he bluntly termed the conflict "punishment" and observed that Americans had "forgotten God," become "intoxicated with unbroken success," and grown "too proud to pray." He called for Americans to "confess our national sins." Lincoln's second inaugural address finally latched onto the penultimate sin of both North and South that caused God's anger: slavery. In sum, jeremiads contributed to civil religion by reinforcing the specialness of America—only the chosen receive God's reproach—and, more broadly, by linking faith to the status of the nation-state. By charging wartime misery to sin and God's anger, jeremiads provided a rationale for the slaughter and bonded church and state. In the end, the nation would be even more blessed by God.[72]

One person and one fellowship—Samuel Simon Schmucker and the Dunkers—particularly illustrate the rising tide of civil religion. While many individuals and most religious organizations changed during the war as they talked more candidly about the earthly kingdom and embraced the great cause, Schmucker and the Dunkers traveled unique roads to a closer relationship between church and state.

Once Schmucker had disapproved of all war. Admittedly, peace was not a major theme in his ministry, but he preached against the Mexican War and repeated the sermon several times, including in Gettysburg during the Antietam campaign. Additionally, on his tour of Europe, Schmucker complained that the "evils of war" were "most impressively seen," especially the ubiquitous presence of soldiers, either standing guard or in transit. Schmucker disapproved, contending that these fighting men produced nothing while requiring the "labor of others" for support.[73] But with war in his nation, and, moreover, in his own town and home, this preeminent Lutheran theologian eventually lined up solidly behind the cause. He served on the relief committee appointed in the opening days of the war to raise money for families of soldiers, and a son, Samuel, a Pennsylvania College student, joined the Emergency Volunteers and stood against Jubal Early. Although Schmucker did not edit his sermon for its 1862 preaching, one wonders if he ad-libbed a softer attitude toward warfare. After the Battle of Gettysburg, Schmucker declared that the victory "in defence of Republican government" came from a "kind Providence." The one-time antiwar preacher now believed that God had chosen his side.[74]

Even more impressive was the power of civil religion to drawn in the Dunkers. Lutherans, after all, could cite Martin Luther, who considered war as a "divine institution and as necessary to mankind as eating and drinking,"[75] but the Dunkers had been nonparticipants in government from their inception in the early eighteenth century and sometimes persecuted for it.

Civil War-era Dunkers still kept the state at bay by refusing to participate in military service. In the early years of the war, Dunkers had little reason to fear that their young men might be compelled to serve. Patriotism motivated many enlistees; then bounties added financial incentive. Communities received quotas, and as filling them became more difficult, the size of the bounties steadily rose. Reluctant warriors could also pay commutation fees of three hundred dollars, a high amount for the poor but manageable for the middle class. Generally, men who did not want to go could stay home. By 1864, however, many who could be persuaded or bought were in uniform, and the gruesome wounds and grim accounts of those who returned and the growing list of those gone forever further discouraged volunteers. As recruits became increasingly scarce, Congress tightened draft laws and eliminated commutation except for conscientious objectors. Although young Dunker men could still pay cash to avoid military service, conscription became a growing concern for the fellowship.[76]

Yearly Meeting held firm. The annual gathering ruled against baptizing soldiers in most cases, opposed paying bounty or hiring substitutes, and instead recommended waiting for the government to compel fines and taxes. Marsh Creek Dunkers enjoyed success in keeping their young men out of uniform even though several had their names called. Raphael Sherfy, son of Joseph and Mary, was in Chambersburg, where the draft procedure took place, to report for Adams County, when a blind man doing the honors pulled Sherfy's name from the wheel. According to an eye-witness, "With mingled surprise and good humor," the startled conscientious objector replied, "'Is that so!' and then shared in the general merriment at his expense." Sherfy along with several other Dunkers paid a commutation fee, which came just months after the battle and must have been difficult. In 1864 Marsh Creek council expelled one who answered the call and suspended another who had declared intent to enlist before drafted to get the bounty. Both of these men had relatives disciplined by the congregation within the previous decade, suggesting that their families were backbenchers reluctant to yield to the council's concept of purity. On the other hand, in 1865, after the war had ended, two more from Marsh Creek followed the counsel of Yearly Meeting and paid a commutation fee. In a show of support for these faithful ones, the congregation tapped into a bequest and in November, six months after Appomattox, contributed towards the expense. By expelling those who took up arms and supporting those who did not, Marsh Creek sustained its traditional values and avoided the influence of the worldly kingdom.[77]

Yet even the Dunkers endorsed the Northern cause and adopted their own form of civil religion. The Yearly Meeting declared discipline for those who preached proslavery principles, even privately, and lest nonvoting and non-resistance cast the Brethren as "indifferent" to or even as opponents of the Union, Yearly Meeting now approved of the effort to "suppress the rebellion." "Suppress" seems a strong word for a nonresistant fellowship to use. Additionally, Yearly Meeting labeled Confederate sympathies as a worldly sin that corrupted the body of believers. Elders and ministers who sided with the South or who voted for secession could not continue in their positions, and voters for secession would "be put away from among us." The gathering also condemned those who "speak evil of the rulers of our land in public." At first blush this appears to reaffirm a long-standing Brethren belief that God ordained civic rulers, but excommunication of those who criticized the government, "especially of President Lincoln," combined with removal of Confederate sympathizers sounds more like an endorsement of Republican policy.[78] In another time a nonresistant faith, repulsed by the carnage, might have joined in the politics of peace, but apparently this generation of Dunkers considered antislavery Unionist Republicanism more attractive than peace Democracy and they edged closer to Big Brother.

In other ways the war encouraged a redefinition of the Brethren relationship with the state. Nonvoting came under severe pressure as rank-and-file Dunkers increasingly wanted to cast ballots, which had been off-limits. Numerous inquiries about voting came to Yearly Meeting. In 1864 one communication reflected that the previous year's decision to continue the ban on political activity had caused "hard feelings and disunion," and in 1865 delegates considered four more questions about voting. Each time denominational leadership ruled against it, but the persistent pressure to relax this position showed growing interest in political activity. In 1864 Marsh Creek council "advised" members "to abstain" from voting, an indication that questions about this had arisen within their fellowship.[79]

Marsh Creek also slipped further into the political mainstream by honoring President Andrew Johnson's request for a day of "humiliation and prayer" a few weeks after Lincoln's assassination. Previously, they had ignored appeals by Buchanan and Lincoln for fasting days, but in 1864 Yearly Meeting approved observing calls from the president and state governors for Thanksgiving and other holidays. This was close enough to Johnson's plea that Marsh Creek scheduled a 10:00 A.M. service. This decision, however, required a special meeting of congregational leadership, which all of the deacons and part of the ministry attended, an indication of the new ground that it broke.[80]

Thus, as might be expected, Marsh Creek Dunkers developed a unique version of church-state faith. True, they never claimed that God was at work on the battlefield or that the nation-state had a millennial destiny, and they retained nonresistance and nonvoting. But pressure to vote mounted, at some cost to cherished unity within the fellowship, and Dunkers heartily stamped their approval on the North's cause. Responding to the state's call to worship, which was also new for them, further represented mainstream political behavior. Of course, for this conservative fellowship dikes to keep out the shifting mainstream had always been works in progress, and the barriers were never leak-proof. But, undeniably the war made it increasingly difficult for Marsh Creek Dunkers to remain aloof from the mainstream, particularly in politics, and although Dunkers did not embrace civil religion as tightly as other fellowships, the extent to which these determined outsiders joined in the intermingling of faith and state brought them a distance as far as anyone and illustrates the remarkable strength of civil religion.

Pacifist Dunkers, however, were an atypical representation of civil religion, only partially imbibing it. The mainstream religious traditions more freely blended their faith with politics, certain that God blessed their side, cursed the other, and caused victory. Smiting foes of the state became the work of God, and church and state were less separate, a significant change in American religion.

CR

In 1865 a visitor to the Sherfy peach orchard found the trees loaded, and Anna, the youngest, selling peaches out of a basket. "They were large and juicy and sweet," the sightseer reported. That year Raphael Sherfy advertised "Peaches from the Battle-Field Orchard" in *The Baltimore Sun*, testament to both change, that is, Gettysburg's fame, and to continuity: the Sherfys had recovered. In 1866 another visitor riding down Emmitsburg Pike Road noted that battle debris, such as hats, shoes, and pieces of equipment, still littered the gullies beside the road and "was scattered everywhere in great profusion." In the peach orchard he reported that "a tangled mass of dead branches still strews the ground." Although the hastily dug graves had disappeared, "the deep green spot in the turf, the few hills of corn more luxuriant than their neighbors, or the dark color of the oats, and the ranker growth of the wheat, told where vegetable life had drawn rich nourishment from the dead." Joseph Sherfy, a lifetime farmer, could hardly have missed the effect this had on his large and juicy peaches.[81]

Like Sherfy and his peaches, Gettysburg religion survived the battle and recovered more or less unchanged. Undoubtedly the wartime tempo of Gettysburg modulated from a peacetime to a martial beat with recruiting, fundraising, garrisoned troops, and invasion scares. But congregations met regularly and struggled with the same antebellum problems of debt and pastoral placement. When the storm broke, life was overturned. Residents evacuated or retreated to their basements, intruding soldiers from both armies shattered the sanctity of the home, and during lulls in the fighting and afterwards, citizens beheld streets littered with battle trash and human and animal corpses. In the aftermath, property damage was extensive, and the care for wounded and the overpowering stench added to an experience never forgotten. The Victorian home may have been a castle but not for three days in July.

Congregations, nevertheless, reinstated normal religious life within weeks and months. By fall 1863, after the mess was cleaned up, most congregations were back to normal, pursuing refinement as before. Only two small faith communities, the AME Zion fellowship with a depleted black population and the immigrant Germans of St. Paul's Lutheran, who closed their doors, suffered permanent damage, and female fundraising in distant locations was different. But sofas for pulpits, discipline for violators of norms, money for strained treasuries, and preachers to provide leadership returned as priorities. In some ways, then, the three-days of bloodletting, for all their disruption of life and enduring impact on the image of the town, changed Gettysburg religion not much.

But if the battle brought limited lasting change, the war itself impacted religion more significantly, especially with the rise of civil religion. This binding together of religion and the nation more tightly than ever before belonged to a broad national trend with enthusiastic participation on both sides of the conflict.[82]

On a simple level, then, the battle changed Gettysburg forever, instantly transforming the little town into a well-known tourist attraction. Raphael Sherfy sold "battle-field" peaches in Baltimore, an interesting adjustment in the family business that capitalized on the famed soil. But the Sherfy family still canned peaches as they had done before the battle, and, likewise, change in religion was measured, except for the altered relationship between church and state. Historians may claim that the Civil War redefined American politics but not its religion.

Conclusion

In late fall 1863, as the days grew shorter, the shadows longer, and all but the most stubborn leaves had dropped, Abraham Lincoln arrived in Gettysburg to dedicate a new national cemetery, a seventeen-acre burial ground adjacent to Evergreen for Union—not Secesh—soldiers who had fallen in the summer battle. The new burial ground was a rural cemetery organized by the state of Pennsylvania and locally by David Wills, a prominent attorney, but it was also a national facility, the result of the new role for government as internment of the countless dead overwhelmed the private sector. African-American work crews, led by Basil Biggs, exhumed bodies, $1.59 per body, from their hasty burials around the battlefield and brought them to the new location.

Lincoln's 3-minute, 9-sentence, 272-word discourse became another powerful Gettysburg memory that touches core religious themes of the nineteenth century. A Greek funeral oration with a biblical rhythm, the speech defined America as a nation that began with the Declaration of Independence and was committed to equality from its birth. "Four score and seven" drew on Psalm 90 ("threescore years and ten"), and "brought forth" is a common biblical phrase, mostly notably in the Christmas story: "and she brought forth her firstborn son" (Luke 2:7). Lincoln's call for a "new birth of freedom" alludes to the doctrine of the new birth and suggests that the nation will experience a cleansing similar to those born again. Other words, such as "hallow" and "consecrate," also have religious implications, and portions of the ceremony felt more religious than political and drew no applause.

Moreover, the Gettysburg Address embodies several strong impulses in American religion. Lincoln did not mention diversity, but the concept nonetheless hovered over the site and the proceedings. The cemetery's layout, which treated all graves equally, aimed to level distinctions between military rank and home state, but it also gave equality to immigrant Catholics of the Irish Brigade and Germans in the Eleventh Corps. Lincoln considered diversity as synonymous with political division and self-interest, but the speech's great emphasis on unity indicates awareness of variety and shows its influence on the short statement. Out of diversity, Lincoln sought a nation, not a union, that is, a *volk* rather than a political combination of diverse elements. More explicitly, Lincoln and the Gettysburg address demonstrated refinement. A choir, drawn from the local talent pool and with a two-to-one female-to-male ratio, sang refined music, and the entire day embraced the rural cemetery movement. The previous year Lincoln had buried his son, Willie, in a rural cemetery in Georgetown, and the president's words at Gettysburg likewise signaled his acceptance of the new style of burial. In typical rural cemetery rhetoric, Lincoln stressed that the new burial ground would memorialize the fallen, especially war heroes, and just as J. H. C. Dosh had preached nine years ago when he dedicated Evergreen, Lincoln promised that the monuments would inspire future generations. Race, another important theme in religion, crept into the speech with its vague but firm call for freedom that in context easily read to mean emancipation for slaves, which is exactly how African Americans took it, and civil religion benefitted from the use of religious words to celebrate the nation-state, including the speech's only ad lib, which described the "one nation" as "under God." Finally, while Lincoln's brief remarks summoned the North to a great cause, they also provided reassurance after a hellish experience. As Gettysburg congregations restored themselves to normalcy in the second half of the summer, so in November the Gettysburg Address brought balance and order to the country after the chaos of July.[1]

❧

Lincoln's unforgettable remarks could hardly have struck such a powerful chord with his audience without solid footing in basic social trends of his day. The Gettysburg Address, then, serves as an eloquent reminder of the vital characteristics of Border North religion, especially refinement, diversity (including race), and the war.

Refinement was as prominent as the steeples that marked nineteenth-century skylines. In Gettysburg the college and seminary disseminated refinement, and Methodists gradually shifted from the emotion and disorder of sudden conversion, especially at camp meetings, to restrained, more dignified Sunday Schools and catechisms. Dunkers resolutely rejected fashion and sophistication, but their effective use of antirefinement to separate from the mainstream ironically confirms the impulse toward sophistication and gentility among the main body of Christians.

In its everyday faith, Gettysburg religion practiced what it preached about refinement. Ecumenical Evergreen Cemetery with its shrubbery, tidiness, and graceful pathways occupied several acres of refinement on the edge of town.

Congregations filled with middle-class consumers, beneficiaries of a changing economy, spent to their capacity and beyond as they improved themselves on a variety of levels, large and small, with furnishings, fixtures, and structures. The individual items all contributed to larger Victorian concepts of achievement, polish, and culture. Refined preaching by seminary graduates and improved music added further decorum. Purchasing power, however, still drew limits, particularly for the poverty-stricken AME Zion, mostly bystanders in the pursuit of refinement. Additionally, many congregations accumulated significant debt as they bought style and taste, and Presbyterian indebtedness became so burdensome that the congregation failed to meet obligations to its pastors. With the exception of the Dunkers and AME Zion, refinement and its cost were ubiquitous.

Diversity, almost as apparent as refinement and just as important, existed in multiple forms. As in Pennsylvania's colonial days, ethnicity and language were varied. German persisted among some who were Pennsylvanians for many generations—including Catholics, Dunkers, Lutherans, and Reformed—while others accepted English without giving up their native tongue. Although many, then, were comfortable with bilingualism, language also had the potential to divide, more so as a new wave of immigrants gave German an additional push. Households of different ethnicity further complicated the mix. The combination formed by the French-born Codoris, who worshipped with Germans and lived with their teen-aged Dutch workers, was unusual, but it illustrates the possibilities and, more importantly, the ordinariness of diversity. Invading Confederates must have heard German on the streets and perhaps even a Dutch oath when they took Nicolas Codori's horse from Charlie Suppan. The roots of those who sat in the pews of Gettysburg stretched to multiple seedbeds.

Doctrinal diversity was equally remarkable. Evangelicalism, for example, was multihued. Although camp meetings and protracted meetings were fading stars in the Methodist universe, Wesleyans still occasionally held these spirit-filled gatherings even as they became more comfortable with Sunday schools and catechisms. A related option was the moderate revivalism of many Lutherans and Reformed who appreciated heart-felt conversion but sought constraint on the disorder of revivalism. Still others, however, completely rejected evangelicalism in favor of the structure of catechism, creeds, and clerical leadership. Individual denominations further contributed to doctrinal diversity. The Associate Reformed/United Presbyterians, descended from Scottish dissent but locally off the Calvinist reservation on creeds and confessions, supplied Gettysburg with a second option for Presbyterians. The dissenters participated in the Evergreen Cemetery and other community projects, and they were not especially nonconformist, except in their rejection of musical innovations. Dunkers and Roman Catholics were more distinctive alternatives. Dunkers reveled in being different, which they achieved in ways no other Protestants did, including trine immersion baptism of adults, plain dress, uneducated, untrained preachers, Love Feasts with feet washing, resistance to consumerism, and nonresistance. Catholics, too, were unusual in special ways, especially with affinity for mysticism, sacramentalism, devotionalism, and hierarchy. Dunkers and Catholics were genuine outsiders, one native-born Protestant and the other foreign-born non-Protestant, and although positioned equidistant from the center, they orbited along very separate paths. Despite these doctrinal disputes, all components of Gettysburg religion usually tolerated each other, and cooperative ventures, including Evergreen Cemetery and union prayer meetings, were routine, though without Dunker, Catholic, or black participation. Only Roman Catholics drew open resistance, but in the grand scheme of things, they, too, benefitted from general broadmindedness as they worshipped openly and built a strong parish. Certainly, Gettysburg offered variety to shoppers in the spiritual marketplace.

Race added another layer of diversity to Gettysburg religion. Race divided Gettysburg as much as any issue with perspectives ranging from race-baiters who respected Southern slavery to activists in the Underground Railroad. The Methodist Baltimore Conference embodied the ideological mosaic by laboring to keep its clergy free of slavery but despising abolitionists and distrusting blacks within its congregations. Dunkers, almost always different, were another voice. They were progressives on race, especially slavery, but pondered how to interact with blacks in one of their distinctive rituals. Nobody else thought about race in quite those terms. Gettysburg also had a significant African-American community, and the overwhelming majority of black churchgoers had their spiritual home with the AME Zion congregation. This society was small, impoverished, undereducated, and short on leadership, hardly the signs of vibrancy, but its survival independent of white leadership made it successful. The popularity of the AME Zion with African Americans testifies to the powerful pull of independent black religion and to the region's ability to make that possible. Although religion was generally segregated, a few blacks worshipped with whites, and whites occasionally visited AME Zion services where they felt welcomed, connected with the worship style, and considered their spiritual growth nourished. Race was multifaceted and important.

Diversity, then, came in many flavors, including an English-language Lutheran congregation for the college and seminary crowd; a second, more German Lutheran fellowship; a third all-German Lutheran society of immigrants;

Scottish Dissenting Presbyterians; mainstream Presbyterians; German Reformed; Methodists; Catholics, many of whom were Germans; Dunkers, descended from Germans; and the AME Zion, who contributed racial diversity. Add doctrinal differences—including Dunkers, Catholics, and a variety of thoughts about evangelicalism—and the continuum was big for a small town.

The battle and the war wrote a violent postscript to the story of antebellum religion. To be sure, wartime Gettysburg was a little different with friendly troops coming and going and enemy soldiers occasionally nearby. Parading men in uniform, military bands, and invasion scares became part of the routine. But at first religion barely noticed the war. Antebellum patterns persisted as everyday details and improvement preoccupied many. In the middle of 1863, however, religious life nearly stopped for a few months, first in anticipation of the battle and then in its aftermath. Fellowships, however, recovered from the conflict, and religion returned to its place. Normal congregational business proceeded as the war continued, except that one congregation, St. Paul's Lutheran, weakened by the battle, closed just days after the war ended, and the AME Zion fellowship suffered from an exodus of refugees. Also, women became more involved in fundraising and saw their status marginally rise. In many ways, however, the religious home front preferred the status quo.

The significant wartime change in Gettysburg religion, the ascent of civil religion, stemmed from the war rather than the battle. The lines between church and state blurred considerably, even for the conscientious-objecting Dunkers, and civil religion became pervasive. God took sides. The Civil War, then, brought some change to Gettysburg religion, but significant continuity remained.

ᚼ

Refinement, diversity, and war in mid-nineteenth-century Gettysburg religion reveal existing national patterns and the future of America. In some cases, Gettysburg and the Border North exemplify broad trends nonspecific to the region, but other times developments unique to Gettysburg religion are windows into America's future.

Refinement, for example, was a widespread impulse with a bright outlook. Education, an essential ingredient of refinement and prominent in Gettysburg, gathered much steam later in the century, especially with the founding of land grant and research universities. Refined doctrine laid a foundation for more genteel, middle-class religion in the late Victorian period when revivalism shed much of its coarseness, acquired polish, and became more rational. The great revivalist of the late nineteenth and early twentieth centuries, D. L. Moody, made his case for salvation in simple, passionate language—after all, he was a revivalist—but he discouraged emotion and enforced self-control among his listeners. Those anxious about their sins retreated to a private inquiry room rather than striding in full view to a conspicuous bench. Antebellum religion, including Gettysburg, sowed the seeds of this restraint.[2] Another aspect of refinement, the marriage of consumerism to religion, was an additional long-term trend. Consumerism has had an extended relationship with Americans, who have been the world's champion consumers from their purchases of status-making, eighteenth-century tea equipage and other "baubles of Britain"[3] to late twentieth-century credit card binges. Consumption, then, has been hand-in-glove with American religion, and its pursuit in antebellum Gettysburg is just one chapter of a long story. In yet another vein, refinement illustrates congregational emphasis on matters small rather than large. To be sure, reforms, such as temperance and mission, had support, and anti-Catholicism and sectional politics stirred passions but mostly outside the meetinghouse. But the congregational prominence of improvement, whether in manners, music, bricks, or baubles, easily matched the power of any social reform or political movement to motivate. Admittedly, maintenance of facilities and organization mandates attention to logistics, but the inclination to keep religion and politics separate left ample room for individuals to compartmentalize their faith and concentrate on routine matters of the congregation, including refinement. This trend would long be part of American religion, and it suggests why reformers in all ages often face frustration. Refinement, then—including education, doctrine, consumerism, improvement, and the nonideological commonplace—was essential to antebellum religion, a trend that continued.

Likewise, Civil War faith in Gettysburg teaches about Civil War America. As the conflict raged, prewar behaviors, especially refinement, exerted a powerful pull, and change generally hung in the background. The effort to repair battle damage and pick up the pieces may simply be dog-bites-man news—a lesson in basic human behavior—but the overall continuance of the routine during a time of upheaval suggests that the Civil War may be less the watershed in religion than in other areas. Civil religion was the exception, a change that gained even more momentum as the modern nation-state matured in succeeding generations. By the late-nineteenth century faith was tightly knit with American imperialism, and the interweaving of church and state had become the peacetime norm. As with refinement, Gettysburg religion during the Civil War was instructive about behavior wider than the Border North.

Diversity was more peculiar to Gettysburg religion and provided a peek into the future. Colonial Pennsylvania had been the most religiously and ethnically varied part of North America, a trait it retained through the antebellum period, and although other regions also had variety, the mix and depth of diversity in Gettysburg and the Border North were striking. By the late Victorian period American religion had so many options—including the Social Gospel, the Gospel of Wealth, muscular Christianity, numerous non-Protestant immigrant religions, liberalism/modernism, and alternative movements like Christian Science and theosophy[4]—that mainstream evangelicalism no longer possessed unquestioned supremacy. Although antebellum Gettysburg religion had only a few of these alternatives, it was so diverse in its own way that it hinted at the late Victorian attack on the mainstream. Antebellum antirevivalists, recent immigrants, Dunkers, Catholics, the AME Zion, and native-born German Americans who clung to the language of the old country all one way or another contrasted with mainstream evangelicalism. From the hindsight of the late Victorians, Gettysburg religion foretold a future of American diversity.[5]

The community's response to its diversity was further predictive. The dominant theme of cooperation mixed with a countermelody of intolerance, sometimes loud and other times fading into the background, foreshadowed American religion in the late Victorian period and into the twentieth century when a swell of immigrants overcame nativist dissonance. America's mixed multitude has usually gotten along with itself, despite the protestations of some, a pattern that became evident early in Gettysburg and the Border North.

Race in antebellum Gettysburg religion also foresaw the future. Because African Americans always preferred to control their own religious life, AME and AME Zion fellowships proliferated in the Border North, in stark contrast to nearby Maryland, which discouraged independent black religion. The popularity of black religious societies in the Border North anticipated the spectacular growth of black denominations in the South during Reconstruction, when autonomous congregations suddenly became possible there. Yet virulent racism also infected the Border North, poverty was endemic among African Americans, and full citizenship illusive. This was Black America's future: emancipation but second class citizenship. Some might question whether African Americans in the South even reached second-class status after Emancipation, but despite Jim Crow and other forms of racial oppression, slavery had ended and black political, educational, and religious institutions had formed. Thus, in race the Border North was prophetic until the civil rights movement brought a second revolution to American society.[6]

Gettysburg religion, then, reveals much about the popular inclination toward refinement and the routine, first in peace and then in war. The religion of this region further instructs about American diversity, which was deep; about race, which had a sad future in America, and about wartime religion, in which change was more a tremor than an earthquake.

Finally, Gettysburg provides a foretaste of modernity. Religion, of course, is deeply embedded in a traditional society, but manufacturing for a semidistant market plus education, consumerism, rational and middle-class–friendly doctrine, complicated but tolerant diversity, compartmentalized faith, and a powerful nation-state contributed to Gettysburg religion. All point to growing modernization and the future of America.

Not bad for a little town in Pennsylvania.

Divertimento

Thaddeus Stevens

The best-known resident of early-nineteenth-century Gettysburg was Thaddeus Stevens. A prominent lawyer and civic leader in Gettysburg, Stevens achieved national fame in the U.S. Congress during the Civil War and Reconstruction periods after he moved to Lancaster.[1]

Born in New England, Stevens came to York, Pennsylvania, in 1815 to join friends who taught at the York Academy. But he studied law and in 1816 relocated to Gettysburg to practice. Soon the newly arrived, twenty-five-year-old attorney defended a prominent murderer, and although losing the case, Stevens performed so skillfully that his practice blossomed. In 1833 voters elected him to the state House of Representatives on an anti-Masonry platform, and in Harrisburg free public education became one of his early crusades.

Stevens also was Gettysburg's most outspoken white advocate for African Americans. Initially, the young lawyer was ambivalent about race and represented both slave owners seeking a return of their property and African Americans litigating for freedom. He avoided an overt, public embrace of abolition that might ill-serve an aspiring politician and instead wrote anonymously on behalf of the cause. Soon, however, the cautious lawyer became a public activist, some say prompted by a free black woman in Maryland who begged him to buy her husband to prevent his sale south. As mentioned, Stevens championed antislavery lecturer Jonathan Blanchard and assisted runaways. In 1837 as a delegate to a state constitutional convention, Stevens argued for jury trials for runaway slaves and when the convention disagreed, he took the argument to the State Senate, where he now sat, but that body was similarly unsympathetic. Stevens also opposed the rollback of suffrage for African Americans, maintaining that blacks deserved equal treatment as human beings and that their "degraded condition" stemmed from their treatment. Now an open supporter of freedom, Stevens condemned bondage as the "most disgraceful institution that the world had ever witnessed."[2]

In 1842 Stevens moved to Lancaster, which in 1848 sent him to Congress as a nativist, antislavery Whig. Congressional colleagues recognized Stevens as leadership timber, and in 1850 and 1852 he received a handful of votes for Speaker of the House. On the increasingly contentious issue of slavery, Stevens promised to block slavery's expansion in the territories and to use congressional authority to eliminate slavery where possible, especially the District of Columbia, but he conceded that the federal government lacked the authority to abolish bondage in the South. Stevens opposed the Compromise of 1850 because he thought it yielded too much to slaveholders.

Stevens's outspoken antislavery position and his participation in the defense of the Christiana Rioters, that is, the runaway slaves who killed a Maryland slave owner attempting to reclaim them, eroded his popularity, and reading the handwriting on the wall, he did not seek reelection in 1852. His law practice, however, flourished. Among his conspicuous cases were the defense of a client accused of selling diseased pork and a bank president charged with embezzlement. Stevens's debts nevertheless mounted, especially from a struggling iron furnace on South Mountain. Stevens remained politically active, joined the Know Nothings, and when the Kansas-Nebraska Act, widely unpopular in the North, shifted the political landscape in his favor, he returned to Congress in 1858, now a Republican.[3]

During the Civil War Stevens urged a vigorous prosecution of the conflict, and as chair of the Ways and Means Committee, he guided measures financing the war through the House. He supported the Conscription Act and initially sought to eliminate the three hundred dollar commutation fee because it discriminated in favor of the wealthy—he favored equal treatment for rich and poor alike—but eventually he accepted cash for exemptions as escape for his pacifist Mennonite, Dunker, and Quaker constituents, whose rights he supported. He thought Abraham Lincoln was too slow on emancipation. Stevens became a victim of the war when Confederate invaders destroyed his forge on South Mountain during the Gettysburg campaign.[4]

After the war Stevens emerged as a leader of the Radical Republicans. In his version of Reconstruction, seceded states would be treated as conquered provinces and placed under military rule supervised by Congress, not the president, and the former Confederates states would re-enter the Union with difficulty. Additionally, Stevens favored confiscation of large plantations and redistribution of much of the land to freedmen. He clashed with President Andrew Johnson over policy, favored his removal from office, and served as a House manager during the president's trial in the Senate. Stevens's great triumph was the Fourteenth Amendment to the Constitution, the definition of citizenship and expansion of due process rights, which he guided through the House.[5]

Throughout his life, Stevens gave little attention to religion. In Gettysburg he rented a pew from the Presbyterians and subscribed to their building fund, but sometimes his obligations were unmet. On his deathbed he received baptism from a Catholic priest although he may not have been aware of it, and Protestants officiated at his funeral and burial, a suggestion that the Catholic ceremony did not take. He never professed conversion or belief.[6]

The Great Commoner, as Stevens was called, is easy to demonize. One biographer proposes that a birth defect, a clubfoot, created Stevens's ambition, anger, and "the faint and ineradicable smell of brimstone." His physical appearance also did not bode well for posterity. Although in his prime Stevens had stood at five feet eleven with thick hair, by the photographic age disease (alopecia; the immune system attacks hair follicles) had claimed his coif—he wore a wig—and his overall health was in serious decline. In Stevens's last years as a Congressman, rheumatism, stomach cramps, and dyspepsia weakened him. He was often bedridden, and he could not climb steps. Given the limits of nineteenth-century medicine, the specific illness is a matter of conjecture; one scholar speculates stomach cancer. For future generations, then, a debilitated Stevens stares austerely at the camera, probably in pain and portraying the classic sourpuss.[7]

Perhaps more importantly, Stevens's advocacy of black rights and willingness to force them on the South remained unpopular long after his passing, and he most lost public favor because his vision of race relations was years ahead of its time. Initially, he and other reformers pushed for abolition, a minority far ahead of the mainstream, but eventually Northern public opinion caught up and emancipation became law. Then, Stevens and other progressives wanted black soldiers, another reform initially unpopular but eventually adopted. For civil rights and voting, reformers once again led public opinion until they cemented the two causes into law with constitutional amendments. Until recently, however, most white southerners despised these changes, and national white opinion generally followed along, making the aggressive, tactless, racial egalitarian an easy target for ridicule.[8]

Consequently, generations of historians have remembered Stevens as an angry, vindictive old man. D. W. Griffith in his popular 1915 film *Birth of a Nation* lampooned Stevens, a.k.a. "Austin Stoneman," as a confident conqueror whose irrational insistence on racial equality led to sexual crimes by black men against white women. Claude G. Bowers, author of an influential, early twentieth-century history of Reconstruction, portrayed Stevens as bitter, cunning, combative, and intolerant. Bowers employed a form of "bitter" four times in two pages to describe his subject. Bowers, a racist, considered Stevens's crusade for equality as an "obsession on negro rights to absolute equality," and he added that Stevens had a mind not "formed for constructive work." Recent writers have been kinder. Hans Trefouse praised Stevens as an "amazing fighter for human rights" who "laid the foundation for the African-American revolution of the twentieth century" through the Fourteenth Amendment. Most recently, Eric Foner describes Stevens as a "lifelong defender of the rights of blacks" who hoped to capitalize on the moment to create a "perfect republic" purged of racial inequality.[9]

Privately, Stevens practiced what he preached. His housekeeper, Lydia Smith, an African American from Gettysburg, was a lifelong companion. He insisted that others address his widowed partner as "Mrs. Smith," a mark of respect for an African American unheard of at this time, and he had her portrait painted, a significant expense indicating her importance to him. Rumors, which Stevens never directly denied, linked the bachelor Stevens romantically to Smith.[10]

Stevens died in 1868. His decline was long and gradual, more than ample advance notice to arrange for his burial. He selected a cemetery in Lancaster that accepted African Americans, final testament to the Great Commoner's lifelong commitment to racial equality.

Coda

Samuel Simon Schmucker resigned as president of the Lutheran Seminary on August 9, 1864. The sixty-five-year-old cited age, but other factors also influenced his decision. Schmucker had lost the doctrinal battle with confessionalists, and his heart-felt, moderate revivalism became a conspicuous minority within the Seminary community. Moreover, the seminary struggled financially, and a controversial president clinging to an unpopular doctrine would not encourage donors. The seminary needed tranquility, and a new president would help. Consequently, Samuel, wife Esther, and Alice, a daughter by a previous marriage, moved from their spacious home on the seminary campus to a newly built, smaller house in the center of town. Freed from teaching, Schmucker's scholarly output increased, and in retirement he quickly published an article, a translation of a Martin Luther work, an address, and two books, one in 1865 that restated his doctrinal position and another in 1870 that advocated Christian unity. He was also active in community organizations, especially Evergreen Cemetery and battlefield memorialization. Samuel and Esther were childless, and after Alice married, Esther spent considerable time with relatives near Philadelphia. In 1869 Schmucker suffered a small stroke that limited activities, and on July 26, 1873, a heart attack took his life. He was buried in Evergreen Cemetery next to his second wife, his soul mate for twenty-two years, Mary Steenbergen Schmucker.[1]

❧

Sallie Myers's life was difficult for a long time. Four cousins—three of them brothers—died in the war, and another shot in the throat barely spoke the rest of his life. Additionally, two girl friends died soon after the battle, perhaps lingering victims, and another suffered from spasms that the doctor blamed on the "trouble." Several of the soldiers Myers nursed back to health became her friends. One died in battle, and another proposed marriage through the mail, then appeared unexpectedly on her doorstep. Myers could not return the affection and justified her refusal by pleading slow-healing wounds from the broken romance with Snyder. The postal-suitor later died in action. Another soldier-correspondent, however, won her heart. Myers developed a relationship with the family of Alexander Stewart, the first wounded combatant she encountered in St. Francis Xavier and whose desperate condition sent her running out of the church. Alexander died in the Myers home a few days after the battle, but Myers met his father when he came to claim the body and she exchanged letters with several members of Stewart's family, including his brother, Harry. The correspondence with Harry flourished, and in 1864 he came to Gettysburg to meet his pen pal. They visited friends, attended church, gathered strawberries, took long walks, and visited the spot on Seminary Ridge where Alexander went down. After they picnicked on one of the Round Tops, smitten Myers wrote that she would "never, never forget" the long walk home. She had found her partner.[2]

On October 17, 1867, Myers and Stewart married. Harry had completed his seminary work and secured a pastorate with the United Presbyterians in Jamestown, Pennsylvania, in the far northwestern part of the state. Tragically, the young husband and pastor died within a year, a victim of an injury he suffered as a soldier in 1863 while chopping wood. The accident cost him his big toe, and erysipelas, a skin infection, appeared and never fully healed. In 1868, almost exactly one year after their marriage, Harry lost the battle with the infection and died. Ten days later Sallie gave birth to their son.[3]

Sallie's in-laws moved to Jamestown to assist the young widow and new mother, but her father-in-law domineered and the situation did not work. She moved back to Gettysburg to help her mother, dying of smallpox, and after the funeral, she stayed. Harry's parents, angry that Sallie left, refused financial support for her son, their grandson, and Myers became a dressmaker, working long hours in one of the few occupations open to women that still provided the flexibility to care for her son. When her child no longer required a mother at home, Myers returned to teaching and secured a position in the Colored School, where the one-time abolitionist served with great success for sixteen years. In 1898 Gettysburg education became integrated, but the reform deeply divided the community and Myers left the Colored School. She taught in a white elementary school building, but the turmoil of integration had somehow tainted her, perhaps she had been a very prominent proponent, and Myers only lasted until November. She remained active as a substitute teacher and a member of several civic organizations, including the Military Nurses Association, which she served as national treasurer. Myers lived to benefit from the Nineteenth Amendment to the U.S. Constitution and in her seventy-eighth year registered to vote. She died in 1922 and was buried in Evergreen Cemetery.[4]

CR

Joseph and Mary Sherfy spent the rest of their lives on their peach farm. One of their daughters, Otelia, later claimed to have heard Lincoln's Gettysburg Address, and maybe other members of the family did, too. Although this did not technically violate Dunker policy, Yearly Meeting banned voting and generally discouraged attendance at community events, making Otelia's presence at the dedication of the National Cemetery a borderline activity, especially for a preacher's daughter. On July 4, 1866, the Sherfys' barn burned, three years to the day plus one after the battle. The Sherfys needed two years after the battle to rebuild the signature structure of a Pennsylvania farm, and, consequently, the building was only one year old when it perished in flames, uninsured. Arson was possible, but chicken thieves were a more plausible explanation.[5]

In 1882 Joseph died of malaria. He was seventy and had just been elevated to elder fifteen months ago after the previous and long-serving senior minister, David Bosserman, passed away. Sherfy's obituary described him as a pioneer in the peach business for his dried and canned fruits.[6]

Tragically, many in the family had the same disease, and a few weeks later it took Sherfy's oldest child, Raphael. The cost of rebuilding after the battle had denied Raphael the opportunity to continue his education, but he managed to become a schoolteacher and an active member of the State Fruit Growers Association, another step into the mainstream for a nonconformist Dunker. Raphael and his wife joined the church when converted during a series of revival meetings, now acceptable for Dunkers.[7]

"Mother" Sherfy, as she was called in later life, remained on the farm and developed a reputation for warm welcomes for returning veterans. One day a large fellow showed up and announced, "I'm the man who ordered you out of your house. What are you going to do with me?" He was the Union officer who ordered their evacuation prior to Sickles's advance to Emmitsburg Road on day two. Another visitor received a tour of the house, and after remarking that his position during the battle was in the cellar, Mary allowed him there. The old cherry tree still stood in the farmyard with the ball in its trunk, a daily reminder of three days in a long ago July. "Mother" Sherfy died in 1904, aged eighty-seven, and was praised for her "gentle manners, her kindness and goodness of her life."[8]

CR

Abraham and Elizabeth Brien stayed on the farm for a few years, then moved into town. White friends aided the illiterate Brien with his damage claim, which he signed with his X. Of the $1,028 he requested, he received only $15 for the hay that Union horses ate. In 1868 Brien sold his farm—perhaps the physical demands of farming taxed the sixty-four-year-old—and he moved into town and found work as a hosteler at a hotel. In small ways African Americans edged closer to equality. The 1870 census described Elizabeth as "keeping house," the same designation home-making white women received, and Abraham and other African-American males were now listed as citizens, again similar to whites. These were little steps but progress nonetheless. In 1879 Abraham Brien died at the age of seventy-five. His epitaph is as follows:

> Blessed are the dead who
> Died in the Lord for they
> Rest from their labors.

Life for Brien, an illiterate, twenty-acre farmer, hosteler, and African American, was indeed one of labor.[9]

CR

Two of the three immigrant Codori brothers died tragically. George Codori, as mentioned previously, after the battle spent almost the rest of the war as a prisoner and then expired a few days after returning home. His wife Regina passed away one month later on April 20, 1865. Antoine/Anthony died the following year. Nicholas, meanwhile, continued to prosper. With his son, Simon, he maintained the slaughterhouse and meat market, while another son, George, established his own butcher house. In 1868 Nicholas sold the farm on Emmittsburg Road, but in 1872 he bought it back and when the town banished slaughterhouses from its limits, Nicholas relocated that part of the business on the Emmitsburg Road property. In 1878 a farming accident claimed his life. A team of colts never previously hitched to a mower were frightened by the noise and bolted. Codori was thrown in front of the blades, his foot severed, and his groin cut severely. Doctors amputated below the knee, but the groin injury proved deadly and a week later he was gone. Nicholas's widow, Elizabeth, died in 1889. Jean Staub never returned to farming. He moved to a nearby village, Bonneauville, and ran a store.[10]

The Codoris still live in Gettysburg. They operate a shop on the Diamond, and some serve as battlefield guides.

Notes

Introduction

1. "Gone with the Wind" (Metro Goldwyn Mayer, 1939).

2. For other studies of religion on the local level during a similar period see Paul E. Johnson, *A Shopkeeper's Millennium: Society and Revivals in Rochester, New York, 1815–1837* (New York: Hill and Wang, 1979); Mary P. Ryan, *Cradle of the Middle Class: The Family in Oneida County, New York, 1790–1865* (New York: Cambridge University Press, 1981), 60–103. Scott, *A Visitation of God, passim*, emphasizes the Civil War from a local or bottom-up perspective in the Old Northwest, but his study became available too late for full incorporation into my manuscript.

3. For a discussion of refinement and particularly the contribution of individual goods to the larger concepts of beauty, polish, and improvement, see Kenneth L. Ames, *Death in the Dining Room and Other Tales of Victorian Culture* (Philadelphia: Temple University Press, 1992); Priscilla J. Brewer, *From Fireplace to Cookstove: Technology and the Domestic Ideal in America* (Syracuse: Syracuse University Press, 2000); Richard L. Bushman, *The Refinement of America: Persons, Houses, Cities* (New York: Alfred A. Knopf, 1992); Howe, *What Hath God Wrought: The Transformation of America, 1815–1848* (New York: Oxford University Press, 2007), 45–47; David Jaffee, *A New Nation of Goods: The Material Culture of Early America* (Philadelphia: University Press of Pennsylvania, 2010); Jaffee, "Peddlers of Progress and the Transformation of the Rural North, 1760–1860," *Journal of American History* 78 (September, 1991): 511–35; John F. Kasson, *Rudeness and Civility: Manners in Nineteenth-Century Urban America* (New York: Hill and Wang, 1990), Jane C. Nylander, *Our Own Snug Fireside: Images of the New England Home, 1760–1860* (New York: Alfred A. Knopf, 1994). For a study of values and consumption in the eighteenth century see John E. Crowley, *The Invention of Comfort: Sensibilities and Design in Early Modern Britain and Early America* (Baltimore: The Johns Hopkins University Press, 2001).

4. Stephanie Grauman Wolf, *Urban Village: Population, Community, and Family Structure in Germantown, Pennsylvania, 1683–1800* (Princeton, N.J.: Princeton University Press, 1976), 8–16, 327–28; "born modern" in Laura Becker, "Diversity and Its Significance in an Eighteenth-Century Pennsylvania Town," in *Friends and Neighbors: Group Life in America's First Plural Society*, ed. Michael W. Zuckerman (Philadelphia: Temple University Press, 1986), 214; Zuckerman, "Introduction: Puritans, Cavaliers, and the Motley Middle," in *Friends and Neighbors*, 3–25. Others have also drawn attention to eighteenth-century Pennsylvania's unique mix of diversity and cooperation, including Sally Schwartz, *"A Mixed Multitude": The Struggle for Toleration in Colonial Pennsylvania* (New York: New York University Press, 1987) and myself in *Tolerance and Diversity: Pennsylvania German Religion, 1700–1850* (Metuchen, N.J.: Scarecrow Press, 1994).

More recent scholars have highlighted tension among eighteenth-century Pennsylvanians, especially resulting from economic conflict and Moravians or because tolerance was limited to white Protestants. See Michael Bradley McCoy, "Absconding Servants, Anxious Germans, and Angry Sailors: Working People and the Making of the Philadelphia Election Riot of 1742," *Pennsylvania History* 74 (Autumn 2007): 440–44; John B. Frantz and William Pencak, eds., *Beyond Philadelphia: The American Revolution in the Pennsylvania Hinterland* (University Park, Pa.: The Pennsylvania State University Press, 1998), xi–ii; Terry Bouton, *Taming Democracy: "The People," the Founders, and the Troubled Ending of the American Revolution* (New York: Oxford University Press, 2007), 21–27; Aaron Spencer Fogleman, *Jesus is Female: Moravians and Radical Religion in Early America* (Philadelphia: University of Pennsylvania Press, 2007), 215–26. These scholars, all with excellent, well-researched histories, who argue that Pennsylvania's cup of tolerance was only half full or less, miss the point that although Pennsylvania was the most diverse colony, it nevertheless was the most tolerant, except perhaps for little Rhode Island. Whatever shortcomings may have existed in colonial Pennsylvania, it did not have established religion, which prevailed in every other colony except Rhode Island, and preachers were unlicensed and generally free to make their case in a marketplace of religion, unique by eighteenth-century standards.

5. In 1860 approximately 7 percent of Gettysburg was foreign born, low compared to urban areas but double the amount for the South. Regarding religious diversity, many counties in New York had Dutch Reformed, German Reformed, Lutherans, Catholics, Scottish Dissenters, and a few African American fellowships. New Jersey had a strong representation of Dutch Reformed and most counties had a few Catholic parishes and African-American congregations, but Lutherans were lightly represented there and German Reformed nonexistent. See United States Census, 1860.

Small countercultural groups were especially well-represented in the Border North. In 1850 Lancaster County, Pennsylvania, for example, had thirty-five Mennonite congregations, who ranked second in denominational size next to forty-one Methodist congregations. Nine Moravian congregations and eleven Friends meetings also met in Lancaster County. Chester and Lebanon Counties, on the other hand, had few minority Germans, but Chester had thirty-seven Friends meetings, second in popularity to the Methodists (forty-five), and of the thirty-three congregations in Lebanon County, twenty-three were Lutheran and Reformed, both of German heritage. York County's mix included ten Mennonite congregations, four Moravian, four Friends meetings, and a Dunker congregation. See United States Census, 1850; J. Matthew Gallman with Susan Baker, "Gettysburg's Gettysburg: What the Battle Did to the Borough," in *The Gettysburg Nobody Knows*, ed. Gabor S. Boritt (New York: Oxford University Press, 1997), 148–49.

6. As with ethnicity and religion, the Border North hardly monopolized racial diversity. New Jersey, for example, had a noticeable African-American presence, according to the 1850 census, with black populations of nearly three percent or more in fifteen of its twenty counties. But Massachusetts was only one percent black and even Suffolk County (Boston) had a population that was merely 1.3 percent African American. Likewise, most New York counties were less than 1.0 percent African American although nine had black populations of approximately 3.0 percent or more. The New York counties with African-

America populations of 3.0 percent or more were Clinton, Dutchess, Green, Kings, Orange, Queens, Richmond, Rockland, Suffolk, Ulster, and Westchester. African-American percentages of the population in southern Pennsylvania counties were Chester County, 7.9 percent; Cumberland, 2.8 percent; Franklin, 4.9 percent; Lancaster, 3.7 percent; and York almost 2.0 percent. United States Census, 1850.

7. Charles Irons, *The Rise of Pro-Slavery Christianity: White and Black Evangelicals in Colonial and Antebellum Virginia* (Chapel Hill: University of North Carolina Press, 2008), 187–90; Henry H. Mitchell, *Black Church Beginnings: The Long-Hidden Realities of the First Years* (Grand Rapids, Mich.: Wm. B. Eerdmans, 2004), 182–92; Edward Ayers, *The Promise of the New South: Life after Reconstruction* (New York: Oxford University Press, 1992), 160–61.

8. Foote quoted in Ken Burns, "1861, The Cause: At the Crossroads of Our Being," *The Civil War* (New York: Time-Life Book Inc., 1989), videocassette, vol. 1. See also George C. Rable, *God's Almost Chosen Peoples: A Religious History of the American Civil War* (Chapel Hill: University of North Carolina Press, 2010), 395; James M. McPherson and William J. Cooper Jr., eds., *Writing the Civil War: The Quest to Understand* (Columbia: University of South Carolina Press, 1998), 1; Garry Wills, *Lincoln at Gettysburg: The Words that Remade America* (New York: Simon and Schuster, 1992), 121–47.

On gender, Drew Gilpin Faust, *Mothers of Invention: Women of the Slaveholding South in the American Civil War* (Chapel Hill: University of North Carolina Press, 1996), believes that the Civil War had little longstanding impact on gender, especially for Southern elite women, but more recently Stephanie McCurry, *Confederate Reckoning: Power and Politics in the Civil War South* (Cambridge, Mass.: Harvard University Press, 2010), suggests that the war was more transformational, particularly for poor Southern white women.

9. Gardiner H. Shattuck Jr., *A Shield and a Hiding Place: The Religious Life of the Civil War Armies* (Macon, Ga.: Mercer University Press, 1987), 35–50, 73–93; Charles Reagan Wilson, *Baptized in Blood: The Religion of the Lost Cause, 1865–1920* (Athens: University Press of Georgia, 1980); Harry S. Stout, *Upon the Altar of the Nation: A Moral History of the American Civil War* (New York: Viking, 2006), xvii–xxii, 248–49; Drew Gilpin Faust, *This Republic of Suffering: Death and the American Civil War* (2008); Mark S. Schantz, *Awaiting the Heavenly Country: The Civil War and America's Culture of Death* (2008); Anne C. Rose, *Victorian America and the Civil War* (New York: Cambridge University Press, 1992), 12–13; Randall M. Miller, Harry S. Stout, and Charles Reagan Wilson, eds., *Religion and the American Civil War* (New York: Oxford University Press, 1998), 1–11; Phillip Shaw Paludan, "Religion and the American Civil War," 21–40; Samuel S. Hill, "Religion and the Results of the Civil War," 371–75, 380; James M. McPherson, "Afterword," 409–12—all in Miller, et al, *Religion and the American Civil War*; Mark A. Noll, *The Civil War as a Theological Crisis* (Chapel Hill: University of North Carolina Press, 2006), 9. Recently George C. Rable has written about civil religion and the Civil War, arguing that the conflict was not a strong turning point in civil religion; Rable, *God's Almost Chosen Peoples*, 3–6.

10. For a similar account of minimal change to Gettysburg see J. Matthew Gallman with Susan Baker, "Gettysburg's Gettysburg: What the Battle Did to the Borough," in *The Gettysburg Nobody Knows*, ed. Gabor S. Boritt (New York: Oxford University Press, 1997),

144–74, and for Gallman's description of modest change on the Northern home front, see his *The North Fights the Civil War: The Home Front* (Chicago: Ivan R. Dee, 1994), *passim*.

11. See Timothy L. Smith, "The Ohio Valley: Testing Ground for America's Experiment in Religious Pluralism," *Church History* 60 (1991): 461–79.

12. Patrick Rael, for example, mentions Columbia and Pittsburgh, Pa., only in passing and concentrates on Philadelphia while "Pennsylvania" does not appear in his index; Rael, *Black Identity & Black Protest in the Antebellum North*, 85, 111, 417–18. Likewise, James Oliver and Lois E. Horton primarily study urban blacks; Horton and Horton, *In Hope of Liberty: Culture, Community, and Protest Among Northern Free Blacks, 1700–1860* (New York: Oxford University Press, 1997). Editors Joe William Trotter Jr. and Eric Ledell Smith in their anthology on African Americans in Pennsylvania include Harrisburg and Lancaster in the discussion of colonial and antebellum Pennsylvania, but most of their articles for this period describe Philadelphia and Pittsburgh; Trotter and Smith, *African Americans in Pennsylvania: Shifting Historical Perspectives* (University Park and Harrisburg, Pa.: Pennsylvania State University and Pennsylvania Historical and Museum Commission, 1997). For an excellent study of a small-town African-American community see Steven B. Burg, "The North Queen Street Cemetery and the African American Experience in Shippensburg, Pennsylvania," *Pennsylvania History* 77 (Winter 2010): 1–36. Another informative source on non-Philadelphia blacks is Carl D. Oblinger, "In Recognition of Their Prominence: A Case Study of the Economic and Social Backgrounds of an Antebellum Negro Business and Farming Class in Lancaster County," *Journal of the Lancaster County Historical Society* 72 (Easter 1968): 65–83. A few scholars have looked at slavery in rural Pennsylvania; see John Alosi, *Shadow of Freedom: Slavery in Post-Revolutionary Cumberland County, 1780–1810* (Shippensburg, Pa.: Shippensburg University Press, 2005), and Christopher Osborne, "Invisible Hands: Slaves, Bound Laborers, and the Development of Western Pennsylvania," *Pennsylvania History* 72 (Winter 2005): 77–99. Gary B. Nash and Jean R. Soderlund, *Freedom by Degrees: Emancipation in Pennsylvania and Its Aftermath* (New York: Oxford University Press, 1991), write mostly about slavery and race in Philadelphia but also describe Chester County. For another scholar who draws similar conclusions about the dearth of work on rural Pennsylvania, see Burg, "The North Queen Street Cemetery," 27n3.

On the Shenandoah Valley see Kenneth E. Koons and Warren R. Hofstra, *After the Backcountry: Rural Life in the Great Valley of Virginia, 1800–1900* (Knoxville: University of Tennessee Press, 2000), and my study on religion, Longenecker, *Shenandoah Religion: Outsiders and the Mainstream, 1715–1865* (Waco, Tx.: Baylor University Press, 2002).

13. Robert J. Brugger, *Maryland: A Middle Temperment, 1634–1980* (Baltimore, Md.: The Johns Hopkins University Press, 1988), 132–248; Barbara Jeanne Fields, *Slavery and Freedom on the Middle Ground: Maryland during the Nineteenth Century* (New Haven, Ct.: Yale University Press, 1985), 1–89; William L. Freehling, *Road to Disunion: Volume II, Secessionists Triumphant, 1854–1861* (New York: Oxford University Press, 2007), 185–98.

14. Edward L. Ayers, *In the Presence of Mine Enemies: War in the Heart of America, 1859–1863* (New York: W. W. Norton & Company, 2003).

15. Margaret S. Creighton, *The Colors of Courage: Gettysburg's Forgotten History: Immigrants, Women, and African Americans in the Civil War's Defining Battle* (New York: Basic

Books, 2005); Gregory A. Coco, *A Strange and Blighted Land; Gettysburg: The Aftermath of a Battle* (Gettysburg, Pa.: Thomas Publications, 1995). William A. Frassanito's *Gettysburg: A Journey in Time* (New York: Charles Scribner's Sons, 1975) describes the antebellum period primarily through images. David L. Valuska and Christian B. Keller study Civil War–era Pennsylvania Germans, especially during the Gettysburg Campaign, in *Damn Dutch: Pennsylvania Germans at Gettysburg* (Mechanicsburg, Pa.: Stackpole Books, 2004).

16. James M. McPherson, "Gettysburg," in *American Places: Encounters with History*, ed. William E. Leuchtenburg (New York: Oxford University Press), 264.

Divertimento: Samuel and Mary Steenbergen Schmucker

1. "most prominent American . . ." in E. Brooks Holifield, *Theology in America: Christian Thought from the Age of the Puritans to the Civil War* (New Haven, Conn.: Yale University Press, 2003), 397; Abdel Ross Wentz, *Pioneer in Christian Unity: Samuel Simon Schmucker* (Philadelphia: Fortress Press, 1967; repr. Lutheran Theological Seminary, 1999), 120–32.

2. Wentz, *Pioneer in Christian Unity*, 1–33, 59–77; Anna Jane Moyer, "A Young Man's Fancy: I, Samuel Simon, Take Thee, Mary Catherine . . . ," in *To Waken Fond Memory: Moments in the History of Gettysburg College* (Gettysburg, Pa.: Friends of Musselman Library, Gettysburg College, 2006), 47–50; John W. Wayland, *A History of Shenandoah County, Virginia* (Strasburg, Va.: Shenandoah Publishing House, 1927), 283, 459, 504.

3. Samuel Simon Schmucker to My dear wife, May 13, 1845, mss., Samuel Simon Schmucker Papers, Special Collections/Musselman Library, Gettysburg College, Gettysburg, Pennsylvania, box 1, folder 3. Emphasis original.

4. "Samuel Simon Schmucker to my dearest wife" (March 3, 1826), MS-023/1-3; United States Census, 1840, 1850.

5. Moyer, *To Waken Fond Memory*, 49–50.

1. Community

1. "blue, distant . . ." in H. C. Bradsby, *History of Adams County Pennsylvania. Originally published as History of Cumberland and Adams Counties: Containing History of the Counties, Their Townships, Towns, Villages, Schools, Churches, Industries, Etc.; Portraits of Early Settlers and Prominent Men: Biographies* (Warner, Beers & Co., 1886; repr. Knightstown, Ind.: The Bookmark, 1977), 203; "great landmark" and "most prominent spot" in *Harper's Weekly*, July 25, 1863, http://www.civilwarliterature.com/2Battles/The14thAtGettysburg/The14th-AtGettysburgHistory.htm, accessed on February 5, 2010; "well-cleared" in E. P. Alexander to J. William Jones, March 17, 1877, http://www.civilwarhome.com/epalexandergettysburg.htm, accessed February 5, 2010. See also Bradsby, 53–54; Robert L. Bloom, *A History of Adams County, Pennsylvania, 1700–1990* (Gettysburg, Pa.: Adams County Historical Society, 1992), 4; United States Geological Survey at http://groundwaterwatch.usgs.gov/AWLSites .asp?S=395846077040601&ncd=crn, accessed May 2, 2011.

2. Bloom, *History of Adams County*, 5, 10–11; Bradsby, *History of Adams County*, 7–11, 36–37. For Jemison's story see James Seaver, *A Narrative of the Life of Mrs. Mary Jemison* (New York: American Scenic & Historical Preservation Society, 1942 edition).

3. Bloom, *History of Adams County*, 49–50, 63–64; Bradsby, *History of Adams County*, 38–41, 182–83.

4. Bradsby, *History of Adams County*, 185–86.

5. J. Howard Wert, "Old Time Notes of Adams County: How Gettysburg Became a Great Carriage Manufacturing Town and How the Industry Died," *Star and Sentinel* 106 (January 3, 1906); J. M. Sheads, "Carriage Making Industry in Gettysburg" (typescript mss., n. d.), Carriage Industry File, Adams County Historical Society; Henry Stewart, "Notes on Gettysburg's Carriage Industry," (typescript mss.; January 1851), Carriage Industry File, Adams County Historical Society; Smith conversation. Albert Russell Erskine, *History of the Studebaker Corporation* (Poole Brothers, 1908), 13–15; "Coachmaking," *Adams Sentinel* 50 (May 27, 1850, advertisement); "H. G. Carr: Carriage Manufacturer," *Republican Compiler* (June 17, 1850; advertisement). Definitions of vehicles from *Encarta Dictionary*.

6. Bradsby, *History of Adams County*, 56.

7. "walking sewers" in Lawrence H. Larsen, "Nineteenth-Century Street Sanitation: A Study of Filth and Frustration," *Wisconsin Magazine of History* 52 (Spring, 1969): 243. See also Larsen, "Nineteenth-Century Street Sanitation," 243–44; Bradsby, *History of Adams County Pennsylvania*, 186–87.

8. Bradsby, *History of Adams County*, 187, 191–92, 195; "Borough Ordinance," *Adams Sentinel* 28 (June 17, 1844).

9. Bradsby, *History of Adams County*, 195; Conversation with Timothy H. Smith, research assistant, Adams County Historical Society. The museum of the Adams County Historical Society has one of the pipes in its collection; it is approximately ten inches in diameter and cut into three pieces, each approximately eight to ten feet in length.

10. Bradley R. Hoch, *Thaddeus Stevens in Gettysburg: The Making of an Abolitionist* (Gettysburg, Pa.: Adams County Historical Society, 2005), 98, 106.

11. "A Letter Writer," *Adams Sentinel* 46 (August 3, 1846). Emphasis in original.

12. Charles H. Glatfelter, *The Churches of Adams County, Pennsylvania* (Biglerville, Pa.: St. Paul's Lutheran Church, 1981), 19.

13. Carlisle Presbytery, Pa.: Minutes, 1756–1794, October, 1788, microfilm mss., Presbyterian Historical Society, Philadelphia, Pa.; Church Book, Gettysburg Presbyterian Church, October 1, 1853, mss., Gettysburg Presbyterian Church, Gettysburg, Pa.; Bradsby, *History of Adams County*, 196–97; Glatfelter, *Churches of Adams County*, 19; Reid W. Stewart, *History of Scottish Dissenting Presbyterianism in Adams County, Pennsylvania* (Lower Burrell, Pa.: Point Pleasant, Ltd., 2003), 16. The records of Upper Marsh Creek are Original Session Minutes, Upper Marsh Creek Presbyterian Congregation, 1776–1788, mss., Gettysburg Presbyterian Church, Gettysburg, Pa.

14. Ray A. King, *A History of the Associate Reformed Presbyterian Church* (Charlotte, N.C.: Board of Christian Education of the Associate Reformed Church, 1966), 1–70; James H. Smylie, *A Brief History of the Presbyterians* (Louisville, Ky.: Geneva Press, 1996), 55–56.

15. King, *History of the Associate Reformed*, 70–72; Smylie, *A Brief History of the Presbyterians*, 82; Stewart, *History of Scottish Dissenting Presbyterianism in Adams County*, 5–19, 25.

16. Glatfelter, *The Churches of Adams County*, 19; D. G. Hart, ed., "Reformed Presbyterian Church in North America, Covenanter Synod and "Reformed Presbyterian Church

in North America, General Synod," *Dictionary of the Presbyterian and Reformed Tradition in America* (Phillipsburg, N.J.: P & R Publishing, 1999), 210; King, *History of the Associate Reformed,* 72–80; Smylie, *A Brief History of the Presbyterians,* 82–83; Stewart, *History of Scottish Dissenting Presbyterianism in Adams County,* 23–34. The subscription lists are "Treasurer's Accounts, Gettysburg Associate Reformed Church, 1841–1842," Stewart, 98–99; "Article of Agreement for Remodeling the Gettysburg United Presbyterian Church, May 12, 1859," Stewart, 106.

17. "History," Minutes of the Leaders Meetings of the Methodist Episcopal Church, Gettysburg, Pennsylvania, typescript copy, Adams County Historical Society (ACHS), 98–108; John H. Wigger, *Taking Heaven by Storm: Methodism and the Rise of Popular Christianity in America* (New York: Oxford University Press, 1998), 80–87. The Methodist Minutes or Church Book began in 1833 as "Official Members of the Methodist Episcopal Church in Gettysburg," then in 1835 it became titled "Official Meetings," and in 1836 "Minutes of the Leaders Meetings."

18. "Membership List, 1854," Minutes of the Leaders Meetings of the Methodist Episcopal Church; United States Census, 1850 and 1860.

19. Daniel Alexander Payne, *Recollections of Seventy Years* (New York: Arno Press and The New York Times, 1968; originally published 1888), 11, 58–65.

20. Minutes of the Leaders Meetings of the Methodist Episcopal Church, September 2, 1840, December 23, 1840, February 3, 1841. See also Quarterly Conference Reports of the Gettysburg Circuit, January 16, 1841; this is also in the Methodist Leaders Meetings book, ACHS; Shelley L. Jones, "St. Paul's A.M.E. Zion Church," *Gettysburg Times* (February 24, 1987); C. Eric Lincoln and Lawrence H. Mamiya, *The Black Church in the African American Experience* (Durham, N.C.: Duke University Press, 1990), 51–52; Steven B. Burg, "The North Queen Street Cemetery and the African-American Experience in Shippensburg, Pennsylvania," *Pennsylvania Magazine* 77 (Winter 2010): 13. In 1787, when Richard Allen and Absalom Jones led blacks out of the Methodist Episcopal congregation in Philadelphia, they called their new fellowship the Bethel African Methodist Episcopal Church.

21. "many seasons . . ." in Frederick Douglass, *My Bondage and My Freedom* (Rochester, N.Y.: 1855) in Frederick Douglass, *Autobiographies* (New York: The Library of America, 1996), 361–62. See also Henry H. Mitchell, *Black Church Beginnings: The Long-Hidden Realities of the First Years* (Grand Rapids, Mich.: William B. Eerdman's Publishing Company, 2004), 69, 110–15.

22. James Oliver Horton and Lois E Horton, *In Hope of Liberty: Cultures, Community, and Protest among Northern Free Blacks, 1700–1860* (New York: Oxford University Press, 1997), 141–42; Lincoln and Mamiya, *The Black Church in the African-American Experience,* 47–58; Mitchell, *Black Church Beginnings,* 113–14; Richard S. Newman, *Freedom's Prophet: Bishop Richard Allen, the AME Church, and the Black Founding Fathers* (New York: New York University Press, 2008), 158–82.

23. David Henry Bradley Sr., *A History of the A.M.E. Zion Church,* 2 vols. (Nashville, Tenn.: Parthenon Press), 2:21; Sandy Dwayne Martin, "African Methodist Episcopal Church," *The Encyclopedia of Protestantism,* 21; Patrick Rael, *Black Identify and Black Protest in the Antebellum North* (Chapel Hill: The University of North Carolina Press, 2002), 87–91; *Pennsylvania Freeman* (February 10, 1841); "To the Christian and Benevo-

lent Public," *Adams County Sentinel* (August 21, 1854); Church Book, St. Paul's AME Zion, no day/month, 1859; private collection; William J. Walls, *The African Methodist Episcopal Zion Church: Reality of the Black Church* (Charlotte, N.C.: A.M.E. Zion Publishing House, 1974), 126–28, 131, 132, 336. I am indebted to Larry Boler for the *Pennsylvania Freeman* source. The Gettysburg AME Zion congregation adopted "St. Paul's" after the Civil War, and its papers are in a private collection.

24. Jones, "St. Paul's"; AME Zion Church Book, October 29, 1859. The parsonage was Ann Chiler's property, given to her by her former master, Thomas Craig Miller, c. 1834.

25. "old union church" in W. R. H. Deatrick, "Reformed Church in Gettysburg, Pa.," Evangelical and Reformed Historical Society, Lancaster, Pa., Gettysburg, Pa., Trinity Reformed folder, 4. See also Joseph Baer Baker, *History of St. James Evangelical Lutheran Church of Gettysburg, Penna., 1775–1921* (Gettysburg, Pa.: Gettysburg Compiler Press, 1921), 9–13; Glatfelter, *Churches of Adams County*, 10; Howard K. Macauley, "A Social and Intellectual History of Elementary Education in Pennsylvania to 1850" (PhD diss.: University of Pennsylvania, 1972), 316–22.

26. "After much reluctance . . ." in Record of the Proceedings of the Council of the Evangelical Lutheran Congregation of St. James' Church, Gettysburg, Pennsyla., May 17, 1847, mss., Wentz Library, Lutheran Theological Seminary, Gettysburg, Pa.; "skillful services . . ." in Deatrick, "Reformed Church in Gettysburg, Pa.," 8; "immediate erection" in Deatrick, 9. See also Deatrick, 8–10; Record of St. James' Church, 1846–1850, passim. Deatrick reported that the Lutherans received $800 for their interest in the building.

27. Glatfelter, *Churches of Adams County*, 12; United States Census, 1850 and 1860. Multiple lists of communicants are in the church books of St. James and Christ Church; see Records of St. James' Church; Minutes of the Proceedings at the Stated and Special Meetings of the Council, Council and Trustees, Congregation and Pew Holders of the English Evangelical Lutheran Church (called Christ Church) at Gettysburg, Adams County, Penn., mss., Lutheran Theological Seminary.

28. J. Walter Coleman, Anthony F. Kane, and Mary Louise Callahan, eds., *A Glorious Heritage of One Hundred Years: A History of St. Francis Xavier Church, Gettysburg, Pennsylvania, 1853–1953* (n.p.: Diocese of Harrisburg, n.d.), 5; Gerald P. Fogarty, "The Origins of the Mission, 1634–1773," Robert Emmett Currant, ed., *The Maryland Jesuits, 1634–1833* (Baltimore, Md.: The Corporation of the Roman Catholic Clergymen, The Maryland Province Society of Jesus, 1976), 25; Mark Häberlein, *The Promise of Pluralism: Congregational Life and Religious Diversity in Lancaster, Pennsylvania, 1730–1820* (University Park, Pa.: The Pennsylvania State University Press, 2009), 154–66; John T. Reily, *Conewago: Centennial Celebration* (Martinsburg, W.Va.: Herald Print, 1887), 13; Reily, *Conewago: A Collection of Catholic Local History* (Martinsburg, W.Va.: Herald Print, 1885; reprinted Westminster, Md.: John William Eckenrode, 1970), 27, 38, 88–118; Sally Schwartz, *"A Mixed Multitude": The Struggle for Toleration in Colonial Pennsylvania* (New York: New York University Press, 1988), 151–52, 240–42, 296.

29. "you will be buried . . ." in Reily, Conewago: A Collection, 155. See also James M. Cole, *For God and Country: A History of St. Francis Xavier Church, 1831–1981: Sesqui-Centennial Anniversary* (Gettysburg, Pa.: St. Francis Xavier Parish), 3–12; Coleman, Kane, and Callahan, eds., *A Glorious Heritage of One Hundred Years*, 5–15; John T. Reily, *Col-*

lections and Recollections in the Life and Times of Cardinal Gibbons (Martinsburg, W.Va.: Herald Print, 1892–93), 2:325; Reily, *Conewago: Centennial Celebration*, 17–19; Reily, *Conewago: A Collection*, 104–6, 155–56, 161–64.

30. Marsh Creek Church of the Brethren Church Book, February 26, 1852; May 20, 1852, mss., ACHS; *Minutes of the Annual Meetings of the Church of the Brethren: Containing All Available Minutes from 1778 to 1909* (Elgin, Ill.: Brethren Publishing House, 1909), 53, 150; J. Linwood Eisenberg, ed., *A History of the Church of the Brethren in Southern District of Pennsylvania by the Historical Committee* (Quincy, Pa.: Quincy Orphanage Press, n.d.), 149–50; "Architecture," ed., Donald F. Durnbaugh, *The Brethren Encyclopedia* (Philadelphia, Pa.: The Brethren Encyclopedia, Inc. 1983), 1:48; Donald F. Durnbaugh, *Fruit of the Vine: A History of the Brethren, 1708–1995* (Elgin, Ill.: Brethren Press, 1997), 104–8. In 1859 Marsh Creek bought a large notebook and recopied its notes into it; Marsh Creek Church Book, May 12, 1859.

31. Glatfelter, *Churches of Adams County*, 7, 9, 14, 22, 23.

32. Larry C. Bolin, "Slaveholders and Slaves of Adams County," *Adams County History* 9 (2003): 7–21, 14–40, 47, 63–64; Gary B. Nash and Jean R. Soderlund, *Freedom by Degrees: Emancipation in Pennsylvania and Its Aftermath* (New York: Oxford University Press, 1991), 14–40; Stewart, *History of Scottish Dissenting Presbyterianism in Adams County*, 124.

33. Nash and Soderlund, *Freedom by Degrees*, 99–113; 183–87.

34. John Alosi, *Shadow of Freedom: Slavery in Post-Revolutionary Cumberland County, 1780–1810* (Shippensburg, Pa.: Shippensburg University Press, 2001), 87–90; Bolin, "Slaves and Slaveholders of Adams County," 17, 63–64; United States Census, 1820.

35. Leroy Hopkins, "Bethel African Methodist Church in Lancaster: Prolegomenon to a Social History," *Journal of the Lancaster County Historical Society* 90 (1986): 207, 209.

36. "Snakes About," 52 (May 10, 1852); n.t., 54 (July 17, 1754); "An Impatient Darkey," 55 (March 19, 1855). For other examples see n. t. 50 (October 28, 1850); n.t. 54 (July 17, 1854): all in *Adams Sentinel*.

37. Christopher Malone, "Rethinking the End of Black Voting Rights in Antebellum Pennsylvania: Racial Ascriptivism, Partisanship and Political Development in the Keystone State," *Pennsylvania History* 72 (2005): 485–99.

38. "well to do" in Charles M. McCurdy, *Gettysburg: A Memoir* (Pittsburgh, Pa.: Reed and Witting Company, 1929), 19. See also Peter C. Vermilyea, "We Did Not Know Where Our Colored Friends Had Gone: The Effect of the Confederate Invasion of Pennsylvania of Gettysburg's African American Community," *Gettysburg Magazine* 24 (2001): 4–6; United States Census, 1860; "Nash and Soderlund, Freedom by Degrees, 187–93; Carl D. Oblinger, "In Recognition of Their Prominence: A Case Study of the Economic and Social Backgrounds of an Antebellum Negro Business and Farming Class in Lancaster County," *Journal of the Lancaster County Historical Society* 72 (Easter, 1968): 65–83; Burg, "The North Queen Street Cemetery," 16.

Black real estate value was $8,650; total community realty value was $899,500. Black realty per capita was $46.50; white reality per capita was $408.12. Black personal property per capita was $18.35; white personal property per capita was $267.32; see Vermilyea, 5.

39. "pretended trial" and "became frantic" in "Another Slave Case," *Star and Banner* 23 (May 28, 1852); this is a lengthy article reprinted from the *Harrisburg Telegraph*. See also

"A Case of Kidnapping at Columbia," *Adams Sentinel* 53 (January 31, 1853); "Kidnapping at Columbia," Star and Banner 23 (January 28, 1853); "Fugitive Slave Case," *Star and Banner* 21 (November 11, 1850); "'Sure Enough," *Star and Banner* 21 (January 10, 1851); n.t., *Adams Sentinel* 52 (May 31, 1852); Margaret S. Creighton, *The Colors of Courage: Gettysburg's Forgotten History; Immigrants, Women and African Americans in the Civil War's Defining Battle* (New York: Basic Books, 2005), 50–58.

40. "Kidnappers," *Star and Banner* 26 (October 5, 1855); Hoch, Thaddeus Stevens in Gettysburg, 241.

41. W. Frank Gorrecht, "The Charity of Thaddeus Stevens," *Historical Papers and Addresses of the Lancaster County Historical Society* (Lancaster, Pa.: Lancaster County Historical Society): 29–31; Thomas P. Slaughter, *Bloody Dawn: The Christiana Riot and Racial Violence in the Antebellum North* (New York: Oxford University Press, 1991), 44–52.

42. Elizabeth Evans, "Appendix," Mary (Goins) Gandy, Guide My Feet, Hold My Hand (published by the author, 1987), 1–4.

43. J. Howard Wert, *Episodes of Gettysburg and the Underground Railroad, As Witnessed and Recorded by Professor J. Howard Wert*, ed. G. Craig Caba (Gettysburg, Pa.: G. Craig Caba Antiques, 1998), 53–54, 58–59,67–72 81, 82, 94, 100–1; Abdel Ross Wentz, *Pioneer in Christian Unity: Samuel Simon Schmucker* (Philadelphia: Fortress Press, 1967; reissued Gettysburg, Pa.: Lutheran Theological Seminary, 1999), 324; "Leading Colored Citizen: Was an Active Agent in the Underground Railroad," *Gettysburg Compiler* (June 13, 1906).

Divertimento: Salome "Sallie" Myers

1. Sarah Sites Rodgers, *The Ties of the Past: The Gettysburg Diaries of Salome Myers Stewart, 1854–1922* (Gettysburg, Pa.: Thomas Publications, 1996), 55.

2. *Report of the Superintendent of Common Schools of Pennsylvania* (Harrisburg, Pa.: A. Boyd Hamilton, State Printer), (1859), 4; (1860), 4; (1861), 3; "The Profession of Teaching: An Essay Read by Mrs. Sallie M. Stewart Before the Adams County Teachers' Institute, Nov. 23, 1897," *Star and Sentinel* (December 7, 1897); untitled note tucked into Myers's 1862 Diary, ACHS.

3. Rodgers, *The Ties of the Past*, 39, 45, 68.

4. "more than I have . . . ," 79; "I must either give him up . . . ," 125; "keeping my thoughts fixed . . . ," 99; "I sometimes feel tempted . . . ," 124; "This is a glorious night . . . ," 96; "my heart is brimful . . . ," 81; "How I love such . . . ," 64: all in Rodgers, *Ties of the Past*; "My Dearest," in Composition Book; "From sport-to-sport . . ." in untitled poem in Composition Book, Sallie Myers Stewart, Diaries file, ACHS; "I'll never forget . . ." in untitled note (June 12, 1862) accompanying 1862 Diary in Diaries file. See also Rodgers, 16–18, 23, 124.

2. Refinement: In Theory

1. Richard L. Bushman, *The Refinement of America: Persons, Houses, Cities* (New York: Alfred A. Knopf, 1992), xi–xix.

2. I have written more extensively on outsiderness in *Shenandoah Religion: Outsiders and the Mainstream, 1719–1865* (Waco, Tx.: Baylor University Press, 2002), 86–96.

3. Bushman, *Refinement of America*, 313–52.

4. "refined and elegant taste," 25; "cultivate the society" and "true refinement," 30; "superior accomplishments . . . ," 31; "refinement of taste," 38: all in Henry L. Smith, *The Education of the Heart: An Address Delivered Before the Phrenakosian Society of Pennsylvania College* (Gettysburg, Pa.: H. C. Neinstedt, 1843).

5. Session Records, May 9, 1845, mss., Gettysburg Presbyterian Church, Gettysburg, Pa.; *Proceedings of the Evangelical Lutheran Synod of West Pennsylvania*, 1859, 39; "Address of the State Sabbath Convention," *Sentinel* 28 (June 24, 1844); "Adams County Temperance Convention," *Sentinel* 28 (August 19, 1844); "To the Friends of Prohibition in Adams County," *Sentinel* 54 (October 2, 1854); "The Sabbath," *Sentinel* 28 (May 20, 1844); Steven Mintz, *Moralists and Modernizers: America's Pre-Civil War Reformers* (Baltimore, Md.: The Johns Hopkins University Press, 1995); Ronald G. Walters, *American Reformers, 1815–1860* (New York: Hill and Wang, 1978).

6. Charles H. Glatfelter, *A Salutary Influence: Gettysburg College, 1832–1985*, 2 vols. (Gettysburg, Pa.: Gettysburg College, 1987), 1:19–57, 205–7; A. Roger Gobbel, *On the Glorious Hill: A Short History in Word and Picture of the Lutheran Theological Seminary at Gettysburg* (Lancaster, Pa.: Pridemark Press, 1990), 4–7; Abdel Ross Wentz, *Pioneer in Christian Unity: Samuel Simon Schmucker* (Philadelphia: Fortress Press, 1967); reissued Gettysburg, Pa.: Lutheran Theological Seminary, 1999), 120–39; "Samuel H. Buehler," *Star and Banner* (September 12, 1856). The count of Lutheran and Reformed congregations is an 1832 statistic; see Glatfelter, 23.

7. George M. Marsden, *The Soul of the American University: From Protestant Establishment to Established Nonbelief* (New York: Oxford University Press, 1994), 79–81.

8. Glatfelter, *A Salutary Influence*, 92–104, 116–17, 157–58; Marsden, *Soul of the American University*, 81. An exact count on colleges is difficult because some never made it off the drawing board and others included precollege training or even performed this exclusively; Marsden, 80. For accounts of student revivals Glatfelter relies on the memory of Joseph B. Bittinger, a professor at the college during this period.

9. "*Ex nihilo, nihil fit*" in John Milligan, "Human Perfection: A Discourse Delivered to Christ's Church, Gettysburg, Pa." (Gettysburg: H. C. Neinstedt, 1851), 12; "ancient Paripatus" in "Discourse Delivered before the Female Bible Society of Gettysburg and Its Vicinity, November 12, 1848," Samuel Simon Schmucker Papers/Special Collections, Musselman Library, Gettysburg College, Gettysburg, Pa, box 5, file 15; and "It would . . ." in "It is a fearful thing to fall into the hand of the living God," Schmucker Papers, box 5, file 19. See also J. H. C. Dosh, "Address Delivered at the Opening Ceremonies of Ever Green Cemetery, Gettysburg, Pa., November 7, 1854" (Gettysburg, Pa.: H. C. Neinstedt, 1855), 4–6. Examples of sermons that include secular knowledge are H. L. Baugher, "The Object of Life: A Discourse Delivered in Christ's Church, Gettysburg, Pa." (Gettysburg, Pa.: H. C. Neinstedt: 1851); Charles Philip Krauth, "Address Delivered on the Anniversary of Washington's Birth-Day" (Gettysburg, Pa.: H. C. Neinstedt, 1846); "But One Thing Is Needful," Schmucker Papers, box 5, file 20. Schmucker's sermons are the only extant sermon notes from this period in Gettysburg.

10. Glatfelter, *A Salutary Influence*, 29, 87, 101, 171–72.

11. William Henry Williams, *The Garden of American Methodism: The Delmarva Peninsula, 1769–1820* (Wilmington, Del.: Scholarly Resources, Inc., 1984), 179–80; John H. Wig-

ger, *Taking Heaven By Storm: Methodism and the Rise of Popular Christianity in America* (New York: Oxford University Press, 1998), 192–95; Christine Leigh Heyrmann, *Southern Cross: The Beginnings of the Bible Belt* (Chapel Hill: University of North Carolina Press, 1997), 26–27; David Hempton, *Methodism: Empire of the Spirit* (New Haven and London: Yale University Press, 2005), 125, 208. Much of the discussion about the loss of Methodist nonconformity focuses on the American South.

12. Longenecker, *Shenandoah Religion*, 109–10.

13. "gracious revival . . ." in Minutes of the Leaders Meetings of the Methodist Episcopal Church, Gettysburg, Pennsylvania, January 16, 1847, typescript, Adams County Historical Society, Gettysburg, Pa., hereafter cited as ACHS; M. L. Ganoe, "History," Church Book, Gettysburg Methodist Church, ACHS; "The Methodist Church in Adams County," *Gettysburg Compiler* (February 26, 1880). Ganoe's "History" is in the same notebook as the Minutes of the Leaders Meetings.

14. "The Methodist Church in Adams County," *Gettysburg Compiler* (February 26, 1880); Russell E. Richey, *Early American Methodism* (Bloomington and Indianapolis: Indiana University Press, 1991), 1–5, 24–32; Wigger, *Taking Heaven By Storm*, 94–97.

15. "Methodism in Adams County"; Sarah Sites Rodgers, *The Ties of the Past: The Gettysburg Diaries of Salome Myers Stewart, 1854–1922* (Gettysburg, Pa.: Thomas Publications, 1996), 33–34; "Camp Meeting," and "Wood and Protracted Meetings," *Star and Banner* 25 (August 18, 1854).

16. "little or no . . ." in *Annual Minutes of the Baltimore Conference*, 1848, 92–93; "did not go . . ." in Rodgers, *Ties of the Past*, 63. See also *Baltimore Conference*, 1851, 577; 1851; 568; Wigger, *Taking Heaven by Storm*, 87, 186, 194; Rodgers, *Ties of the Past*, 34, 36, 37, 38, 43, 50, 63, 64, 71, 98, 109, 110; James E. Kirby, Russell E. Richey, and Kenneth E. Rowe, *The Methodists*, Denominations in America Series (Westport, Conn.: Greenwood Press, 1996), 177–79, 221.

17. "Quarterly Conference Reports," *Baltimore Conference*, November 11, 1854, 38; Ganoe, "History"; Kirby, *The Methodists*, 180–85, 187–88, 201–3; Anne M. Boylan, *Sunday School: The Formation of an American Institution* (New Haven and London: Yale University Press, 1988), 6–21.

18. "To S.S . . ." in Rodgers, *Ties of the Past*, 85. See also Rodgers, 44, 69, 84, 103; Boylan, *Sunday School*, 114–26; Kirby, *The Methodists*, 221–22.

19. "left in disgust . . ." in Rodgers, *Ties of the Past*, 87; "foolish plays" in Minutes of the Leaders Meetings of the Methodist Episcopal Church, October 22, 1835, 15. See also Rodgers, 21; Minutes of the Leaders Meetings, October 13, 1837.

20. "My First Love," newspaper clipping in pocket of 1862 Diary. The poem is undated and without an author. Myers's authorship is assumed but without final proof.

21. Quarterly Conference Reports, August 29 and November 5, 1854, Methodist Church Book. For Hoffman's membership on a building committee, see May 10, 1851. Hoffman's property value was $4,000 and Barrett's $4,600; United States Census, 1850.

22. Carl F. Bowman, *Brethren Society: The Cultural Transformation of a "Peculiar People"* (Baltimore: The Johns Hopkins University Press, 1995), 77–80; Donald F. Durnbaugh, *Fruit of the Vine: A History of the Brethren, 1708–1995* (Elgin, Ill.: The Brethren Press,

1996), 211–13; Marsh Creek Church of the Brethren Church Book, February 8, 1851, February 24, 1853, February 22, 1855, May 21, 1857, February 24, 1859, mss., ACHS.

23. "unsafe places . . ." (1853), 138–39; "to the humble . . ." (1833), 54; "cautious" (1852), 140: all in *Minutes of the Annual Meetings of the Church of the Brethren: Containing All Available Minutes from 1778 to 1909* (Elgin, Ill.: Brethren Publishing House, 1909). See also J. Linwood Eisenberg, ed., *A History of the Church of the Brethren in Southern District of Pennsylvania by the Historical Committee* (Quincy, Pa.: Quincy Orphanage Press, n.d.), 150–52.

24. "unnecessary ornaments" from *Minutes of the Annual Meetings*, 150. See also (1859), 187. The description of the Friends Grove Meetinghouse is in Marsh Creek Church Book, February 26 and May 20, 1852. See also *Minutes of Annual Meetings*, 53; Eisenberg, ed., *Church of the Brethren in the Southern District*, 149–50; "Architecture," ed., Donald F. Durnbaugh, *The Brethren Encyclopedia* 4 vols. (Philadelphia, Pa.: The Brethren Encyclopedia, Inc., 1984), 1:48; Durnbaugh, *Fruit of the Vine*, 104–8.

25. "building and ornamenting . . ." in (1845), 85; "tinkling of bells . . ." (1840), 70; "God made man . . ." and "not to mar . . ." (1804), 26; "in conformity to . . ." (1853), 135; "high and fashionable clothing . . ." (1835), 58; "after the fashion . . ." (1847), 94–95; "high fashions" (1822), 46–47: all in *Minutes of Annual Meetings*. See also (1822), 45–46; (1827), 51; (1828), 53; (1840), 70; (1845), 85; (1846), 91; (1849), 104; (1853), 135; (1853), 135, 138; (1856), 156; (1861), 201.

26. "shamefully bad," in *Minutes of Annual Meeting* (1822), 46; "so many men . . ." (1828), 52; "excessive . . ." (1864), 228.

3. Refinement: In Practice

1. "Lost and Found . . ." in *Republican Compiler* (January 14, 1856); " 'Know Nothing' Meeting" and "Know Nothings," *Star and Banner* (June 16, 1854); *Sentinel* (November 1, 1852).

Charles Sellers, *The Market Revolution: Jacksonian America, 1815–1846* (New York: Oxford University Press, 1991) argues for sweeping, shocking changes in the early nineteenth-century economy that transformed society, mostly for the worse. Others, especially Daniel Walker Howe, point out that significant change took place much earlier or that economic change benefitted many even as its transformation hurt some. My thoughts are that although consumption began in the eighteenth century, enough change happened in the next century to use the term *market revolution*. A new round of change, especially mechanization, canals, railroads, and boom and bust cycles, caused adjustments and pain for some but brought increased opportunity for others, especially the middle class. For examples of eighteenth-century market activity, see Karin Calvert, "The Function of Fashion in Eighteenth-Century America," eds., Cary Carson, Ronald Hoffman, and Peter J. Albert, *Of Consuming Interests: The Style of Life in the Eighteenth Century* (Charlottesville: University Press of Virginia, 1994), 252–83; Jack P. Greene, *Pursuits of Happiness: The Social Development of Early Modern British Colonies and the Formation of American Culture* (Chapel Hill: University of North Carolina Press, 1988), 31–35, 107–40; Greene, *Impera-*

tives, Behaviors, and Identities: Essays in Early American Cultural History (Charlottesville: University Press of Virginia, 1992), 192–94, 221–23. For nineteenth-century adjustments, see Paul E. Johnson, *A Shopkeeper's Millennium: Society and Revivals in Rochester, New York, 1815–1837* (New York: Hill and Wang, 1978), 38–48; Carol Sheriff, *The Artificial River: The Erie Canal and the Paradox of Progress, 1817–1862* (New York: Hill and Wang, 1996), 96–97, 126–27; Merritt Roe Smith, *Harpers Ferry Armory and the New Technology: The Challenge of Change* (Ithaca, N.Y.: Cornell University Press, 1977), 254–56, 271–73. The best argument for positive change coming from the market revolution is Daniel Walker Howe, "The Market Revolution and the Shaping of Identity in Whig-Jacksonian America," in *The Market Revolution in American: Social Political, and Religious Expressions, 1800–1880*, ed. Melvin Stokes and Stephen Conway (Charlottesville: University Press of Virginia, 1996), 259–77. Howe more succinctly rebuts Sellers in *What Hath God Wrought: The Transformation of America, 1815–1848* (New York: Oxford University Press, 2007), 5.

The advertisers who borrowed from politics are particularly interesting because their customers included women, even though politics was outside women's domain. A few abolitionist women used consumerism to make political statements by boycotting slave-made goods and organizing alternative free produce shops and networks. This movement, however, involved a very small minority and was almost exclusively Quaker. No evidence of this activity appears in Gettysburg. See Julie Roy Jeffrey, *The Great Silent Army of Abolitionism: Ordinary Women in the Antislavery Movement* (Chapel Hill: University of North Carolina Press, 1998), 20–22, 48; Stacey M. Robertson, *Hearts Beating for Liberty: Women Abolitionists in the Old Northwest* (Chapel Hill: University of North Carolina Press, 2010), 67–90.

2. "ceremonialized coming . . ." in Kenneth L. Ames, *Death in the Dining Room and Other Tales of Victorian Culture* (Philadelphia: Temple University Press, 1992), 20; "miniature museum . . ." in John F. Kasson, *Rudeness and Civility: Manners in Nineteenth-Century Urban America* (New York: Hill and Wang, 1990), 176. See also Ames, 1–8, 17–32, 41–43, 233–41; Richard L. Bushman, *The Refinement of America: Persons, Houses, Cities* (New York: Alfred A. Knopf, 1992), 262–79; David Jaffee, *A New Nation of Goods: The Material Culture of Early America* (Philadelphia: University Press of Pennsylvania, 2010), xiii, 314–25; Kasson, 173–81; Jane C. Nylander, *Our Own Snug Fireside: Images of the New England Home, 1760–1860* (New York: Alfred A. Knopf, 1994), 251–56. For a study of values and consumption in the eighteenth century see John E. Crowley, *The Invention of Comfort: Sensibilities and Design in Early Modern Britain and Early America* (Baltimore, Md.: Johns Hopkins University Press, 2001), ix–xi, 290–92.

3. "present state" and "expedient" in Evergreen Cemetery Minutes, November 29, 1853, Records of Evergreen Cemetery, typescript copy, Evergreen Cemetery, Gettysburg, Pa. See also Trustees Book, November 2, 1846, May 19, and June 19, 1849, February 18, 1851, June 2, 1855, Gettysburg Presbyterian Church, Gettysburg, Pa.; Mary Margaret Stewart, "Black's Graveyard: A History," mss., Gettysburg Presbyterian Church, Gettysburg, Pa.; Minutes of the Leaders Meetings of the Methodist Episcopal Church, Gettysburg, Pennsylvania, May 8, 1846, typescript, Adams County Historical Society, Gettysburg, Pa.

4. "civilization and refinement," R. [Reuben] Hill, *Discourse at the Laying of the Cornerstone* (Gettysburg, Pa.: H. C. Neinstedt, 1855), 14; "lowest races," Hill, 13; "Hottentot,"

Hill, 15. See also Stanley French, "The Cemetery as Cultural Institution: The Establishment of Mount Auburn and the 'Rural Cemetery' Movement," *American Quarterly* 26 (March, 1974): 46, 48–49.

5. Evergreen Cemetery Minutes, November 29, 1853; Samuel Simon Schmucker to Beale Schmucker, December 31, 1855, Samuel Simon Schmucker Papers/Special Collections, Musselman Library, Gettysburg College, Gettysburg, Pa., box 1, folder 5.

6. J. H. C. Dosh, *Address Delivered at the Opening Ceremonies of Ever Green Cemetery, Gettysburg, Pa., November 7, 1854* (Gettysburg, Pa.: H. C. Neinstedt, 1855), 4–6. The Norton poem was "Weep Not for Him That Dieth."

7. "fall asleep . . ." in Dosh, "Address Delivered at the Opening Ceremonies of Ever Green Cemetery," 4.

8. "adorn . . ." and "high and holy . . ." in Hill, *Discourse at the Laying of the Cornerstone*, 15.

9. "not only know . . ." in William D. Kelley, *Characteristics of the Age: An Address Delivered Before the Linnaean Association of Pennsylvania College, At the Annual Commencement, Sept. 18th, 1850* (Gettysburg, Pa.: H. C. Neinstedt, 1850), 16; Story quoted in French, "The Cemetery as Cultural Institution," 58. Hill in *Address Delivered at the Opening Ceremonies of Ever Green Cemetery, Gettysburg, Pa., November 7, 1854* (Gettysburg, Pa.: H. C. Neinstedt, 1855), 4–6.

10. "the vast chain . . ." and "sleep . . . last trump . . ." in Dosh, *Address Delivered at the Opening Ceremonies of Ever Green Cemetery*, 5; "maternal wisdom" in Kelley, *Characteristics of the Age*, 4; "nowhere else," "hidden recesses," "gigantic wonders," and "microscopic beauties" in Daniel M. Smyser, *The Study of Natural History: An Address Delivered Before the Linnæan Association of Pennsylvania College, Gettysburg, Pa.* (Gettysburg, Pa.: H. C. Neinstedt, 1849), 14. See also Stanley French, "The Cemetery as Cultural Institution," 39–40, 46–49, 52, 57, 59; Smith, *Education of the Heart*, 8–9; Mark S. Schantz, *Awaiting the Heavenly Dead: The Civil War and America's Culture of Death* (Ithaca, N.Y.: Cornell University Press, 2008), 70–96; David Charles Sloane, *The Last Great Necessity: Cemeteries in American History* (Baltimore, Md.: Johns Hopkins University Press, 1991), 44–95; Garry Wills, *Lincoln at Gettysburg: The Words That Remade America* (New York: Simon and Schuster, 1992), 62–75; "Ever Green Cemetery," *Adams Sentinel* 54 (January 6, 1854).

11. "friends of the dead deposited there" in "Ever-Green Cemetery" (June 22, 1857). See also "Ever Green Cemetery" (June 29, 1857); David M'Conaughy, "The Sentinel and the Cemetery" and [Robert G. Harper], "A Few Remarks in Reply" (July 6, 1857): all in *Adams Sentinel* 57; Evergreen Cemetery Minutes, June 24, 1857; Margaret S. Creighton, *The Colors of Courage: Gettysburg's Forgotten History; Immigrants, Women, and African Americans in the Civil War's Defining Battle* (New York: Basic Books, 2005), 36–37.

12. "all sects" in Evergreen Cemetery Minutes, November 29, 1853. See also Meeting of Managers, April 5, 1854, Evergreen Cemetery Minutes; Schmucker to Beale Schmucker, December 31, 1855; Dosh, *Address Delivered at the Opening Ceremonies of Ever Green Cemetery*, 6; "Ever Green Cemetery," *Republican Compiler* 37 (March 19, 1955); "Ever-Green Cemetery," *Star and Banner* 26 (September 7, 1855).

13. *Minutes of the Annual Meetings* (1855), 149.

14. "hundreds of . . ." in Evergreen Cemetery Minutes, September 1, 1855; "modest charge" in "The New Cemetery," *Republican Compiler* 37 (November 11, 1854). See also Rodgers, *Ties of the Past*, 42, 43, 54. The Myers composition is not extant.

15. "filthy practice . . ." in Minutes of the Leaders Meeting of the Methodist Episcopal Church, February 21, 1844, 16. See also August 5, 1842.

16. Council and Trustees Minutes, Minutes of Proceedings at the Stated and Special Meetings of the Council, Council and Trustees, Congregation and Pew Holders of the English Evangelical Lutheran Church (Called Christ Church) at Gettysburg, Adams County, Penn., January 22, 1852; May 30, 1854; January 5, 1856, mss., Wentz Library, Lutheran Theological Seminary; Minutes and Proceedings of the Congregation of Christ Church, January 5, 1856, Minutes and Proceedings at the Stated and Special Meetings.

17. Records of the Proceedings of the Council of the Evangelical Lutheran Congregation of St. James' Church, Gettysburg, Pennsyla. May 3, 1852, mss., Wentz Library, Lutheran Theological Seminary, Gettysburg, Pa.

18. W. R. H. Deatrick, "Reformed Church in Gettysburg, Pa.," mss., Gettysburg Pa., Trinity Reformed folder, Evangelical and Reformed Historical Society, Lancaster, Pa., 11–12.

19. Joseph Enders to Reverend and Dear Father, October 15, 1852, Archives, Maryland Province, Society of Jesus, Lauinger Library, Special Collections Research Center, Georgetown University, Washington, D.C., box 73–10; Minutes of the Leaders Meeting of the Methodist Episcopal Church, February 23, 1841, February 11, 1848, December 18, 1848; Quarterly Conference Report of the Gettysburg Circuit, January 26, 1850, May 10, 1851; Council and Trustees Minutes, June 17, 1850, December 19, 1856, Gettysburg Presbyterian Church; Records of the Proceedings of the Council of St. James' Church, August 12, and September 16, 1850.

20. "very nice" in Rodgers, *Ties of the Past*, 64. See also Rodgers, 63, 65; Minutes and Proceedings of the Congregation of Christ's Church, January 29, and September 1, 1860; Proceedings of the Council, St. James Lutheran, June 16 and December 16, 1860, March 23, 1861; Council and Trustees Minutes, August 31, 1861, Gettysburg Presbyterian Church; Proceedings of the Evangelical Lutheran Synod of West Pennsylvania, 1861, 11; John T. Reily, *Conewago: A Collection of Local History* (Martinsburg, W.Va.: Herald Print, 1885; repr. Westminster, Md.: John William Eckenrode, 1970), 164; Harold F. Wilson and Arnold R. Daum, *American Petroleum Industry: The Age of Illumination, 1859–1899* (Westport, Conn.: Greenwood Press, 1981; originally published by Northwestern University Press, 1959), 38–42.

21. "more better . . ." in Samuel Simon Schmucker to Beale Schmucker, November 17, 1848, Schmucker Papers, box 1, folder 5. See also "Singing School," *Star and Banner* 21 (January 10, 1851); Record of Zion's Classis, vol. 2, 1849–1863, 1853 mss., Evangelical and Reformed Historical Society, Lancaster, Pa.: 146; William T. Dargan, *Lining Out the Word: Dr. Watts Hymn Singing in the Music of Black Americans* (Berkeley: University of California Press, 2006), 27. German-heritage congregations may have sung more melodically, but sources in Gettysburg do not differentiate between the musical ability of German and English congregations. I am indebted to Larry Taylor for much of my understanding of congregational singing in early America.

22. Minutes of the Leaders Meeting of the Methodist Episcopal Church, January 28, 1842; Joseph Enders to Reverend and Dear Father Stonestreet, December 2, 1852, Archives, Maryland Province, Society of Jesus, Lauinger Library, Special Collections, Georgetown University, Washington, D.C., box 73, folder 9; Reily, *Conewago; A Collection*, 162; James M. O'Toole, *The Faithful: A History of Catholics in America* (Cambridge, Mass.: The Belknap Press of Harvard University Press, 2008), 75, 80–82; Trustees Book, May 20, 1844, Gettysburg Presbyterian Church.

23. "Correct singing" in *Minutes of the Annual Meetings*, (1849), 108; "serious contemplation" and "tickling of the outward ear" (1844), 82; "have nothing to do . . ." (1852), 49; "abuses . . ." (1862), 206. See also (1857), 165; (1859), 183.

24. Reid W. Stewart, *History of Scottish Dissenting Presbyterianism in Adams County, Pennsylvania* (Lower Burrell, Pa.: Point Pleasant, 2003), 16.

25. "New Lutheran Church," *Star and Banner* 19 (April 28, 1848).

26. "better the . . ." in Minutes of the Leaders Meeting of the Methodist Episcopal Church, November 19, 1841; See also Trustees Book, November 1, 1847, February 18, 1851, January 12, 1852, Gettysburg Presbyterian Church.

27. Proceedings of the Council, St. James' Lutheran, August 11, 1848, March 12, 1849, April 16, 1849, February 20, 1850, January 13, 1851, March 10, 1851.

28. Enders to Stonestreet; Trustees Book, June 27 and November 14, 1844, January 19, 1846, Gettysburg Presbyterian Church.

29. "fair actresses," "only elderly matrons," and "charms" in John W. Nevin, "Fancy Fairs" (Mercersburg, Pa.: n.p., 1843), 13. See also Nevin, 12.

30. "other eatables . . ." in Mary Catherine Steenbergen Schmucker to Caroline Schmucker Sadtler (December 28, 1845), Samuel Simon Schmucker Collection, Special Collections/Musselman Library, Gettysburg College, Gettysburg, Pennsylvania, box 2, folder 3; "feasting their eyes" in Samuel Simon Schmucker to Beale Schmucker (December 31, 1855), box 1, folder 5. See also Beverly Gordon, *Bazaars and Fair Ladies: The History of the American Fundraising Fair* (Knoxville: University of Tennessee Press, 1998), 35–57.

31. Gordon, *Bazaars and Fair Ladies*, 36.

32. "present income . . ." and "for their greater . . ." in Proceedings of the Council, St. James' Lutheran, April 16, 1849; Council and Trustees, January 31, 1861, March 2, 1862, Christ Church Lutheran; Trustees Book, June, n.d., and July 6, 1852, Gettysburg Presbyterian Church; Deatrick, "Reformed Church in Gettysburg, Pa.," 12; Reily, *Conewago: A Collection*, 162.

33. Proceedings of the Council, St. James' Church, November 8, 1852, June 13, 1853; Council and Trustees, January 11, 1853, Christ Church Lutheran.

34. "our funds . . ." in Trustees Book, November 1, 1847, Gettysburg Presbyterian Church. See also May 22, 1843, December 4, 1858, March 28 and June 20, 1859.

35. "Meeting of the Alumni of the Seminary, Gettysburg," *Lutheran Observer*, n.d.; Minutes and Proceedings of the Congregation of Christ's Church, September 6 and November 29, 1852, November 30, 1857, December 13, 1858, December 12, 1859, February 4, 1861; Council and Trustees Minutes, January 11, March 23 and 27, 1853, Christ Church.

36. Proceedings of the Council, St. James' Church, May 28 and November 11, 1849, August 12, 1850.

37. Proceedings of the Council, St. James' Church, November 7, 1857, May 7, June 12, July 31, November 20, 1858.

38. Proceedings of the Council, St. James' Church, October 13, 1860, May 4, 1861.

39. Leaders Book, St. Paul's AME Zion Church, February 23 and 24, 1863. mss., private collection, Jean Odom.

Divertimento: The Codoris

1. United States Census, 1850 and 1860; Pam Newhouse, *The Codori Family and Farm: In the Path of Battle* (Gettysburg, Pa.: Friends of the National Parks at Gettysburg, Inc., 1999), 1–2; http://codorifamily.com/the_codori's_1, accessed July 10, 2007. I am also indebted to Ann-Marie Codori and Bill Codori for their assistance. I am unable to locate Catherine and John Staub in the 1860 census.

2. United States Census, 1850 and 1860; Newhouse, *Codori Family and Farm*; 2–3; http://codorifamily.com/index.htm, accessed January 27, 2011; Helen Tangires, *Public Markets and Civic Culture in Nineteenth-Century America* (Baltimore, Md.: Johns Hopkins University Press, 2003), 61–63; "Democratic County Committee," *Compiler* 41 (June 27, 1859); "Staubs and Codoris," typescript mss., Staub Farm and Sherfy Tenant House, File 2–16, Gettysburg National Military Park.

3. United States Census, 1860.

4. John T. Reily, *Conewago: A Collection of Local History* (Martinsburg, W.Va.: Herald Print, 1885; repr. Westminster, Md.: John William Eckenrode, 1970), 162; *Republican Compiler* (December 22, 1851); James M. Cole, *For God and Country: A History of St. Francis Xavier Church, 1831–1981: Sesqui-Centennial Anniversary* (Gettysburg, Pa.: St. Francis Xavier Parish), 9; http://codorifamily.com/index.htm; United States Census, 1850 and 1860; Baptisms, 1843–1943, St. Francis Xavier, Roman Catholic Church. Gettysburg, photocopied mss., Adams County Historical Society, Gettysburg, Pa.

4. Diversity: Ethnicity and Doctrine

1. "A Letter Writer," *Adams Sentinel* 46 (August 3, 1846).

2. Steven M. Nolt, *Foreigners in Their Own Land: Pennsylvania Germans in the Early Republic* (University Park: Pennsylvania State University Press, 2002), 129–43.

3. Marsh Creek Church Book, mss, Adams County Historical Society; Carl F. Bowman, *Brethren Society: The Cultural Transformation of a "Peculiar People"* (Baltimore, Md.: Johns Hopkins University Press, 1995), 97; "Brüderbote, Der," "Hymnals," "Language Shift," *The Brethren Encyclopedia*, ed. Donald F. Durnbaugh, 4 vols. (Philadelphia, Pa., and Oak Brook, Ill.: Brethren Encyclopedia, Inc., 1983), 1:218, 1:641–42, 2:724–25; *Minutes of the Annual Meetings of the Church of the Brethren: Containing All Available Minutes from 1778 to 1909* (Elgin, Ill.: Brethren Publishing House, 1909), (1841) 72, (1845) 87. The conclusion that Marsh Creek was almost entirely native-born comes from names culled from the church book and searched in the United States Census, 1850 and 1860. Henry Kurtz privately published *The Gospel Visitor*, but Yearly Meeting sanctioned its distribution.

4. "natural . . ." and "German from . . ." in *Proceedings of the Evangelical Lutheran Synod of West Pennsylvania*, 1859, 39–40; "exclusive" in J. H. B., "Hindrances to Our Church," *Lutheran Observer* 28 (November 23, 1860).

5. "enrich" in Philip Schaff, *Anglo-Germanism or the Significance of the German Nationality in the United States, an address delivered March 10, 1846, before the Schiller Society of Marshall College*, trans. J. S. Ermentrout (Chambersburg, Pa.: Publication Office of the German Reformed Church, 1846), 15; "almost unintelligible . . ." in Schaff, 10; "living conjunction . . ." and "petrification" in Schaff, 20. See also Schaff, 10–22; "Lutheranism in Somerset County, Pa.," *Lutheran Observer* 20 (March 1, 1852): 676. For another example of an advocate of English who still favored retention of German, see J. H. B. "Hindrances to Our Church."

6. Linn Harbaugh, *Life of the Reverend Henry Harbaugh, D. D.* (Philadelphia: Reformed Church Publication Board, 1900), 63–72, 74, 89; Nolt, *Strangers in Their Own Land*, 131–43.

7. *Acts and Proceedings of the West Pennsylvania Lutheran Synod*, 1859, 27; 1861, 34; *The Acts and Proceedings of the Synod of the German Reformed of the United States*, 1854, 20; 1857, 23; 1859, 104; Records of Zion's Classis, vol. 2, 1849–1863, May 1849, 13; 1851, 87–89, mss., Evangelical and Reformed Historical Society, Lancaster, Pa.

8. "try to comprehend . . ." in *Proceedings of the Evangelical Lutheran Synod of West Pennsylvania*, 1856, 28; Nolt, *Foreigners in Their Own Land*, 67–88, 133, 193n10.

9. Joseph Enders to Reverend and Dear Father Stonestreet (December 2, 1852), Archives, Maryland Province, Society of Jesus, Lauinger Library, Special Collections Research Center, Georgetown University, Washington, D.C., box 73, folder 9; Records of Zion's Classis, 1852, 104; 1859, 365; May 13, 1859, 352–53; 1860, 392; 1861, 429; Aaron Spangler, "Pastors," *Register of the German Branch of the First Reformed Church of York and of Zion Reformed Church, 1852–1907* (York, Pa.: typescript, York County Historical Society, 1945), 52–54. The membership numbers are 1859 figures.

10. *Proceedings of the Evangelical Lutheran Synod of West Pennsylvania*, 1859, 6–7, 15; 1860, 13; 1861, 11; St. Paul's Lutheran Church Book, mss. Wentz Library, Lutheran Theological Seminary, Gettysburg, Pa.; R. H. Deatrick "Reformed Church in Gettysburg, Pa.," mss., Evangelical and Reformed Historical Society, Gettysburg, Pa., Trinity Reformed folder, 6, 11.

11. For an astute discussion of the argument over revivalism, see James D. Bratt, "Religious Anti-Revivalism in Antebellum America," *Journal of the Early Republic* 24 (Spring 2004): 65–106.

12. Patricia U. Bonomi, *Under the Cope of Heaven: Religion, Society, and Politics in Colonial America* (New York: Oxford University Press, 1986), 139–49; E. Brooks Holifield, *Theology in America: Christian Thought from the Age of the Puritans to the Civil War* (New Haven, Ct.: Yale University Press, 2003), 91–101.

13. Holifield, *Theology in America*, 376; Mark A. Noll, *America's God: From Jonathan Edwards to Abraham Lincoln* (New York: Oxford University Press, 2002), 254, 308–11; James H. Smylie, *A Brief History of the Presbyterians* (Louisville, Ky.: Geneva Press, 1996), 78–80.

14. A second center of Pietism in southwestern Germany emphasized private, superior faith that withdrew from the larger society. Halle, in contrast, stressed state support and involvement in society that produced broad reform. Both taught inward faith and renewal of the church; A. G. Roeber, *Palatines, Liberty and Property: German Lutherans in Colonial British America* (Baltimore, Md.: Johns Hopkins University Press, 1993, 1998), 63–64. See also Holifield, *Theology in America*, 398–402.

15. "directed almost . . ." in Nolt, *Foreigners in Their Own Land*, 58; "a set time . . ." in Records of Zion's Classis (1856), 260; "revival church" in "Lutheranism in Somerset County, Pa.," *Lutheran Observer* 20 (March 19, 1852): 676. Emphasis original. See also "Revival," *Lutheran Observer* 20 (April 9, 1852): 688; *Proceedings of the Evangelical Lutheran Synod of West Pennsylvania* (1858), 23; (1861), 20; Nolt, 50–65.

16. "crying, shouting, . . ." in Nolt, *Foreigners in Their Own Land*, 62; "The brother who . . ." in L. K., "Revivals," *Lutheran Observer* 26 (May 28, 1858); "God is not . . ." Records of Zion's Classis, May 13, 1859, 355–56; "find their hearts," in Samuel Simon Schmucker to Beale Schmucker, February 12, 1863, Samuel Simon Schmucker Collection, Special Collections/Musselman Library, Gettysburg College, Gettysburg, Pennsylvania, box 1, file 5. See also Holifield, *Theology in America*, 402–8; Nolt, *Foreigners in Their Own Land*, 50–65; Henry Harbaugh, *The Fathers of the German Reformed Church in Europe and America*, 2 vols. (Lancaster, Pa.: J. M. Westhaeffer, 1857; 2nd ed., 1872), 2:302–4. Runkel retired in Gettysburg and died in 1832.

17. "must Lutheranisn . . ." in Holifield, *Theology in America*, 411.

18. "rest their hopes . . ." in Record of Zion's Classis, May 10, 1850, 50; "mechanical" and "shallow" in John W. Nevin, *The Anxious Bench: A Tract for the Times* (Chambersburg, Pa.: Publication Office of the German Reformed, 1844; 2nd ed.), vi; "rude . . ." in Nevin, 108; "the whole . . ." in Nevin, ix; "channels of life" in Zion's Classis, 1852, 116; "ordinary means" in Zion's Classis, 1856, 259; " convulsing influence" in *Acts and Proceedings of the Synod of the German Reformed*, 1853, 30; "ordinary course . . ." and "extraordinary change . . ." in *Acts and Proceedings of the Synod of the German Reformed Church* (1856), 25; "pure, unadulterated . . ." in Holifield, *Theology in America*, 410. See also Nevin, *The Anxious Bench*, vi, vii, ix, 103, 104–8, 119–20, 128–29; Record of Zion's Classis, 1857, 284; *Acts and Proceedings of the Synod of the German Reformed* (1856), 23–28; 1859, 34–35; Holifield, *Theology in America*, 408–14; 468–69. I have written more extensively on Lutheran and Reformed Pietism in *Piety and Tolerance: Pennsylvania German Religion, 1700–1850*, Pietist and Wesleyan Studies Series (Metuchen, N.J.: Scarecrow Press, 1994), 71–103.

19. Bowman, *Brethren Society*, 23–92; Donald F. Durnbaugh, *Fruit of the Vine: A History of the Brethren, 1708–1995* (Elgin, Ill.: Brethren Press, 1997), 45–50.

20. *Minutes of the Annual Meeting*, (1842) 75, (1848) 98, (1849) 104, (1855) 151; Stephen L. Longenecker, "Emotionalism Among Early American Anabaptists," in *The Dilemma of Anabaptist Piety: Strengthening or Straining the Bonds of Community*, ed. Longenecker (Bridgewater, Va.: Forum for Religious Studies, Bridgewater College, 1997), 61–67; Longenecker, *Shenandoah Religion: Outsiders and the Mainstream, 1716–1865* (Waco, Tx.: Baylor University Press, 2002), 66, 75–76.

21. Bowman, *Brethren Society*, 86–87; Durnbaugh, *Fruit of the Vine*, 110–12; St. Paul's AME Zion Church Book, October 29, 1859, mss., private collection.

22. Mack, "Rights and Ordinances," in *European Origins of the Brethren: A Source Book on the Beginnings of the Church of the Brethren in the Early Eighteenth Century*, ed. Donald F. Durnbaugh (Elgin, Ill.: The Brethren Press, 1958), 363–64; Marsh Creek Church Book, August 31, 1854, August 30, 1855, May 13 and August 26, 1858, February 27, 1862; Bowman, *Brethren Society*, 58–64; Durnbaugh, *Fruit of the Vine*, 119–20; Roger E. Sappington, *The Brethren in the New Nation: A Source Book on the Development of the Church of the Brethren, 1785–1865* (Elgin, Ill.: Brethren Press, 1976), 168–92.

23. Marsh Creek Church Book, December 12, 1850, February 8, 1851, August 28, 1851, November 27, 1851, September 25, 1852, November 23, 1854, May 22, 1862; Bowman, *Brethren Society*, 85–92.

24. Marsh Creek Church Book, May 5, 1853, May 9, 1861, November 28, 1861, February 27, 1862, November 13, 1862.

25. For marital discord see Marsh Creek Church Book, December 12, 1850, May 13, 1858, May 19, 1860. For sexual transgressions see July 26 and August 28, 1851. For public drunkenness see May 9, 1861. For expulsion for associating with other denominations see November 27, 1851, May 22, 1862. See also Bowman, *Brethren Society*, 85–91.

26. A list of those interred in the Catholic Cemetery records includes German-born; John T. Reily, *Collections in the Life and Times of Cardinal Gibbons* (McSherrystown, Pa.: n.p., 1902), 7:1356–61, in the St. Francis Xavier file/John Timons Reily Historical Society, Conewago, Pa. See also Reily, *Conewago: Centennial Celebration*, 13, 17; J. Walter Coleman, Anthony F. Kane, and Mary Louise Callahan, eds., *A Glorious Heritage, One Hundred Years: A History of St. Francis Xavier Church* (n.p.: Diocese of Harrisburg, n.d.), 10–11; United States Census, 1850 and 1860; John T. Reily, *Conewago: A Collection of Local Catholic History* (Martinsburg, W.Va.: Herald Print, 1885; reprinted Westminster, Md.: John William Eckenrode, 1970), 150, 155, 162.

27. Holifield, *Theology in America*, 427–30.

28. Francis X. DeNeckere, "On the Three Classes of Men" and "Means of Salvation," mss., untitled journal book, the Rev. Francis X. DeNeckere Papers, Lauinger Library, Special Collections Research Center, Georgetown University, Washington, D.C.

29. DeNeckere, "Means of Salvation"; Holifield, *Theology in America*, 431–32.

30. Holifield, *Theology in America*, 432.

31. Jay P. Dolan, *In Search of an American Catholicism: A History of Religion and Culture in Tension* (New York: Oxford University Press, 2002), 51–53; Reily, *Conewago*, 152.

32. "by order of . . ." in *Republican Compiler* (December 22, 1851), quoted in Cole, *For God and Country*, 9. See also Cole, 9–10; Dolan, *In Search of an American Catholicism*, 41–51; James M. O'Toole, *The Faithful: A History of Catholic America* (Cambridge, Mass.: Belknap Press of Harvard University Press, 2008), 78–79, 81, 85–89.

33. Dolan, *In Search of an American Catholicism*, 56–59; O'Toole, *The Faithful*, 86–87; Sean Wilentz, *The Rise of American Democracy: Jefferson to Lincoln* (New York: W. W. Norton and Company, 2005), 680; Richard J. Carwardine, *Evangelicals and Politics in Antebellum America* (New Haven, Ct.: Yale University Press, 1993), 81–84.

34. Tyler Anbinder, *Nativism and Slavery: The Northern Know Nothings and the Politics of the 1850s* (New York: Oxford University Press, 1992), 20–51; Carwardine, *Evangelicals*

and Politics in Antebellum America, 218–27; Wilentz, *Rise of American Democracy*, 680–81, 682–84.

35. "Americanism is . . ." in Anbinder, *Nativism and Slavery*, 238. See also Anbinder, 57–68, 150–54, 238–40, 261–64.

36. "Romish superstition" and "neglect of . . ." in *Proceedings of the Evangelical Lutheran Synod of West Pennsylvania*, 1859, 24; n.t. *Adams Sentinel* 54 (October 2, 1854); "The Claims of the Pope," *Lutheran Observer* 20 (April 9, 1852). The description of the "cathedral" was a reprint.

37. Samuel Simon Schmucker, "The Papal Hierarchy, Viewed in the Light of Prophecy and History" (Gettysburg, Pa.: H. C. Neinstedt, 1845).

38. "mass of undesireable . . ." and "studding the allies . . ." in "Mr. McClean on the American Movement," *Star and Banner* 26 (April 13, 1855); references to the Adams County poor house in "Tax-Payers of Adams County, Look at This!" *Star and Banner* 26 (September 7, 1855).

39. "Germans in America," *Star and Banner* 26 (October 5, 1855; reprinted from the *New York Journal of Commerce*).

40. "Mr. McClean on the American Movement," *Star and Banner* 26 (April 13, 1855); "Mr. Brownson and the Temporal Power of the Pope," *Star and Banner* 26 (July 27, 1855). "The Foreign Vote," *Star and Banner* 27 (November 14, 1856).

41. "True Americanism," *Star and Banner* 26 (July 27, September 7, and October 5, 1855).

42. "The Removal of Mr. Weikert," *Star and Banner* 26 (October 5, 1855).

43. "true-blue Americans candidates" and "whether 'Americans . . . ' " in "Vote the Settled Ticket," *Star and Banner* 26 (October 5, 1855). See also "Mr. Brownson and the Temporal Power of the Pope," *Star and Banner* 26 (July 27, 1855). "Anti-American Ticket" listed candidates of the opposition beneath the endorsed candidates of the *Star and Banner* (October 5, 1855).

44. "fond" in Sarah Sites Rodgers, *The Ties of the Past: The Gettysburg Diaries of Salome Myers Stewart, 1854–1922* (Gettysburg, Pa.: Thomas Publications, 1996), 111; "splendid music" in Rodgers, 79; "silly" in Rodgers, 123. See also Rodgers, 44, 88, 94, 106.

45. "midnight plot" in "The Know Nothing Ticket," *Republican Compiler* 37 (September 25, 1854). See also *Minutes of Annual Meeting*, (1855) 148; Anbinder, *Nativism and Slavery*, 24; Carwardine, *Evangelicals and Politics in Antebellum America*, 227–33; "Riot and Bloodshed at Washington," *Compiler* 40 (June 8, 1857); "The Proof Demanded!" *Compiler* 42 (October 17, 1859); "The Democracy," *Republican Compiler* 38 (September 24, 1855).

Divertimento: Abraham and Elizabeth Brien

1. "Brien Farm," Gettysburg National Military Park, Gettysburg, Pa.,VI-11; Marcella Sherfy, "The Brien Farm and Family," June, 1972, GNMP, I-11d,: 4–5, 9; Margaret S. Creighton: *The Colors of Courage: Gettysburg's Forgotten History; Immigrants, Women, and African Americans in the Civil War's Defining Battle* (New York: Basic Books, 2005), 51, 54, 64–65; United States Census, 1850 and 1860.

2. Leaders Book, AME Zion Church, Gettysburg, Pa., July 23, 1877, mss., private collection; Church Book, AME Zion Church, Gettysburg, Pa., October 29, 1859, n.d., n.m., 1862, mss., private collection; Creighton, *Colors of Courage*, 61.

5. Diversity: Race

1. Session Book, January 4, 1851, mss., Gettysburg Presbyterian Church, Gettysburg, Pa. For lists of members and communicants, see "Communicanten auf den 12ten April, 1851," and "Communicants of Easter Sunday, April 20th, 1851," mss., St. James Church Book, Wentz Library, Lutheran Theological Seminary, Gettysburg, Pa.; "List of Communicants," September 16, 1860, mss., Christ Church Book, Wentz Library; St. Paul's Lutheran Church Book, Wentz Library; Trinity Reformed Church Book, Adams County Historical Society, Gettysburg, Pa.; Records of Zion's Classis, vol. 2, 1849–1863, mss., Evangelical and Reformed Historical Society, Lancaster, Pa.,1851, 93; 1857, 314. Hannah and James Johnston appear in the U.S. Census, 1870.

2. Presbyterian Church Book, Gettysburg, June 22, 1841, for the Erection of Church Ediface, June 22 and 25, August 8, 12, and 16, 1842, mss., Gettysburg Presbyterian Church, Gettysburg, Pa.; United States Census, 1850.

3. United States Census, 1860.

4. "Membership List, 1854," typescript, Methodist Episcopal Church Book, Adams County Historical Society, Gettysburg, Pa.; United States Census, 1850 and 1860.

5. "Parochial Report," *Proceedings of the Evangelical Lutheran Synod of West Pennsylvania*; Records of Zion's Classis, 1859, 365; *Annual Minutes of the East Baltimore Conference*, 1860, 46, 47, 51. For Methodists I included fourteen probationers as members. The nine Methodist congregations are Carlisle, Chambersburg, Hampstead, Hanover, Shippensburg, Waynesboro, Wrightsville, York, and York Springs.

6. United States Census, 1850 and 1860.

7. Mark A. Noll, *The Civil War as a Theological Crisis* (Chapel Hill: University of North Carolina Press, 2006), 125–55; George C. Rable, *God's Almost Chosen Peoples: A Religious History of the American Civil War* (Chapel Hill: University of North Carolina Press, 2010).

8. M. Mielziner, "The Institution of Slavery among the Ancient Hebrews, According to the Bible and the Talmud," trans. H. I. Schmidt, *Evangelical Review* 13 (January, 1862): 311–55; *Proceedings of the Evangelical Lutheran Synod of West Pennsylvania*, (1857) 27–31, (1858) 20–24, (1859), 69–42; *The Acts and Proceedings of the Eastern Synod of the German Reformed Church in the United States*, (1853) 30, (1854) 18–19, (1857) 22; Records of Zion's Classis, (1849) 24, (1853) 157, (1856) 259–60, (1857) 284; (1858) 314, 316; (1859) 355–56. Other synodical conventions during this period expressed similar concerns.

9. "Tax-Payers Be Warned! The Mammoth at Work," *Compiler* 40 (October 5, 1857). For another example, see "Who Shall Govern?" *Compiler* 40 (October 12, 1857).

10. "superiority of slavery . . ." in "The Dignity of bein' Niggers," *Compiler* 42 (June 18, 1860). The quotation is Stahle's, but the slave's observation on his value is reprinted from the *Petersburg Express* (Virginia); "The Night Funeral of a Slave," reprinted from the *Home Journal*; *Compiler* 38 (December 31, 1855).

11. "To the Senate and House of Representatives of the State of Pennsylvania" (January 15, 1847), in David G. Smith, "On the Edge of Freedom: The Fugitive Slave Issue in South Central Pennsylvania, 1820–1870" (Ph.D. diss., Pennsylvania State University, 2006), 391–92.

12. "African Candor," *Star and Banner* 16 (October 17, 1845). Emphasis in original.

13. "Another Slave Case," *Star and Banner* 23 (May 28, 1852), reprint from *Harrisburg Telegraph*; N.t., *Adams Sentinel* 52 (May 31, 1852). For another example see "Fugitive Slave Case," *Compiler* 33 (January 6, 1851).

14. N.t., 17 (August 7, 1846); "Conflict with Fugitive Slaves" 21 (January 1, 1851); "A Chase" 21 (June 14, 1850); n.t. 24 (June 16, 1854): all in *Star and Banner.*

15. Buehler used "darkies" to describe several runaways in n.t., *Star and Banner* 24 (June 16, 1854).

16. "severity," "degradation," and "wrong in principle," in Samuel Simon Schmucker, *The Christian Pulpit, The Rightful Guardian of Morals in Political No Less Than Private Life* (Gettysburg, Pa.: H. C. Neinstedt, 1846), 20; "would send us . . ." in Schmucker, *Elements of Popular Theology; with Occasional Reference to the Doctrines of the Reformation, as Avowed Before the Diet at Augsburg in MDXXX* (Philadelphia: E. W. Miller, 1848), 332–36; "in the spirit . . ." in Abdel Ross Wentz, *Pioneer in Christian Unity: Samuel Simon Schmucker* (Philadelphia: Fortress Press, 1967; reissued Lutheran Theological Seminary, 1999), 322. See also Schmucker, *Memorial of Professor S. S. Schmucker, Relative to Binding Out Minor Colored Children* (Harrisburg, Pa.: Boas and Coplan, 1839); Schmucker, *Elements of Popular Theology*, 332–36; Schmucker, "Sermon on Matthew 25:34–40," Samuel Simon Schmucker Collection, Special Collections, Musselman Library, Gettysburg College, Gettysburg, Pa., box 6, file 28; Schmucker, "The Christian Pulpit," 17–20; Wentz, *Pioneer in Christian Unity*, 316–24; Paul P. Kuenning, *The Rise and Fall of American Lutheran Pietism: The Rejection of an Activist Heritage* (Macon, Ga.: Mercer University Press, 1988), 151–63.

17. Daniel Alexander Payne, *Recollections of Seventy Years* (New York: Arno Press and New York Times, 1968; originally published 1888), 11, 44–46, 56–65.

18. *Minutes of the Annual Meetings of the Brethren: Containing All Available Minutes from 1778 to 1909* (Elgin, Ill. The Brethren Publishing House, 1909), (1782) 7–8, (1797) 18–19, (1812) 30, (1813) 31–32, (1838) 65, (1845) 85, (1853) 136.

19. *Minutes of the Annual Meetings*, (1853) 135–36, (1854) 142–43; Denise D. Kettering, "'Greet One Another with a Holy Kiss': The Evolution of the Holy Kiss in the Church of the Brethren," in *Line, Places, and Heritage: Essays Commemorating the 300th Anniversary of the Church of the Brethren*, ed. Steve Longenecker and Jeff Bach, (Penobscot, Me.: Church of the Brethren Higher Education Association, 2008), 197–21.

20. *Minutes of the Annual Meetings* (1835) 58, (1835) 60, (1845) 85, (1849) 110–11.

21. "by the right hand . . ." in Marsh Creek Church Book, August 28, 1851, mss., Adams County Historical Society, Gettysburg, Pa. See also November 27, 1851; February 26, 1852.

22. "How is a . . ." in Marsh Creek Church Book, May 17, 1855; "Finding him . . ." and "in love . . ." in Annual Meeting (Henry Kurtz, clerk) to Marsh Creek Brethren, May 30, 1855, Marsh Creek Church Book; "owing to . . ." in Marsh Creek Church Book, May 12, 1859.

23. "Well, bos . . ." in "A Slave Refusing Her Liberty," 54 (August 21, 1854); "The 'Dignity of Bein' Niggers,'" 60 (June 4, 1860); "a giant Negro" in n.t., (March 3, 1856); "extend the limits . . ." in "Lynch Law—High-handed Measure" 50 (July 29, 1850), repr. from the *Baltimore Clipper*: all in *Sentinel*. See also n.t., *Sentinel* 50 (August 30, 1852); "Fugitive Slave Law," *Sentinel* 50 (October 28, 1850).

24. The annual conference of 1785 quoted in Robert Emory, *History of the Discipline of the Methodist Episcopal Church* (New York: G. Lane and C. B. Tippett, 1845), 80. See also Emory, 34–36, 43–45, 80, 274–76; Donald G. Mathews, *Slavery and Methodism: A Chapter in American Morality, 1780–1845* (Princeton, N.J.: Princeton University Press), 10–12, 19–27.

25. "bishop Andrew and . . ." in Horace Holland, Darnestown, Md., to Dear Sister Harriet Gist, Westminster, Md., (November 4, 1844), Horace Holland Papers, Lovely Lane Museum and Archives, Baltimore, Md. See also "Lynch Law in the Church," *Star and Banner* 16 (October 24, 1845); James E. Kirby, Russell E. Richey, and Kenneth E. Rowe, *The Methodists* (Westport, Conn.: Greenwood Press, 1996), 32–37, 110–12, 259–60; "Methodism in Adams Co.," *Gettysburg Compiler* (February 19, 1880).

26. *Annual Minutes of the East Baltimore Conference* (1859), 30; (1860), 41–42.

27. Annual Minutes of the Baltimore Conference, mss., Lovely Lane, (1845), 446; (1855), 449; Homer L. Calkin, "The Slavery Struggle, 1780–1865," in *Those Incredible Methodists: A History of the Baltimore Conference of the United Methodist Church*, ed. Gordon Pratt Baker (Baltimore, Md.: Commission on Archives and History, The Baltimore Conference, 1972), 197, 198–99, 206–10, 216–17. The Baltimore Conference had become the largest Methodist judicatory in the nation, and in 1857 it split into two with most of Baltimore City, northern Maryland, and Pennsylvania between the Susquehanna River and the high point of the Alleghenies forming the East Baltimore Conference. The Shenandoah Valley, portions of Baltimore City, and southern Maryland remained within the Baltimore Conference. In 1868 most of East Baltimore became part of the Central Pennsylvania Conference, but the Maryland circuits and a few congregations in the Pennsylvania mountains along the Maryland border went back to Baltimore. See Edwin Schell, "East Baltimore and Central Pennsylvania Conferences," in Baker, *Those Incredible Methodists*, 249–50, 257.

28. "source of ungovernable . . ." in Minutes of the Baltimore Conference (1855), 480; the phrase appears in a statement on colonization. Other quotations are from "Report on the Condition of Colored People" and "Resolutions on the Condition of Colored People," Annual Minutes of the Baltimore Conference, 1844. See also Charles F. Irons, *The Origins of Proslavery Christianity: White and Black Evangelicals in Colonial and Antebellum America* (Chapel Hill: University of North Carolina Press, 2008), 187–90, 200–4.

29. "would send us . . ." in Schmucker, *Elements of Popular Theology*, 335; "Departure of Mr. and Mrs. Wilson," *Star and Banner* 26 (May 4, 1855). See also Schmucker, *Popular Theology*, 332–36. Margaret Creighton believes that Buehler and his *Star and Banner* strongly supported colonization. The examples she cites are from 1848 through 1851, suggesting that as the sectional crisis deepened, Buehler moved away from colonization. See Creighton, *Colors of Courage*, 57, 252n26.

30. "energetic, brave . . ." in "Colonization," *Sentinel* 28 (January 15, 1844; repr. from the *Biblical Repository*). See also Minutes of the Baltimore Conference, passim; "Coloniza-

tion in Africa," *Sentinel* 50 (May 13, 1850; repr. from *The New York Tribune*); "1861 Adams County Pro-Colonization Petition," in Smith, "On the Edge of Freedom," 398–402. There were two identical petitions.

31. "civilization" and "infernal" in "Colonization in Africa," *Sentinel*; "natural prejudices," 1857; "to the last . . . ," 1857; "peaceable separation . . . ," 1851; "whole continent . . . ," 1851: all in the Minutes of the Baltimore Conference. See also "Colonization," *Sentinel*; Minutes of the Baltimore Conference, 1855; "1861 Adams County Pro-Colonization Petition," in Smith, *On the Edge of Freedom*, 398–402.

32. "one of the most . . ." in Daniel Walker Howe, *What Hath God Wrought: The Transformation of America, 1815–1848* (New York: Oxford University Press, 2007), 265; "so farfetched . . ." in William W. Freehling, *The Road to Disunion: Secessionists at Bay, 1776–1854* (New York: Oxford University Press, 1990), 160.

33. "the most glorious enterprise . . ." and "ranks among . . ." in Minutes of the Baltimore Conference, 1856; "most important enterprize . . ." in "Colonization," *Sentinel*. See also Minutes of the Baltimore Conference, 1852.

34. St. Paul's AME Zion Church Book, October 29, 1859; April 13, 1860, mss., private collection.

35. AME Zion Church Book, February 9, 1853, February 6, 1854.

36. AME Zion Leaders Book, February 23 and 24, 1863, mss., private collection; "To the Christian and Benevolent Public," *Sentinel* 54 (August 21, 1854).

37. United States Census, 1850 and 1860; Peter C. Vermilyea, "'We Did Not Know Where Our Colored Friends Had Gone': The Effect of the Confederate Invasion of Pennsylvania on Gettysburg's African American Community," *Gettysburg Magazine*, 24 (2001): 8. All of the Rideouts were born in Maryland, except the ten-month-old baby, indicating arrival sometime between the births of their two youngest children.

38. AME Zion Church Book; Marsh Creek Church Book; United States Census, 1850 and 1860. To compile a Dunker membership list, I used the Marsh Creek Church Book, which contains names of leadership and members subject to discipline. The Dunkers did not list members who neither achieved leadership nor suffered discipline. I assumed that adult households, especially wives, were members. The primary source of names for the Zion is the 1859 list of donors to the pastor's salary. If the donor was male, I included the wife on the assumption that the male made the donation on behalf of the household. If the name was female, I assumed that husband was not a member. Discipline and leadership also added names to the Zion's list.

39. "a comitee . . ." in AME Zion Church Book, July 21, 1854; "it was . . ." in September 11, 1852.

40. AME Zion Church Book, September 11, 1852, July 21, 1854; Presbyterian Church Book Gettysburg, June 22, 1842, for the erection of Church Ediface [*sic*], July 4, August 6, August 12, 1842, September 1, and September 12, 1842, November 20, 1843, mss., Gettysburg Presbyterian Church, Gettysburg, Pa.

41. United States Census, 1860; AME Zion Church Book, April 13 and 14, 1860. The census lists Biggs's birthplace as Pennsylvania rather than Maryland. Perhaps he was born in Pennsylvania, and then moved to Maryland, or perhaps the census is erroneous.

42. AME Zion Church Book, September 25, 1857, to June 4, 1858. This book also has a gap from February 9, 1858 to April 17, 1859.

43. AME Zion Church Book, August 8, 1854, June 24, October 2, and October 29, 1859, March 16, 1860, undated 1862.

44. For nonattendance see AME Zion Leaders Book, September 11, 1852, Church Book, November 11, 1852; for alcohol see Church Book, February 9, 1858, August 7, 1860; for "imprudent conduct" see Church Book, November 10, 1851, September 11, 1852, February 13, 1854; for O'Brien, see April 3, 1861. Both cases of nonattendance deal with the same individual.

45. AME Zion Church Book, November 10, 1851, April 7, 1852.

46. "justified themselves . . ." in AME Zion Church Book, September 24, 1859. See also March 16, 1860. For another example of dancing, see n.d., 1862.

47. "rebuked sharply . . ." in AME Zion Church Book, October 1, 1859. For other adjudicated disputes see June 24, 1853, January 8, 1862.

48. "yellow bitch . . ." in AME Zion Church Book, November 21, 1859. See also September 11, 1852.

49. James Oliver Horton and Lois E. Horton, *In Hope of Liberty: Culture, Community, and Protest among Northern Free Blacks, 1700–1860* (New York: Oxford University Press, 1997), 146; Patrick Rael, *Black Identity and Black Protest in the Antebellum North* (Chapel Hill: University of North Carolina Press, 2002).

50. John Wesley taught that after conversion the born-again could progress towards a second experience in which they became free from overt sin and followed more perfectly Christ's way.

51. Zilpha Elaw, *Memoir of the Life, Religious Experience, Ministerial Travels and Labors of Mrs. Zilpha Elaw, An American Female of Color* (London: 1846) in ed. and into., *Sisters of the Spirit: Three Black Women's Autobiographies of the Nineteenth Century*, ed. William L. Andrews (Bloomington: Indiana University Press, 1986), 66–67; Horton and Horton, *In Hope of Liberty*, 132–37.

52. Sarah Sites Rodgers, *The Ties of the Past: The Gettysburg Diaries of Salome Myers Stewart, 1854–1922* (Gettysburg, Pa.: Thomas Publications, 1996), 49. Myers expressed interest in worshipping with the AME Zion more frequently than she actually did. Either it was "too late," 35; she was ill, 35; she went and there was no meeting, 41, or it was raining, 41–42. For Myers's attendance see 42, 49; and for attendance by her friends, 44: all in Rodgers, *Ties of the Past*.

53. Samuel M. Giles, Christopher Rush, and Joseph P. Thompson, *Hymns for the Use of the African Methodist Episcopal Zion Church* (New York: D. Fanshaw, 1858), 17, 137, 201, 217, 228, 328, 354, 375, 394.

54. William T. Dargan, *Lining Out the Word: Dr. Watts Hymn Singing in the Music of Black Americans* (Berkeley: University of California Press, 2006), 27; Horton and Horton, *In Hope of Liberty*, 134–35, 145; Payne, *Recollections of Seventy Years*, 255; Patrick Rael, "The Market Revolution and Market Values in Antebellum Black Protest Thought," in *Cultural Change and the Market Revolution in America, 1789–1860*, ed. Scott C. Martin (Lanham, Md.: Rowman and Littlefield Publishers, 2005), 28–35; Rodgers, *Ties of the Past*, 49.

55. Myers in Rodgers, *Ties of the Past*, 136–37; Payne, *Recollections of Seventy Years*, 253–55.

56. According to evangelicals, the antediluvian period was a time of great sin between the Fall and the Flood.

57. Rodgers, *Ties of the Past*, 136–37.

58. "To the Christian and Benevolent Public," *Sentinel* 54 (August 21, 1854).

59. "Notice," *The Examiner* 48 (August 1, 1855); Nina Honemond Clarke, *History of the Nineteenth-Century Black Churches in Maryland and Washington, D.C.* (New York: Vantage Press, 1987), 13–17, 22–25, 28–30; David Smith, *Biography of Rev. David Smith, of the A.M.E. Church, Being a Complete History, Embracing Over Sixty Years' Labor in the Advancement of the Redeemer's Kingdom on Earth* (Xenia, Oh.: Xenia Gazette Office, 1881), 39. Leroy Hopkins, "Bethel African Methodist Church in Lancaster: Prolegomenon to a Social History," *Journal of the Lancaster County Historical Society* 90 (1986): 218–20, identifies other black preaching points, including Martic and Little Britain Townships (Lancaster County) and Mt. Vernon, Russellville, and Penningtonville (Chester County.)

Frederick County had 8,200 blacks, including slaves and free; Washington County, 3,112; and Carroll County, 1,908. Adams County had 474 blacks; Franklin County, 1,799; and York County, 1,366. United States Census, 1860.

60. Irons, *Origins of Proslavery Christianity*, 184–90, 200–4.

61. *Star and Banner* 17 (August 7, 1846); "Negro Jubilees," *Examiner* 47 (June 7, 1854); "Unlawful Meetings," 47 *Examiner* (January 18, 1854); Jarena Lee, *Religious Experience and Journal of Mrs. Jarena Lee, giving an account of her call to preach the gospel, revised and corrected from the original manuscript written by herself* (Philadelphia: 1836), 60. Jarena Lee reported that the incident in Frederick took place in 1830.

62. *Annual Minutes of the East Baltimore Conference*, 1860, 46–51. I included probationers as members.

Divertimento: Mary and Joseph Sherfy

1. Kathleen R. Georg, "The Sherfy Farm and the Battle of Gettysburg," mss., Gettysburg National Military Park, 1977, 1–6.

2. Gregory A. Coco, *A Strange and Blighted Land; Gettysburg: The Aftermath of a Battle* (Gettysburg, Pa.,: Thomas Publications, 1995), 47; United States Census, 1860 and 1870.

3. Marsh Creek Church Book, October 4, 1851, May 29, 1853, mss., Adams County Historical Society; Carl F. Bowman, *Brethren Society: The Cultural Transformation of a "Peculiar People"* (Baltimore, Md.: The Johns Hopkins University Press, 1995), 86–87; Donald F. Durnbaugh, *Fruit of the Vine: A History of the Brethren, 1708–1995* (Elgin, Ill.: The Brethren Press, 1995), 110–13.

4. Marsh Creek Church Book, February 23, 1854.

5. Marsh Creek Church Book, February 26, 1852; February 24, 1853; February 28, 1856; February 26, 1857; February 25, 1858.

6. Marsh Creek Church Book, August 25, 1859.

7. Marsh Creek Church Book, May 21, 1857.

8. "Rare Souvenirs Lost in Battle," undated newspaper clipping, Sherfy Family File, ACHS.

9. *Minutes of the Annual Meetings*, 107, 164, 178, 617, 793.

6. War

1. "War Commenced," *Compiler* 43 (April 22, 1861); "Commencement of Civil War," *Adams Sentinel* 61 (April 17, 1861).

2. J. Matthew Gallman with Susan Baker, "Gettysburg's Gettysburg: What the Battle Did to the Borough," in *The Gettysburg Nobody Knows*, ed. Gabor S. Boritt (New York: Oxford University Press, 1997), 148, 150, 170–73.

3. [Editorial], *Compiler* 42 (July 2, 1860); "Secession," *Sentinel* 60 (October 31, 1860); "Wide Awakes in Gettysburg!" *Compiler* 42 (October 8, 1860); "The 'Wide Awakes,'" *Compiler* (October 15, 1860); "Wide Awake Jolification," *Compiler* (October 29, 1860); "Gettysburg Wide Awakes" and "Additional Meeting," *Sentinel* 60 (September 26, 1860); "The Torch-Light Procession," and "The Wide Awake Club," *Sentinel* 60 (October 24, 1860); n.t., *Sentinel* 60 (October 31, 1860); Douglas R. Egerton, *Year of Meteors: Stephen Douglas, Abraham Lincoln, and the Election That Brought on the Civil War* (New York: Bloomsburg Press, 2010), 182–84; Charles H. Glatfelter, "Adams County Votes for President, 1804–2008," *Adams County History* 15 (2009): 38–39, 58; Ayers, *In the Presence of Mine Enemies*, 82–83; "Presidential Election in Adams County," *Adams Sentinel* 61 (November 14, 1860); William G. Thomas III and Edward L. Ayers, *The Differences Slavery Made: A Close Analysis of Two American Communities*, http://www2.vcdh.virginia.edu/AHR/, accessed April 4, 2011.

4. *Compiler* 43 (January 7, 1861); *Sentinel* 61 (January 9, 1861); "Important News: The War Commenced," *Sentinel* 61 (January 16, 1861). For identification of Smyser see United States Census, 1860, which lists him as "President Judge" in Norristown, Pa. The *Sentinel* printed Buchanan's proclamation of a national day of fasting; "To the People of the United States," *Adams Sentinel* 61 (December 19, 1860).

5. "anti-slavery radicals" in "Startling News! War To Be Inaugurated!" and "Black Republicans" in "Who Are for the Union?" in *Compiler* 43 (April 15, 1861); "stand by . . ." in "War Commenced," *Compiler* (April 15); "left in the cars," in untitled news item, *Sentinel* 61 (April 24, 1861); "called forth . . ." in "Great Union Meeting," *Sentinel* (April 24.) See also "Gettysburg Patriotism Alive," *Sentinel* (April 17, 1861), and untitled news briefs in the April 17 *Sentinel* and April 22 *Compiler*; "The Relief Association" and "A Home Guard," *Sentinel* (April 24); "Stand by the Old Flag," *Compiler* 43 (April 29, 1861; repr. from *Lancaster Intelligencer*).

6. "Men of Adams . . ." in Gallman and Baker, "Gettysburg's Gettysburg," 150–51; "made a very . . ." in Rodgers, *Ties of the Past*, 81. See also "The Troop of Cavalry" and "Zouaves in Gettysburg," *Sentinel* 61 (May 1, 1861); Gallman and Baker, 151–55, 158.

7. Roger D. Hunt, *Colonels in Blue: Union Army Colonels of the Civil War; The Mid-Atlantic States* (Mechanicsburg, Pa.: Stackpole Books, 2007), 160; Osceola Lewis, *History of the One Hundred and Thirty-Eighth Regiment, Pennsylvania Volunteer Infantry* (Norristown, Pa.: Wills, Iradell and Jenkins, 1866), 12–13, 22–23; Thomas P. Lowry, *Tarnished*

Eagles: The Courts-Martial of Fifty Union Colonels and Lieutenant Colonels (Mechanics-burg, Pa.: Stackpole Books, 1997), 116–20; "Fifty Years Ago Today," *Baltimore Sun* (May 19, 1913): 6.

8. Gallman and Baker, "Gettysburg's Gettysburg," 152–53; Rodgers, *Ties of the Past*, 81–92.

9. "Rebels are coming" in Charles M. McCurdy, *Gettysburg: A Memoir* (Pittsburgh, Pa.: Reed and Witting Company, 1929), 9; "comical" in Tillie Pierce Alleman, *At Gettysburg; Or, What a Girl Saw and Heard of the Battle* (New York: W. Lake Borland, 1889), 18–19; "partly prepared" in "The Adams Dragoons," *Star and Banner* 23 (September 11, 1862). See also "Arrival of Refugees," and "Excitement," *Star and Banner* 23 (September 4, 1862); "Latest!" (September 8, 1862) and "Rumors of War," September 15, 1862), both in *Compiler* 44; "Home Guard," *Sentinel* 62 (September 9, 1862); Robert Bloom, "'We Never Expected a Battle': The Civilians at Gettysburg, 1863," *Pennsylvania History* 55 (October 1988): 164.

10. Ayers, *In the Presence of Mine Enemies*, 322–27; Bloom, "We Never Expected a Battle,"164; John W. Thompson IV, *Horses, Hostages, and Apple Cider: J.E.B. Stuart's 1862 Pennsylvania Raid* (Mercersburg, Pa.: Mercersburg Printing, 2002), 58–83.

11. Bloom, "'We Never Expected a Battle," 164–65.

12. "in view of . . ." in Records of Zion's Classis, vol. 2, 1849–1863, March 10, 1861, 430–32, May 9, 1862, 466, mss., Evangelical and Reformed Historical Society, Lancaster, Pa.; *Proceedings of the Evangelical Lutheran Synod of West Pennsylvania*, 1861, 30–31; George C. Rable, *God's Chosen Peoples; A Religious History of the American Civil War* (Chapel Hill: University of North Carolina Press, 2010), 95–98; David Rolfs, *No Peace for the Wicked: Northern Protestant Soldiers and the American Civil War* (Knoxville: University of Tennes-see Press, 2009), 172–77; Minutes, Presbytery of Carlisle, 1861–70, April 8 and 9, 1862, 46, 50–51, mss., Presbyterian Historical Society, Philadelphia, Pa.; Rodgers, *Ties of the Past*, 82; "Communion Postponed," *Compiler* 44 (September 22, 1862); "Historical Sketch of Trinity Reformed Church, Gettysburg, Pa., *Directory: Trinity Reformed Church*, Trinity Reformed Church folder, Evangelical and Reformed Historical Society, 31–32.

13. *Proceedings of the Evangelical Lutheran Synod of West Pennsylvania*, 1862, 9–10, 21, 22; Rable, *God's Almost Chosen Peoples*, 98–106.

14. *Annual Register of the East Baltimore Conference*, 1863, 12, Juniata District, 13; Records of Zion's Classis; May 9, 1962, 466; Session Records, Gettysburg Presbyterian Church, September 6, 1861, January 11, 1862, May 3, 1862, August 30, 1862, January 9, 1863, and May 9, 1863, mss., Gettysburg Presbyterian Church, Gettysburg, Pa.; Trustees Book, August 31, 1861, Gettysburg Presbyterian Church; "Communion," *Sentinel* 62 (Septem-ber 9, 1862); "Festival," *Sentinel* 63 (June 16, 1863); Minutes of Proceedings at the Stated and Special Meetings of the Council, Council and Trustees, Congregation, and Pew Holders of the English Evangelical Lutheran Church (called Christ Church) at Gettysburg, Ad-ams County, Penn., Council and Trustees, March 19, 1862, mss., Wentz Library, Lutheran Theological Seminary, Gettysburg, Pa.; Record of the Proceedings of the Council of the Evangelical Lutheran Congregation of St. James' Church, Gettysburg, Pennsyla., March 15, 1862, December 13, 1862, mss., Lutheran Theological Seminary; Proceedings of the Evan-

gelical Lutheran Synod of West Pennsylvania, 1861, 11; Marsh Creek Church Book, May 14, 1863, mss., Adams County Historical Society, Gettysburg, Pa.

15. Trustees Book, Christ Church, January 18, 1861; Minutes of the Congregation, Christ Church, December 24, 1860, February 4 and December 27, 1861, January 27, 1862, February 2 and 24, 1863; Council, St. James' Church, November 10 and December 16, 1860, March 23 and May 4, 1861, March 15, 1862.

16. Ayers, *In the Presence of Mine Enemies*, 391–412; Harry W. Pfanz, *Gettysburg—The First Day* (Chapel Hill: University of North Carolina Press, 2001), 2–14, 19–20.

17. "bought" in Ayers, *In the Presence of Mine Enemies*, 402. See also Ayers, 401–5; Pfanz, *Gettysburg—The First Day*, 15–16. For a persuasive discussion of limited warfare during the Civil War see Mark E. Neely Jr., *The Civil War and the Limits of Destruction* (Cambridge, Mass.: Harvard University Press, 2007), passim.

18. "almost stripped," in Philip Schaff, "The Gettysburg Week," *Scribner's Magazine* 16 (July-December, 1894): 24. See also "Report of Capt. E. B. Brunson, C. S. Artillery" (July 31, 1863), *The War of the Rebellion: A Compilation of the Official Records Official Records of the Union and Confederate Armies*, 128 vols. (Washington, D.C.: U.S. Government Printing Office, 1890–1901): Series I, Volume 27 (2): 677; C. G. Chamberlayne, ed., *Ham Chamberlayne—Virginian: Letters and Papers of an Artillery Officer in the War for Southern Independence, 1861–1865* (Richmond, Va.: Dietz Printing Co., 1932), 191–92; "The Invasion: Occupation of York by the Enemy," *The York Gazette* (June 30, 1863); Pfanz, *Gettysburg— The First Day*; 15–17; James O. Lehman and Steven M. Nolt, *Mennonites, Amish, and the American Civil War* (Baltimore, Md.: Johns Hopkins University Press, 2007), 133; Ayers, *In the Presence of Mine Enemies*, 395–405, 407–9; D.P. Saylor, "Correspondence," *Gospel Visitor* 13 (September 1863): 284–87.

19. "driving them off . . ." (Rachel Cormany) in Ayers, *In the Presence of Mine Enemies*, 405–6. See also Ayers, 105, 397–98, 405–7; Schaff, "The Gettysburg Week," 22, 24; Schaff, *Slavery and the Bible: A Tract for the Times* (Chambersburg, Pa.: M. Kieffer and Company, 1861), *passim*; Peter C. Vermilyea, "'We Did Not Know Where Our Colored Friends Had Gone': The Effect of the Confederate Invasion of Pennsylvania on Gettysburg's African American Community," *Gettysburg Magazine* 24 (2001): 11; Margaret S. Creighton, *The Colors of Courage: Gettysburg's Forgotten History: Immigrants, Women, and African Americans in the Civil War's Defining Battle* (New York: Basic Books, 2005), 126–32. For a summary of invading Confederates and African Americans see David G. Smith, "Race and Retaliation: The Capture of African Americans during the Gettysburg Campaign," in *Virginia's Civil War*, ed. Peter Wallenstein and Bertram Wyatt-Brown (Charlottesville: University of Virginia Press, 2005), 137–151.

20. "worse than ever," in Rodgers, *Ties of the Past*, 160. See also Rodgers, 161; Vermilyea, "We Did Not Know Where Our Colored Friends Had Gone," 12–14; "The Visit of Jenkins's Cavalry to McConnellsburg and Mercersburg" *Compiler* 45 (June 29, 1863); "Invasion of the North," *Sentinel* 63 (June 23, 1863); "Excitement in York—Apprehended Rebel Invasion," *York Gazette* (June 23, 1863).

21. Alleman, *At Gettysburg*, 19–20. See also Vermilyea, "We Did Not Know Where Our Colored Friends Had Gone," 11–12.

22. David A. Murdoch, ed., "Catherine May White Foster's Eyewitness Account of the Battle of Gettysburg," *Adams County History* 1 (1995): 45–46, 48–49; Rodgers, *Ties of the Past*, 161.

23. "well uniformed . . ." in Pfanz, *Gettysburg—The First Day*, 14. See also Bloom, "We Never Expected a Battle," 165–66.

24. Buehler's account in "The Rebels in Gettysburg," *Star and Banner* 34 (July 2, 1863); "In Rebeldom," in Rodgers, *Ties of the Past*, 161; "not to drive fast," in Clifton Johnson, *Battlefield Adventures: The Stories of Dwellers on the Scenes of Conflict in Some of the Most Noble Battles of the Civil War* (Boston and New York: Houghton Mifflin, 1915), 160; the source was only eight years old at the time of the battle. "did not know . . ." in Mary Warren Fastnacht, *Memories of the Battle of Gettysburg: Year 1863* (New York: Princely Press, 1941), n.p. See also, Rodgers, 160–61; Pfanz, *Gettysburg—The First Day*, 14; Gerald R. Bennett, *Days of "Uncertainty and Dread": The Ordeal Endured by the Citizens at Gettysburg* (Littlestown, Pa.: published by the author, 1994), 11–15; Bloom, "We Never Expected a Battle," 166–68; Edwin B. Coddington, *The Gettysburg Campaign: A Study in Command* (New York: Charles Scribner's Sons, 1968), 167–68; Murdoch, ed., "Catherine May White Foster's Eyewitness Account, 48.

25. Pfanz, *Gettysburg—The First Day*, 21–39.

26. "very ominous" in Johnson, *Battleground Adventures*, 177. See also Pfanz, *Gettysburg—The First Day*, 39–50; Rodgers, *Ties of the Past*, 162; M. Jacobs, "The Battle of Gettysburg," *Evangelical Review* 15 (April, 1864): 228.

27. "old gentleman" in Pam Newhouse, *The Codori Family and Farm: In the Path of Battle* (Gettysburg, Pa.: Friends of the National Parks at Gettysburg, 1999), 4. See also Pfanz, *Gettysburg—The First Day*, 51–79; Bloom, *"We Never Expected a Battle,"* 171–72; Kathleen R. Georg, "The Sherfy Farm and the Battle of Gettysburg," (Gettysburg National Military Park Archives, 1977, typescript), 6–8; Robert L. Brake, "The Joseph Sherfy Family at the Battle of Gettysburg," typescript, Sherfy Family File, ACHS; Timothy H. Smith, "The Sherfy House," (May 10, 1995, typescript), Civilian Accounts of the Battle of Gettysburg, ACHS; Pfanz, *Gettysburg—The First Day*, 74–75. Brake excerpted "The Joseph Sherfy Family and the Battle of Gettysburg" from William Emory Sherfey, *The Sherfey Family in the United States, 1751–1948* (Greensburg, Ind.); Sherfey relied heavily on the account of Otelia Sherfy, a daughter, whom he interviewed. "The Sherfy House" is a typescript of a handwritten account written by an unnamed family member; Smith describes the document as "undated" but it carries the date "1916."

28. Pfanz, *Gettysburg—The First Day*, 294–349.

29. Vermilyea, "We Did Not Know Where Our Colored Friends Had Gone," 12–13; "Leading Colored Citizen: Was an Active Agent in the Underground Railroad," *Gettysburg Compiler* (June 13, 1906); Jean Bohn, "Abram Brien," typescript, May 2003, GNMP, VI-11.

30. Myers's recollections in Johnson, *Battleground Adventures*, 178–79. See also "Resignation of Rev. A. Essick," *Lutheran Observer* 32 (October 7, 1864); Newhouse, *The Codori Family and Farm*, 5. Nicholas's whereabouts are family lore.

31. Bloom, "We Never Expected a Battle," 175; Clifton Johnson, *Battleground Adventures: The Stories of Dwellers on the Scenes of Conflict in Some of the Most Notable Battles of the Civil War* (New York: Houghton Mifflin, 1915), 177; Rodgers, *Ties of the Past*, 162;

Jacobs, "Battle of Gettysburg," 233; "Gettysburg," *Lutheran Observer* (July 31, 1863); Abdel Ross Wentz, *Pioneer in Christian Unity: Samuel Simon Schmucker* (Philadelphia: Fortress Press, 1967; repr. Gettysburg: Lutheran Theological Seminary, 1999), 326–27, 329.

32. Bloom, "We Never Expected a Battle," 168–69; Creighton, *Colors of Courage*, 135–139; Vermilyea, "We Did Not Know Where Our Colored Friends Had Gone," 16–17.

33. Harry W. Pfanz, *Gettysburg—The Second Day* (Chapel Hill: University of North Carolina Press, 1987), 64–65.

34. "everywhere...," "nothing...," and "she was too busy..." in Johnson, *Battleground Adventures*, 179.

35. "Claim of Joseph Sherfy," Federal Claims, National Archives, RG 92, 214–849; Georg, "The Sherfy Farm," 8–9; Pfanz, *Gettysburg: The Second Day*, 137–38.

36. Newhouse, *The Codori Family and Farm*, 4. Both scenarios for Catherine Staub's shelter during the battle are family lore without documentation. Another family story places Staub in Carlisle with her fleeing family, but the Codoris probably would not have taken a nine-months-pregnant woman on this twenty-five-mile trip, which also required their horses to pass through Confederate lines without being confiscated.

37. "pretty well hardened..." in Gregory A. Coco, *A Vast Sea of Misery: A History and Guide to the Union and Confederate Field Hospitals at Gettysburg, July 1-November 20, 1863* (Gettysburg, Pa.: Thomas Publications, 1988), 18. See also Coco, 12–21.

38. "riddled" in Georg, "The Sherfy Farm," 24. See also Georg, 10–26; "The Joseph Sherfy Family at the Battle of Gettysburg"; Pfanz, *Gettysburg: The Second Day*, 94–95, 303–35, 364; "History of the 114th (Zouaves d'Afrique) Regiment Infantry-Pa. Volunteers," Gettysburg National Military Park, Sherfy Farm and the Battle of Gettysburg File.

39. Jeffry D. Wert, *Gettysburg: Day Three* (New York: Simon and Schuster, 2001), 205–10, 237; Noah Andre Trudeau, *Gettysburg: A Testing of Courage* (New York: Harper-Collins, 2002), 494–95. The term *Pickett's Charge* is controversial because units other than Pickett's division participated in the assault.

40. "everything was quiet . . ." in Johnson, *Battleground Adventures*, 180; "skin, seeds . . ." in Bloom, "We Never Expected a Battle, 167. See also Bennett, *Days of "Uncertainty and Dread*," 67–72; Kent Masterson Brown, *Retreat from Gettysburg: Lee, Logistics, and the Pennsylvania Campaign* (Chapel Hill: University of North Carolina Press, 2005), 75–76, 105; Coddington, *The Gettysburg Campaign*, 535–37; Jacobs, "Battle of Gettysburg," 241; George Sheldon, *When the Smoke Cleared at Gettysburg: The Tragic Aftermath of the Bloodiest Battle of the Civil War* (Nashville, Tenn.: Cumberland House Publishing, 2003), 107–11.

41. Coco, *Strange and Blighted Land*, 257; Newhouse, *The Codori Family and Farm*, 3–6.

42. Bloom, "We Never Expected a Battle," 182; Jacobs, "Battle of Gettysburg," 243; Catherine Duncan to Beale Schmucker, July 17, 1863, Samuel Simon Schmucker Collection, Special Collections/Musselman Library, Gettysburg College, Gettysburg, Pennsylvania, box 1, file 7; Coco, *Strange and Blighted Land*, 5–79, 84, 165, 186; John Walker Jackson, "Visit to the Battle-field," *Christian Advocate and Journal* 38 (August 13, 1863): 258; L. L. Crouse, "to the editor of *The New York Times*," *York Gazette* (July 7, 1863). For confirmation that Jackson was an African American clergyman, see John Walker Jackson, *The Union—The*

Constitution—Peace: A Thanksgiving Sermon (Harrisonburg, Pa.: "Telegraph" Steam Book and Job Office, August 6, 1863); Harry C. Silcox, "Nineteenth-Century Philadelphia Black Militant: Octavius v. Catto (1839–1871)," in *African Americans in Pennsylvania: Shifting Historical Perspectives*, ed. Joe William Trotter Jr. and Eric Ledell Smith (University Park: Pennsylvania University Press, 1997), 215; *Coco, Vast Sea of Misery*, 20. I identify Jackson as a Methodist because he preached his Thanksgiving Day sermon in a Methodist church and published the description of his visit to Gettysburg in the Methodist periodical.

43. "Claim of Abraham Brien," 214/798, Gettysburg National Military Park; Harry Pfanz, *Gettysburg—Second Day*, 64.

44. "J. G. Beardon . . ." in Wentz, *Pioneer of Christian Unity*, 330. See also Wentz, 327–31; "Gettysburg," *Lutheran Observer*; Catherine Duncan to Beale Schmucker. Paul P. Kuenning argues that slavery politics motivated systematic trashing of the Schmucker household; Kuenning, *The Rise and Fall of American Lutheranism: The Rejection of an Activist Heritage* (Macon, Ga.: Mercer University Press, 1988), 177. Wentz includes an extensive quotation from Schmucker's report to the seminary board of directors; the Civilian Accounts collection of the Adams County Historical Society has a briefer version.

45. "clothes, bonnets, towels . . ." in Brown, *Retreat from Gettysburg*, 76, and Coco, *A Strange and Blighted Land*, 42–43. See also Sherfy War Claims; Georg, "The Sherfy Farm," 27–28; "Rare Souvenirs Lost in Battle," undated newspaper clipping, Sherfy Family File, ACHS; "The Joseph Sherfy Family at the Battle of Gettysburg"; "The Sherfy House"; Thomas W. Knox, "The Battle Field at Gettysburg: Scenes after the Battle," Gettysburg Newspaper Clippings File, GNMP; Coco, *A Strange and Blighted Land*, 38–52, 379n27. Knox published his account in *New York Herald* (July 9, 1863); it was reprinted in *Berks and Schuylkill Journal* (July 18, 1863).

46. Catherine Duncan to Beale Schmucker; Myers quoted in Johnson, *Battleground Adventures*, 180.

47. Two residents used the phrase "have a Sunday" in Bloom, "We Never Expected a Battle," 185–86. See also Gregory A. Coco, *A Strange and Blighted Land, Gettysburg: The Aftermath of a Battle* (Gettysburg, Pa.: Thomas Publications, 1995), 190–91, 226–37; "School Matters," *Sentinel* 63 (September 8, 1863).

48. Church Book, St. Paul's German Lutheran Congregation, mss., Wentz Library, Lutheran Theological Seminary, Gettysburg, Pa.; *Proceedings of the Evangelical Lutheran Synod of West Pennsylvania*, 1864, 15; Council of the Congregation, St. James Lutheran, April 28, 1865.

49. Church Book, AME Zion, August 16 and 25, 1863, December 26, 1863; Leaders Book, AME Zion, October 18, 1863; Vermilyea, "We Did Not Know Where Our Colored friends Had Gone," 21–22, United States Census, 1860.

50. Coco, *Vast Sea of Misery*, 17–18; J. Walter Coleman, Anthony F. Kane, and Mary Louise Callahan, eds., *A Glorious Heritage, One Hundred Years: A History of St. Francis Xavier Church, Gettysburg, Pennsylvania, 1853–1953* (n.p.: Diocese of Harrisburg, n.d.), 15–17; James M. Cole, *For God and Country: A History of St. Francis Xavier Church, 1831–1981* (Gettysburg, Pa.: St. Francis Xavier Parish, 1981), 18–21; Baptisms, 1843–1943, St. Francis Xavier Roman Catholic Church, photocopied mss., Adams County Historical Society, Gettysburg, Pa., 23.

51. Marsh Creek Church Book, August 13 and November 12, 1863, February 27, 1864.

52. Marsh Creek Church Book, August 13, 1863; Henry Utz Claims File, National Archives, 214–726; Michael Bushman, Pennsylvania, Claims File, GNMP; Sherfy Claims File, National Archives. Other Dunkers who sustained losses were Michael Bushman, who had a farm along the Confederate line of march towards Little Round Top and who claimed $717.50, and John Trostle, whose farm was a hospital behind Union lines, who asked for $1574.

53. "A Brief Synopsis of Br. [John] Hunsacker's Journal," *Gospel Visiter* (May 1864): 157–58.

54. Session Records, Gettysburg Presbyterian Church, January 10, 1864; Trustees Book, Gettysburg Presbyterian Church, July 27 and September 2, 1863; *Sentinel* 63 (October 6, 1863); Council of the Congregation, St. James, August 29 and October 17, 1863; "Religious," *Sentinel* 64 (December 15, 1863).

55. *Annual Minutes of the East Baltimore Conference* (1860), 46, (1861), 33, (1862), 41, (1863), 47, (1864), 46; *Proceedings of the Evangelical Lutheran Synod of West Pennsylvania*, (1860), 33; (1861), 39, (1862), 33, (1863), n.p., (1864), n.p., (1865), 33. Methodist figures include the Gettysburg circuit, which included Adams County congregations. Many Lutheran pastors claimed communicants in suspiciously round figures that were multiples of fifty, raising questions about the reliability of their reports.

56. Minutes and Proceedings of the Congregation of Christ's Church, November 23 and December 5, 1863, January 18, 1864.

57. Trustees Book, Gettysburg Presbyterian Church, July 27 and September 2, 1863, February 13 and May 4 and 7, 1864. The Trustees Book incorrectly identifies the date of the September 2 meeting as 1864, but the context and chronology of the minutes indicate that it should be 1863.

58. Gallman and Baker, "Gettysburg's Gettysburg," 154–55. Gallman and Baker believe that gender divisions remained high during and after the war, but George Frederickson, Anne Firor Scott, and Nancy Hewitt have written that women's voluntarism during the war expanded their public role. Gallman briefly discusses the historiography of female voluntarism in "Voluntarism in Wartime: Philadelphia's Great Central Fair," in *Toward a Social History of the Civil War: Exploratory Essays*, ed. Maris A. Vinovskis (Cambridge: Cambridge University Press, 1990), 94–95, 110–16.

59. Church Book, AME Zion, June 29 and December 23, 1964, June 29 and September 21, 1865; Council of the Congregation, St. James, August 27, and November 12, 1864, April 28, 1865, n.d. 1865; Trustees Book, Gettysburg Presbyterian, May 30, 1864; "some" in Minutes, Presbytery of Carlisle, April 13, 1864, 127; Council and Trustees, Christ Church, January 8, 1864; Marsh Creek Church Book, March 26, 1864.

60. Drew Gilpin Faust, *This Republic of Suffering: Death and the American Experience* (New York: Alfred A. Knopf, 2008), xi–xviii, 171–265. Faust's examples of those who questioned traditional faith because of large-scale death are Ambrose Bierce, Emily Dickinson, Oliver Wendell Holmes Jr., and Herman Melville, all New England intellectuals. Faust also describes evangelicals who relied on traditional assumptions to somehow explain God's role in the carnage.

61. "hand of God" in H. L. Baugher, *The Christian Patriot: A Discourse Addressed to the Graduating Class of Pennsylvania College, September 15, 1861* (Gettysburg, Pa.: A. D.

Buehler, 1861), 8; "there is no . . ." in "Abraham Lincoln," *Evangelical Review* 16 (July, 1865): 422–23; "final results" in "The United States Christian Commission," *Evangelical Review* 16 (April, 1865): 258–59. See also Stout, xvii–xxii, 248–51, 282–83, 459; Mark A. Noll, *The Civil War as a Theological Crisis* (Chapel Hill: University of North Carolina Press, 2006), 18, 22–23; Rable, *God's Chosen Peoples*, 25–26, 34, 41–44; "Our National Crisis," *Evangelical Review* 13 (July, 1861):149–50. Richard Carwardine, *Evangelicals and Politics in Antebellum America* (New Haven, Ct.: Yale University Press, 1993), passim, emphasizes the role of religion in public policy debates before the Civil War.

62. "we are not . . ." in *Annual Register of the East Baltimore Conference*, 1862, 32; "patriotism is . . ." in *Annual Register*, 31; "with great enthusiasm," *Annual Register*, 1863, 7. See also *Annual Register*, 6–7; Henry Ziegler, "Politics and the Pulpit," *Evangelical* Review 16 (April 1865): 245–58.

63. Christian B. Keller, "The Pennsylvania Dutch and 'the Hard Hand of War,'" in *Damn Dutch: Pennsylvania Germans at Gettysburg*, ed. David L Valuska and Christian B. Keller (Mechanicsburg, Pa.: Stackpole Books, 2004), 56–73; "Historical Sketch of Trinity Reformed Church," 33; Jackson, "Visit to the Battle-field," 258.

64. "armor" and "victory in . . ." in G. A. Lintner, "The Crusades," *Evangelical Review* 14 (October, 1862): 131; "holiest cause . . ." in "Our National Crisis," 150; "will of God," in *The Christian Patriot*, 7. See also *The Christian Patriot*, 19; *Proceedings of the Evangelical Lutheran Synod of West Pennsylvania Synod*, 1863, 22–23.

65. "If the president . . ." in *Annual Minutes of the East Baltimore Conference*, 1862, 7; "treasonable," "wise," and "patriotic," 1862, 31; "crime against God . . . ," "enemies of society . . . ," and "profound gratitude . . ." in 1864, 40. See also 1860, 41, 42; 1862, 6–7, 10, 31–33. For the pre-war conservatism of border Methodists, especially the Baltimore Conference, see Robert D. Clark, "Methodist Debates and Union Sentiment on the Border, 1860–1861," in *Antislavery and Disunion, 1858–186: Studies in the Rhetoric of Compromise and Conflict*, ed. J. Jeffery Auer (New York: Harper & Row, 1963), 152–70.

66. "baptism of . . ." in J. H. Brown, S. Keples, and J. H. C. Dosh, "Missionary Correspondence," *Christian Advocate and Journal* 38 (April 23, 1863): 134; Nevin quoted in Noll, *The Crisis over Providence*, 76; "profound gratitude . . ." in *Annual Minutes of the East Baltimore Conference*, 1864, 40. See also *East Baltimore*, 1865, 13; Noll, 77. The Methodist preachers burst into song "on motion" rather than spontaneously.

67. *Proceedings of the Evangelical Lutheran Synod of West Pennsylvania* (1863), 22–23.

68. "hollow of God's hand" in F. W. Conrad, "The Hand of God in War," *Evangelical Review* 16 (April 1865): 234. See also Conrad, 225–45. An editorial in the *Lutheran Observer* made exactly the same points as Conrad, namely that the change in command, the selection of positions, motivation to defend home soil, etc., were all divinely inspired; "God Giving Victory at Gettysburg," *Lutheran Observer* (August 14, 1863).

69. "profound gratitude . . ." in *Proceedings of the East Baltimore Conference*, 1864, 40. See also Rable, *God's Almost Chosen Peoples*, 54–55. The East Baltimore preachers burst into song "on motion" rather than spontaneously.

70. F. W. Conrad, "The Hand of God in War," *Evangelical Review* 16 (April 1865): 245; Rable, *God's Almost Chosen Peoples*, 88, 358–59.

71. Rolfs, *No Peace for the Wicked*, 126–29; Stout, *Upon the Altar of the Nation*, xix–xx; "Our National Crisis," *Evangelical Review* 13 (July, 1861): 136.

72. "martyrdom" and "baptism of blood" were commonly used, but the specific quotations here are Horace Bushnell and Philip Schaff, respectively, in Harry S. Stout, *Upon the Altar of the Nation: A Moral History of the Civil War* (New York: Viking, 2006), 250; Payne in Noll, *The Civil War as a Theological Crisis*, 78; Lutherans in *Proceedings of the Evangelical Lutheran Synod of West Pennsylvania*, 1865; Lincoln's proclamations in Rolfs, *No Peace for the Wicked*, 140. See also Baugher, *The Christian Patriot*, 11; Rable, *God's Almost Chosen Peoples*, 54, 80–81, 87, 234–35; Rolfs, 126–29, 133–34, 139–43;

73. Schmucker to Mary Steenbergen Schmucker, Vienna, June 6, 1846, mss., Schmucker Collection, box 1, file 4.

74. "in defense . . ." in Schmucker to David McConaughy, Esq., Gettysburg, August 14, 1863, mss., Schmucker Collection, box 1, file 7. See also Schmucker, "Then Shall the King Say to Them on His Right," Schmucker Collection, box 5, file 70; "The Relief Committee," *Compiler* 43 (April 29, 1861); Abdel Ross Wentz, *Pioneer in Christian Unity: Samuel Simon Schmucker* (Philadelphia: Fortress Press, 1967; reissued by Lutheran Theological Seminary, 1999), 339. Schmucker's "Then Shall the King" sermon described the "character of true Disciples of Christ" and criticized unjust wars and conquest through war.

75. G. A. Wenzel, "The Bearing of Ministers of the Gospel in Time of War—A Voice from Luther to His Contemporaries," *Evangelical Review* 13 (April, 1862): 463. The quotation is from Luther's "Civil Government."

76. J. Matthew Gallman, *The North Fights the Civil War: The Home Front* (Chicago: Ivan R. Dee, 1994), 166–67; James W. Geary, *We Need Men: The Union Draft in the Civil War* (DeKalb: Northern Illinois Press, 1991), 111–39; Lehman and Nolt, *Mennonites, Amish, and the American Civil War*, 143–57.

77. "with mingled surprise . . ." in "Local Items," *Franklin Repository* (August 26, 1863); *Minutes of the Annual Meetings*, (1864) 230, 231–32; *Gettysburg Compiler* (November 23, 1863); Marsh Creek Church Book, March 26, 1864, April 17, 1865.

78. "indifferent . . ." in *Minutes of the Annual Meetings* (1864), 231–32; "rebels in this bloody rebellion" (1865) 238; "speak evil . . . ," 238; "especially of President Lincoln" (1865), 242. See also 239.

79. "hard feelings . . ." in *Minutes of the Annual Meetings* (1864), 225. See also *Minutes*, 236, 241, 242, 244; Marsh Creek Church Book, March 26, 1864.

80. *Minutes of the Annual Meetings*, 238; Marsh Creek Church Book, May 7, 1865.

81. "They were . . ." in J. T. Trowbridge, "The Field of Gettysburg," *Atlantic Monthly* 16 (November, 1865): 622. Also quoted in Coco, *A Strange and Blighted Land*, 48. "was scattered" in Coco, *A Strange and Blighted Land*, 52. See also *The Baltimore Sun* (September 11, 1865): 3; Sherfy Farm and the Battle of Gettysburg File, GNMP, archives 2–11b.

82. Stout, *Upon the Altar of the Nation*, xxi–xxii.

Conclusion

1. Gabor Boritt, *The Gettysburg Gospel: The Lincoln Speech that Nobody Knows* (New York: Simon & Schuster, 2006), 47–48, 91–123; Drew Gilpin Faust, *This Republic of Suffer-*

ing: *Death and the American Civil War* (New York: Alfred A. Knopf, 2008), 99–101; David Goldfield, *America Aflame: How the Civil War Created a Nation* (New York: Bloomsbury Press, 2011), 293–94; Allen C. Guelzo, *Abraham Lincoln: Redeemer President* (Grand Rapids, Mich.: William B. Eerdmans Company, 2003), 369–74; George C. Rable, *God's Almost Chosen Peoples: A Religious History of the American Civil War* (Chapel Hill: University of North Carolina Press, 2010), 276–77; Mark S. Schantz, *Awaiting the Heavenly Kingdom: The Civil War and America's Culture of Death* (Ithaca, N.Y.: Cornell University Press, 2008), 92–96; Garry Wills, *Lincoln at Gettysburg: The Words that Remade America* (New York: Simon & Schuster, 1992), 41–147. Biblical quotations are King James Version.

2. William G. McLoughlin Jr., *Modern Revivalism: Charles Grandison Finney to Billy Graham* (New York: Ronald Press Company, 1959), 239–46, 249–62; Lyle W. Dorsett, *A Passion for Souls: The Life of D. L. Moody* (Chicago: Moody Press, 1997), 187–94. David Goldfield argues that post–Civil War evangelicalism, including Moody, remained entertaining but was much less fervent and that science replaced evangelicalism as America's compass; *America Aflame: How the Civil War Created a Nation* (New York: Bloomsbury Press, 2011), 4–8, 12–14, 510–13.

3. T. H. Breen, " 'Baubles of Britain': The American and Consumer Revolutions of the Eighteenth Century," *Past and Present* (May 1988): 73–104.

4. The Social Gospel applied religion to the problems of industrialization and encouraged the faithful to work for the improvement of society rather than for individual salvation. The Gospel of Wealth taught that the discipline required to acquire a fortune built character but that God wanted the money returned to society. Muscular Christianity articulated the faith to appeal directly to men, chiefly through action and service. The huge increase in immigration in the late nineteenth and early twentieth centuries added innumerable variety to American religion, including Catholics, Jews, and Eastern Orthodox, with each great faith tradition also contributing ethnic diversity. Liberalism, also known as modernism, departed from orthodox Protestantism by urging religion to change with the times and for each generation should develop its own truths. One aspect of liberalism applied modern knowledge to biblical interpretation, thereby challenging long-held and popular assumptions about the Bible. Christian Science believed that matter and spirit are part of the same world and that proper thinking directed by God can overcome pain and illness, which are not real. Theosophy drew from Hinduism and Buddhism and claimed that every individual possessed the single universal religious consciousness. Charles H. Lippy, *Introducing American Religion* (London and New York: Routledge, 2009).

5. William R. Hutchinson, *Religious Pluralism in America: The Contentious History of a Founding Ideal* (New Haven, Ct.: Yale University Press, 2003), 84–138; Martin E. Marty, *Righteous Empire: The Protestant Experience in America* (New York: The Dial Press, 1970), 144–209.

6. Marty, *Righteous Empire*, 142–43.

Divertimento: Thaddeus Stevens

1. Other famous residents of Gettysburg are Eddie Plank, a Hall of Fame baseball player; Francis X. Bushman, a silent film star; and retired President Dwight D. Eisenhower.

2. "degraded condition" and "most disgraceful . . ." in Bradley R. Hock, *Thaddeus Stevens in Gettysburg: The Making of an Abolitionist* (Gettysburg, Pa.: The Adams County Historical Society, 2005), 117. See also Hock, 1–7, 18–22, 98, 115–18, 227–45; Fawn M. Brodie, *Thaddeus Stevens: Scourge of the South* (New York: W.W. Norton and Company, 1959), 63–68; Hans L. Trefousse, *Thaddeus Stevens: Nineteenth-Century Egalitarian* (Chapel Hill: University of North Carolina Press, 1997), 50–52.

3. Brodie, 105–31. Trefousse, *Thaddeus Stevens*, 75–99.

4. Trefousse, *Thaddeus Stevens*, 112–15; James O. Lehman and Steven M. Nolt, *Mennonites, Amish, and the American Civil War* (Baltimore: Johns Hopkins University Press, 2007), 144–47.

5. Trefousse, *Thaddeus Stevens*, 138–40, 161–88.

6. Trustees Book, January 19, 1846, Gettysburg Presbyterian Church; Trefousse, *Thaddeus Stevens*, 215, 240, 242.

7. "the faint . . ." in Brodie, *Thaddeus Stevens*, 19. See also Brodie, 23–26, 31; Trefousse, *Thaddeus Stevens*, 5, 7–8, 16, 161, 213, 214–15.

8. Eric Foner, *A Short History of Reconstruction, 1863–1877* (New York: Harper and Row, 1990), 108.

9. "bitter" and "bitterness" in Claude G. Bowers, *The Tragic Era: The Revolution after Lincoln* (New York: Houghton Mifflin Company, 1929, 1957 printing), 66–67; "obsession on . . ." and "formed for . . . ," 83. See also Bowers, 65–84; Hans Trefouse, *Thaddeus Stevens*, xi, xiii; Eric Foner, *Forever Free: The Story of Emancipation and Reconstruction* (New York: Alfred A. Knopf, 2005), 46–47.

10. Brodie, *Thaddeus Stevens*, 86–93.

Coda

1. Wentz, *Pioneer in Christian Unity*, 334, 343–52, 363–64; A. Roger Gobbel with Donald N. Matthews and Elaine C. Matthews, *On the Glorious Hill: A Short History in Word and Picture of the Lutheran Theological Seminary at Gettysburg* (Lancaster, Pa.: Pridemark Press, 1990), 26, Schmucker to F. H. Weaver, December 8, 1870, mss., Special Collections, Musselman Library, Gettysburg College, box 1, file 7. Schmucker's publications in retirement were "Historical Development of the Contrast Between the Two Grand Aspects of the World, in its Religious Character and Relations, as Viewed from the Standpoint of Christianity and Infidelity," *Evangelical Review* 16 (April 1865): 156–72; "Human Depravity," *Evangelical Review* 17 (January 1866): 100–13; *The Church of the Redeemer, as Developed in the General Synod of the Lutheran Church in America* (Baltimore: T. N. Kurtz, 1867); "Holman Lecture on the Augsburg Confession, Lecture on Article III: The Incarnation, the Christology and Soteriology," *Evangelical Review* 19 (October 1868): 489–531; *The True Unity of Christ's Church: Being a Renewed Appeal to the Friends of the Redeemer, on Primitive Christian Union, and the History of its Corruption* (New York: Anson D. F. Randolf & Company, 1870).

2. Rodgers, *Ties of the Past*, 197–204.

3. Ibid., 205–10.

4. Ibid., 262–71.

5. "Mrs. Hereter Expires; Heard Lincoln Speak," *Gettysburg Times* (May 13, 1939): 1; "Barn Burnt," *Republican Compiler* (July 9, 1866): 2.

6. *Compiler* (October 1, 1882, and October 11, 1882)—Sherfy Family File, ACHS.

7. B. F. Kittinger, "Death of Raphael Sherfy," *The Primitive Christian* (January 7, 1883), Sherfy Family File, ACHS.

8. "Mother Sherfy" in K. Ployd, "At Gettysburg: What Was Recalled by a Tramp Over Part of the Battlefield," *The National Tribune* (July 28, 1898), Newspaper Clipping File, v. 2, GNMP. "I'm the man . . ." in n.a., "The Sherfy House," typescript, 1916, Civilian Accounts of the Battle of Gettysburg, ACHS; transcribed by Timothy H. Smith from a handwritten account by a member of the Sherfy family. See also I. H. Dean to Mrs. [Mary] Sherfy (March 4, 1891), Sherfy Family File, ACHS; "Mary H. Sherfy" obituary, undated, Sherfy Family File, ACHS.

9. Marcella Sherfy, "The Brien Farm and Family," typescript (GNMP, June 1972), 5; Abraham Brien Claims File 214/798 typescript copy, United States Census, 1870. The epitaph comes from personal observation.

10. Newhouse, *Codori Family and Farm*, 6–7, 12–16. For newspaper account of Nicholas's accident and his obituary, see Newhouse, 68.

Bibliography

Newspapers and Periodicals

Adams Sentinel, Sentinel (Gettysburg, Pa.)
Baltimore Sun (Baltimore, Md.)
Compiler, Republican Compiler (Gettysburg, Pa.)
Evangelical Review (Gettysburg, Pa.)
Examiner (Frederick, Md.)
Franklin Repository (Chambersburg, Pa.)
Gettysburg Times (Gettysburg, Pa.)
Gospel Visitor (Philadelphia, Pa.)
Lutheran Observer (Baltimore, Md.)
Pennsylvania Freeman (Philadelphia, Pa.)
Primitive Christian
Star and Banner, Star and Republican Banner (Gettysburg, Pa.)
York Gazette (York, Pa.)

Congregational Records

Christ Evangelical Lutheran Church, Gettysburg. A. R. Wentz Library, Lutheran Theological Seminary at Gettysburg (LTS).
Gettysburg Presbyterian Church. Gettysburg Presbyterian Church, Gettysburg, Pa.
Marsh Creek Church of the Brethren Church Book. Adams County Historical Society (ACHS), Gettysburg, Pa.
Methodist Episcopal Church in Gettysburg. ACHS.
St. Francis Xavier, Roman Catholic Church. ACHS.
St. James' Evangelical Lutheran Church, Gettysburg, Pennsyla. LTS.
St. Paul's African Methodist Episcopal Zion, Gettysburg, Pa. Jean Odom (private collection).
St. Paul's German Lutheran Congregation. LTS.
Upper Marsh Creek Presbyterian Congregation, 1776–1788. Gettysburg Presbyterian Church, Gettysburg, Pa.

Manuscript Collections

Adams County Historical Society, Gettysburg, Pa.
    Ganoe, M. L. "History," Church Book, Gettysburg Methodist Church.
    Quarterly Conference Reports of the Gettysburg Circuit.
    Stewart, Salome Myers. "Diary," Diaries File. Adams County Historical Society.
    Stewart, Salome Myers. "Composition Book."

Evangelical and Reformed Historical Society, Lancaster, Pa.
　Deatrick, W. R. H. "Reformed Church in Gettysburg, Pa."
　Record of Zion's Classis, vol. 2, 1849–1863.
Evergreen Cemetery, Gettysburg, Pa.
　Records of Evergreen Cemetery.
Gettysburg College, Special Collections/Musselman Library, Gettysburg, Pa.
　Samuel Simon Schmucker Papers.
Lauinger Library, Special Collections Research Center, Georgetown University, Washington, D.C.
　The Rev. Francis X. DeNeckere Papers.
　Society of Jesus, Archives, Maryland Province.
Lovely Lane Library and Archives, Baltimore, Md.
　Annual Minutes of the Baltimore Conference [Methodist].
　Annual Minutes of the East Baltimore Conference [Methodist].
　Holland, Horace Papers.
Presbyterian Historical Society, Philadelphia, Pa.
　Presbytery of Carlisle, Minutes, 1861–70.

Publications

The Acts and Proceedings of the Synod of the German Reformed of the United States.
Alleman, Tillie Pierce. *At Gettysburg; Or, What a Girl Saw and Heard of the Battle.* New York: W. Lake Borland, 1889.
Annual Register of the East Baltimore Conference.
Baugher, H. L. *The Christian Patriot: A Discourse Addressed to the Graduating Class of Pennsylvania College, September 15, 1861.* Gettysburg, Pa.: A. D. Buehler, 1861.
———. *The Object of Life: A Discourse Delivered in Christ's Church, Gettysburg, Pa.* Gettysburg, Pa.: H. C. Neinstedt, 1851.
Chamberlayne, C. G., ed. *Ham Chamberlayne—Virginian: Letters and Papers of an Artillery Officer in the War for Southern Independence, 1861–1865.* Richmond, Va.: Dietz Printing Co., 1932.
Dosh, J. H. C. *Address Delivered at the Opening Ceremonies of Ever Green Cemetery, Gettysburg, Pa., November 7, 1854.* Gettysburg, Pa.: H. C. Neinstedt, 1855.
Douglass, Frederick. *Autobiographies.* New York: Library of America, 1996.
Elaw, Zilpha. *Memoir of the Life, Religious Experience, Ministerial Travels and Labors of Mrs. Zilpha Elaw, An American Female of Color.* London: 1846. Ed. and intro., William L. Andrews. *Sisters of the Spirit: Three Black Women's Autobiographies of the Nineteenth Century.* Bloomington: Indiana University Press, 1986.
Fastnacht, Mary Warren. *Memories of the Battle of Gettysburg: Year 1863.* New York: Princely Press, 1941.
Giles, Samuel M., Christopher Rush, and Joseph P. Thompson. *Hymns for the Use of the African Methodist Episcopal Zion Church.* New York: D. Fanshaw, 1858.
Hill, R. [Reuben]. *Address Delivered at the Opening Ceremonies of Ever Green Cemetery, Gettysburg, Pa., November 7, 1854.* Gettysburg, Pa.: H. C. Neinstedt, 1855.

———. *Discourse at the Laying of the Cornerstone*. Gettysburg, Pa.: H. C. Neinstedt, 1855.

Jackson, John Walker. *The Union—The Constitution—Peace: A Thanksgiving Sermon*. Harrisonburg, Pa.: "Telegraph" Steam Book and Job Office, August 6, 1863.

———. "Visit to the Battle-field." *Christian Advocate and Journal* 38 (August 13, 1863): 258.

Johnson, Clifton. *Battlefield Adventures: The Stories of Dwellers on the Scenes of Conflict in Some of the Most Noble Battles of the Civil War*. Boston and New York: Houghton Mifflin, 1915.

Kelley, William D. *Characteristics of the Age: An Address Delivered Before the Linnaean Association of Pennsylvania College, At the Annual Commencement, Sept. 18th, 1850*. Gettysburg, Pa.: H. C. Neinstedt, 1850.

Knox, Thomas W. "The Battle Field at Gettysburg: Scenes after the Battle." *New York Herald* (July 9, 1863).

Krauth, Charles Philip. *Address Delivered on the Anniversary of Washington's Birth-Day*. Gettysburg, Pa.: H. C. Neinstedt, 1846.

Lee, Jarena. *Religious Experience and Journal of Mrs. Jarena Lee, giving an account of her call to preach the gospel, revised and corrected from the original manuscript written by herself*. Philadelphia: 1836.

Mack, Alexander Sr. "Rights and Ordinances." In *European Origins of the Brethren: A Source Book on the Beginnings of the Church of the Brethren in the Early Eighteenth Century*, edited by Donald F. Durnbaugh. Elgin, Ill.: Brethren Press, 1958.

Minutes of the Annual Meetings of the Church of the Brethren: Containing All Available Minutes from 1778 to 1909. Elgin, Ill.: Brethren Publishing House, 1909.

McCurdy, Charles M. *Gettysburg; A Memoir*. Pittsburgh, Pa.: Reed and Witting Company, 1929.

Milligan, John. *Human Perfection: A Discourse Delivered to Christ's Church, Gettysburg, Pa*. Gettysburg: H. C. Neinstedt, 1851.

Nevin, John W. *The Anxious Bench: A Tract for the Times*. Chambersburg, Pa.: Publication Office of the German Reformed, 1844; second ed.

———. *Fancy Fairs*. Mercersburg, Pa.: n.p., 1843.

Payne, Daniel Alexander. *Recollections of Seventy Years*. New York: Arno Press and The New York Times, 1968; originally published 1888.

"The Profession of Teaching: An Essay Read by Mrs. Sallie M. Stewart before the Adams County Teachers' Institute, Nov. 23, 1897." *Star and Sentinel* (December 7, 1897).

Proceedings of the Evangelical Lutheran Synod of West Pennsylvania.

Report of the Superintendent of Common Schools of Pennsylvania. Harrisburg: A. Boyd Hamilton, State Printer, 1859, 1860, 1861.

Rodgers, Sarah Sites. *The Ties of the Past: The Gettysburg Diaries of Salome Myers Stewart, 1854–1922*. Gettysburg, Pa.: Thomas Publications, 1996.

Schaff, Philip. *Anglo-Germanism or the Significance of the German Nationality in the United States, an address delivered March 10, 1846, before the Schiller Society of Marshall College*. Translated by J. S. Ermentrout. Chambersburg, Pa.: Publication Office of the German Reformed Church, 1846.

Schaff, Philip. "The Gettysburg Week." *Scribner's Magazine* 16 (July–December, 1894): 21–30.

Schmucker, Samuel Simon. *The Christian Pulpit, The Rightful Guardian of Morals in Political No Less Than Private Life*. Gettysburg, Pa.: H. C. Neinstedt, 1846.

———. *Elements of Popular Theology; with Occasional Reference to the Doctrines of the Reformation, as Avowed Before the Diet at Augsburg in MDXXX*. Philadelphia: E. W. Miller, 1848.

———. *Memorial of Professor S. S. Schmucker, Relative to Binding Out Minor Colored Children*. Harrisburg, Pa.: Boas and Coplan, 1839.

———. *The Papal Hierarchy, Viewed in the Light of Prophecy and History*. Gettysburg, Pa.: H. C. Neinstedt, 1845.

Seaver, James. *A Narrative of the Life of Mrs. Mary Jemison*. New York: American Scenic & Historical Preservation Society, 1942.

Smith, David. *Biography of Rev. David Smith, of the A.M.E. Church, Being a Complete History, Embracing Over Sixty Years' Labor in the Advancement of the Redeemer's Kingdom on Earth*. Xenia, Oh.: Xenia Gazette Office, 1881.

Smith, Henry L. *The Education of the Heart: An Address Delivered Before the Phrenakosian Society of Pennsylvania College*. Gettysburg, Pa.: H. C. Neinstedt, 1843.

Smyser, Daniel M. *The Study of Natural History: An Address Delivered Before the Linnæan Association of Pennsylvania College, Gettysburg, Pa.* Gettysburg, Pa.: H. C. Neinstedt, 1849.

Trowbridge, J. T. "The Field of Gettysburg." *Atlantic Monthly* 16 (November, 1865): 616–24.

United States Census.

United States Department of War. *The War of the Rebellion: A Compilation of the Official Records Official Records of the Union and Confederate Armies*. 128 vols. Washington, D.C.: U.S. Government Printing Office, 1890–1901.

Secondary Sources

Alosi, John. *Shadow of Freedom: Slavery in Post-Revolutionary Cumberland County, 1780–1810*. Shippensburg, Pa.: Shippensburg University Press, 2005.

Ames, Kenneth L. *Death in the Dining Room and Other Tales of Victorian Culture*. Philadelphia: Temple University Press, 1992.

Anbinder, Tyler. *Nativism and Slavery: The Northern Know Nothings and the Politics of the 1850s*. New York: Oxford University Press, 1992.

Ayers, Edward L. *In the Presence of Mine Enemies: War in the Heart of America, 1859–1863*. New York: W. W. Norton & Company, 2003.

———. *The Promise of the New South: Life after Reconstruction*. New York: Oxford University Press, 1992.

Baker, Gordon Pratt. *Those Incredible Methodists: A History of the Baltimore Conference of the United Methodist Church*. Baltimore: Commission on Archives and History, The Baltimore Conference, 1972.

Baker, Joseph Baer. *History of St. James Evangelical Lutheran Church of Gettysburg, Penna., 1775–1921*. Gettysburg, Pa.: Gettysburg Compiler Press, 1921.

Bennett, Gerald R. *Days of "Uncertainty and Dread": The Ordeal Endured by the Citizens at Gettysburg*. Littlestown, Pa.: published by the author, 1994.

Bloom, Robert. "We Never Expected a Battle: The Civilians at Gettysburg, 1863." *Pennsylvania History* 55 (October, 1988): 161–200.

Bloom, Robert L. *A History of Adams County, Pennsylvania, 1700–1990*. Gettysburg, Pa.: Adams County Historical Society, 1992.

Bohn, Jean. "Abram Brien." Typescript, May 2003, Gettysburg National Military Park, VI–11.

Bolin, Larry C. "Slaveholders and Slaves of Adams County." *Adams County History* 9 (2003): 4–92.

Bonomi, Patricia U. *Under the Cope of Heaven: Religion, Society, and Politics in Colonial America*. New York: Oxford University Press, 1986.

Boritt, Gabor. *The Gettysburg Gospel: The Lincoln Speech that Nobody Knows*. New York: Simon & Schuster, 2006.

Bouton, Terry. *Taming Democracy: "The People," the Founders, and the Troubled Ending of the American Revolution*. New York: Oxford University Press, 2007.

Bowers, Claude G. *The Tragic Era: The Revolution after Lincoln*. New York: Houghton Mifflin Company, 1929, 1957 printing.

Bowman, Carl F. *Brethren Society: The Cultural Transformation of a "Peculiar People."* Baltimore, Md.: Johns Hopkins University Press, 1995.

Boylan, Anne M. *Sunday School: The Formation of an American Institution*. New Haven and London: Yale University Press, 1988.

Bradsby, H. C. *History of Adams County Pennsylvania. Originally published as History of Cumberland and Adams Counties: Containing History of the Counties, Their Townships, Towns, Villages, Schools, Churches, Industries, Etc.; Portraits of Early Settlers and Prominent Men: Biographies*. Warner, Beers & Co., 1886. Reprint, Knightstown, Ind.: The Bookmark, 1977.

Brake, Robert L. "The Joseph Sherfy Family at the Battle of Gettysburg." Typescript, Sherfy Family File, Adams County Historical Society.

Bratt, James D. "Religious Anti-Revivalism in Antebellum America." *Journal of the Early Republic* 24 (Spring 2004): 65–106.

Breen, T. H. "'Baubles of Britain': The American and Consumer Revolutions of the Eighteenth Century." *Past and Present* (May 1988): 73–104.

"Brien Farm." Gettysburg National Military Park, Gettysburg, Pa., VI–11.

Brodie, Fawn M. *Thaddeus Stevens: Scourge of the South*. New York: W.W. Norton and Company, 1959.

Brown, Kent Masterson. *Retreat from Gettysburg: Lee, Logistics, and the Pennsylvania Campaign*. Chapel Hill: University of North Carolina Press, 2005.

Brugger, Robert J. *Maryland: A Middle Temperment, 1634–1980*. Baltimore, Md.: Johns Hopkins University Press, 1988.

Burg, Steven B. "The North Queen Street Cemetery and the African American Experience in Shippensburg, Pennsylvania." *Pennsylvania History* 77 (Winter, 2010): 1–36.

Bushman, Richard L. *The Refinement of America: Persons, Houses, Cities*. New York: Alfred A. Knopf, 1992.

Calvert, Karin. "The Function of Fashion in Eighteenth-Century America." In *Of Consuming Interests: The Style of Life in the Eighteenth Century*, edited by Cary Carson, Ronald Hoffman, and Peter J. Albert. Charlottesville: University Press of Virginia, 1994.

Carwardine, Richard J. *Evangelicals and Politics in Antebellum America*. New Haven, Ct.: Yale University Press, 1993.

Clarke, Nina Honemond. *History of the Nineteenth-Century Black Churches in Maryland and Washington, D.C.* New York: Vantage Press, 1987.

Clark, Robert D. "Methodist Debates and Union Sentiment on the Border, 1860–1861." In *Antislavery and Disunion, 1858–186: Studies in the Rhetoric of Compromise and Conflict*, edited by J. Jeffery Auer, 152–70. New York: Harper & Row, 1963.

Coco, Gregory A. *A Strange and Blighted Land; Gettysburg: The Aftermath of a Battle*. Gettysburg, Pa.: Thomas Publications, 1995.

Coddington, Edwin B. *The Gettysburg Campaign: A Study in Command*. New York: Charles Scribner's Sons, 1968.

Cole, James M. *For God and Country: A History of St. Francis Xavier Church, 1831–1981: Sesqui-Centennial Anniversary*. Gettysburg, Pa.: St. Francis Xavier Parish, 1981.

Coleman, J. Walter, Anthony F. Kane, and Mary Louise Callahan, eds., *A Glorious Heritage of One Hundred Years: A History of St. Francis Xavier Church, Gettysburg, Pennsylvania, 1853–1953*. N.p.: Diocese of Harrisburg, n.d.

Creighton, Margaret S. *The Colors of Courage: Gettysburg's Forgotten History: Immigrants, Women, and African Americans in the Civil War's Defining Battle*. New York: Basic Books, 2005.

Crowley, John E. *The Invention of Comfort: Sensibilities and Design in Early Modern Britain and Early America*. Baltimore: Johns Hopkins University Press, 2001.

Dargan, William T. *Lining Out the Word: Dr. Watts Hymn Singing in the Music of Black Americans*. Berkeley: University of California Press, 2006.

Dolan, Jay P. *In Search of an American Catholicism: A History of Religion and Culture in Tension*. New York: Oxford University Press, 2002.

Dorsett, Lyle W. *A Passion for Souls: The Life of D. L. Moody*. Chicago: Moody Press, 1997.

Durnbaugh, Donald F., ed. *The Brethren Encyclopedia*. 4 vols. Philadelphia, Pa.: Brethren Encyclopedia, Inc., 1983.

———. *Fruit of the Vine: A History of the Brethren, 1708–1995*. Elgin, Ill.: Brethren Press, 1995.

Egerton, Douglas R. *Year of Meteors: Stephen Douglas, Abraham Lincoln, and the Election That Brought on the Civil War*. New York: Bloomsburg Press, 2010.

Eisenberg, J. Linwood, ed. *A History of the Church of the Brethren in Southern District of Pennsylvania by the Historical Committee*. Quincy, Pa.: Quincy Orphanage Press, n.d.

Erskine, Albert Russell. *History of the Studebaker Corporation*. Poole Brothers, 1908.

Faust, Drew Gilpin. *Mothers of Invention: Women of the Slaveholding South in the American Civil War*. Chapel Hill: University of North Carolina Press, 1996.

———. *This Republic of Suffering: Death and the American Civil War*. New York: Alfred A. Knopf, 2008.

Fields, Barbara Jeanne. *Slavery and Freedom on the Middle Ground: Maryland during the Nineteenth Century*. New Haven, Ct.: Yale University Press, 1985.

Fogarty, Gerald P. "The Origins of the Mission, 1634–1773." In *The Maryland Jesuits, 1634–1833*, edited by Robert Emmett Curran, 9–27. Baltimore, Md.: Corporation of the Roman Catholic Clergymen, Maryland Province Society of Jesus, 1976.

Fogleman, Aaron Spencer. *Jesus is Female: Moravians and Radical Religion in Early America*. Philadelphia: University of Pennsylvania Press, 2007.

Foner, Eric. *Forever Free: The Story of Emancipation and Reconstruction*. New York: Alfred A. Knopf, 2005.

———. *A Short History of Reconstruction, 1863–1877*. New York: Harper and Row, 1990.

Frantz, John B., and William Pencak, eds. *Beyond Philadelphia: The American Revolution in the Pennsylvania Hinterland*. University Park, Pa.: Pennsylvania State University Press, 1998.

French, Stanley. "The Cemetery as Cultural Institution: The Establishment of Mount Auburn and the 'Rural Cemetery' Movement." *American Quarterly* 26 (March, 1974): 37–59.

Freehling, William L. *Road to Disunion: Volume II, Secessionists Triumphant, 1854–1861*. New York: Oxford University Press, 2007.

Gallman, J. Matthew. *The North Fights the Civil War: The Home Front*. Chicago: Ivan R. Dee, 1994.

———. "Voluntarism in Wartime: Philadelphia's Great Central Fair." In *Toward a Social History of the Civil War: Exploratory Essays*, edited by Maris A. Vinovskis, 93–116. Cambridge: Cambridge University Press, 1990.

Gallman, J. Matthew, with Susan Baker, "Gettysburg's Gettysburg: What the Battle Did to the Borough." *The Gettysburg Nobody Knows*, edited by Gabor S. Boritt, 144–74. New York: Oxford University Press, 1997.

Geary, James W. *We Need Men: The Union Draft in the Civil War*. DeKalb: Northern Illinois Press, 1991.

Georg, Kathleen R. "The Sherfy Farm and the Battle of Gettysburg." Typescript, Gettysburg National Military Park, 1977.

Glatfelter, Charles H. "Adams County Votes for President, 1804–2008." *Adams County History* 15 (2009).

———. *A Salutary Influence: Gettysburg College, 1832–1985*. 2 vols., Gettysburg, Pa.: Gettysburg College, 1987.

———. *The Churches of Adams County, Pennsylvania*. Biglerville, Pa.: St. Paul's Lutheran Church, 1981.

Gobbel, A. Roger. *On the Glorious Hill: A Short History in Word and Picture of the Lutheran Theological Seminary at Gettysburg*. Lancaster, Pa.: Pridemark Press, 1990.

Goldfield, David. *America Aflame: How the Civil War Created a Nation*. New York: Bloomsbury Press, 2011.

Gordon, Beverly. *Bazaars and Fair Ladies: The History of the American Fundraising Fair*. Knoxville: University of Tennessee Press, 1998.

Gorrecht, W. Frank. "The Charity of Thaddeus Stevens." In *Historical Papers and Addresses of the Lancaster County Historical Society,* 21–35. Lancaster, Pa.: Lancaster County Historical Society.

Greene, Jack P. *Imperatives, Behaviors, and Identities: Essays in Early American Cultural History.* Charlottesville: University Press of Virginia, 1992.

———. *Pursuits of Happiness: The Social Development of Early Modern British Colonies and the Formation of American Culture.* Chapel Hill: University of North Carolina Press, 1988.

Guelzo, Allen C. *Abraham Lincoln: Redeemer President.* Grand Rapids, Mich.: William B. Eerdmans Company, 2003.

Häberlein, Mark. *The Promise of Pluralism: Congregational Life and Religious Diversity in Lancaster, Pennsylvania, 1730–1820.* University Park, Pa.: Pennsylvania State University Press, 2009.

Harbaugh, Linn. *Life of the Reverend Henry Harbaugh, D. D.* Philadelphia: Reformed Church Publication Board, 1900.

Hempton, David. *Methodism: Empire of the Spirit.* New Haven and London: Yale University Press, 2005.

Heyrmann, Christine Leigh. *Southern Cross: The Beginnings of the Bible Belt.* Chapel Hill: University of North Carolina Press, 1997.

"Historical Sketch of Trinity Reformed Church, Gettysburg, Pa." *Directory: Trinity Reformed Church,* Trinity Reformed Church folder, Evangelical and Reformed Historical Society.

Hoch, Bradley R. *Thaddeus Stevens in Gettysburg: The Making of an Abolitionist.* Gettysburg, Pa.: Adams County Historical Society, 2005.

Holifield, E. Brooks. *Theology in America: Christian Thought from the Age of the Puritans to the Civil War.* New Haven, Conn.: Yale University Press, 2003.

Hopkins, Leroy. "Bethel African Methodist Church in Lancaster: Prolegomenon to a Social History." *Journal of the Lancaster County Historical Society* 90 (1986): 1–32.

Horton, James Oliver and Lois E. Horton. *In Hope of Liberty: Culture, Community, and Protest Among Northern Free Blacks, 1700–1860.* New York: Oxford University Press, 1997.

Howe, David Walker. "The Market Revolution and the Shaping of Identity in Whig-Jacksonian America." In *The Market Revolution in American: Social Political, and Religious Expressions, 1800–1880,* edited by Melvin Stokes and Stephen Conway. Charlottesville: University Press of Virginia, 1996, 259–77.

———. *What Hath God Wrought: The Transformation of America, 1815–1848.* New York: Oxford University Press, 2007.

Hunt, Roger D. *Colonels in Blue: Union Army Colonels of the Civil War; The Mid-Atlantic States.* Mechanicsburg, Pa.: Stackpole Books, 2007.

Hutchinson, William R. *Religious Pluralism in America: The Contentious History of a Founding Ideal.* New Haven, Ct.: Yale University Press, 2003.

Irons, Charles. *The Rise of Pro-Slavery Christianity: White and Black Evangelicals in Colonial and Antebellum Virginia.* Chapel Hill: University of North Carolina Press, 2008.

Jaffee, David. *A New Nation of Goods: The Material Culture of Early America*. Philadelphia: University Press of Pennsylvania, 2010.

———. "Peddlers of Progress and the Transformation of the Rural North, 1760–1860." *Journal of American History* 78 (September, 1991): 511–35.

Jeffrey, Julie Roy. *The Great Silent Army of Abolitionism: Ordinary Women in the Antislavery Movement*. Chapel Hill: University of North Carolina Press, 1998.

Johnson, Paul E. *A Shopkeeper's Millennium: Society and Revivals in Rochester, New York, 1815–1837*. New York: Hill and Wang, 1979.

Kasson, John F. *Rudeness and Civility: Manners in Nineteenth-Century Urban America*. New York: Hill and Wang, 1990.

Kettering, Denise D. " 'Greet One Another with a Holy Kiss': The Evolution of the Holy Kiss in the Church of the Brethren," In *Line, Places, and Heritage: Essays Commemorating the 300th Anniversary of the Church of the Brethren*, edited by Steve Longenecker and Jeff Bach. Penobscot, Me.: Church of the Brethren Higher Education Association, 2008.

King, Ray A. *A History of the Associate Reformed Presbyterian Church*. Charlotte, N.C.: Board of Christian Education of the Associate Reformed Church, 1966.

Kirby, James E., Russell E. Richey, and Kenneth E. Rowe. *The Methodists*, Denominations in America Series. Westport, Conn.: Greenwood Press, 1996.

Koons, Kenneth E. and Warren R. Hofstra. *After the Backcountry: Rural Life in the Great Valley of Virginia, 1800–1900*. Knoxville: University of Tennessee Press, 2000.

Kuenning, Paul P. *The Rise and Fall of American Lutheran Pietism: The Rejection of an Activist Heritage*. Macon, Ga.: Mercer University Press, 1988.

Larsen, Lawrence H. "Nineteenth-Century Street Sanitation: A Study of Filth and Frustration." *Wisconsin Magazine of History* 52 (Spring, 1969): 239–47.

Lehman, James O., and Steven M. Nolt. *Mennonites, Amish, and the American Civil War*. Baltimore: Johns Hopkins University Press, 2007.

Lewis, Osceola. *History of the One Hundred and Thirty-Eighth Regiment, Pennsylvania Volunteer Infantry*. Norristown, Pa.: Wills, Iradell and Jenkins, 1866.

Lippy, Charles H. *Introducing American Religion*. London and New York: Routledge, 2009.

Lincoln, C. Eric, and Lawrence H. Mamiya, *The Black Church in the African American Experience*. Durham, N.C.: Duke University Press, 1990.

Longenecker, Stephen L. "Emotionalism Among Early American Anabaptists." In *The Dilemma of Anabaptist Piety: Strengthening or Straining the Bonds of Community*, edited by Longenecker, 61–68. Bridgewater, Va.: Forum for Religious Studies, Bridgewater College, 1997.

———. *Shenandoah Religion: Outsiders and the Mainstream, 1715–1865*. Waco, Tx.: Baylor University Press, 2002.

———. *Tolerance and Diversity: Pennsylvania German Religion, 1700–1850*. Metuchen, N.J.: Scarecrow Press, 1994.

Lowry, Thomas P. *Tarnished Eagles: The Courts-Martial of Fifty Union Colonels and Lieutenant Colonels*. Mechanicsburg, Pa.: Stackpole Books, 1997.

Macauley, Howard K. "A Social and Intellectual History of Elementary Education in
    Pennsylvania to 1850." Ph.D. diss., University of Pennsylvania, 1972.
McCoy, Michael Bradley. "Absconding Servants, Anxious Germans, and Angry Sailors:
    Working People and the Making of the Philadelphia Election Riot of 1742." *Pennsyl-
    vania History* 74 (Autumn 2007): 427–51.
McCurry, Stephanie. *Confederate Reckoning: Power and Politics in the Civil War South.*
    Cambridge, Mass.: Harvard University Press, 2010.
McLoughlin, William G., Jr. *Modern Revivalism: Charles Grandison Finney to Billy Gra-
    ham.* New York: Ronald Press Company, 1959.
McPherson, James M., and William J. Cooper Jr., eds. *Writing the Civil War: The Quest t
    o Understand.* Columbia: University of South Carolina Press, 1998.
McPherson, James M. "Gettysburg." In *American Places: Encounters with History,*
    edited by William E. Leuchtenburg, 261–68. New York: Oxford University
    Press, 2000.
Malone, Christopher. "Rethinking the end of Black Voting Rights in Antebellum
    Pennsylvania: Racial Ascriptivism, Partisanship and Political Development in the
    Keystone State." *Pennsylvania History* 72 (2005): 466–504.
Marsden, George M. *The Soul of the American University: From Protestant Establishment
    to Established Nonbelief.* New York: Oxford University Press, 1994.
Marty, Martin E. *Righteous Empire: The Protestant Experience in America.* New York:
    Dial Press, 1970.
Mathews, Donald G. *Slavery and Methodism: A Chapter in American Morality, 1780–
    1845.* Princeton, N.J.: Princeton University Press.
Miller, Randall M., Harry S. Stout, and Charles Reagan Wilson, eds., *Religion and the
    American Civil War.* New York: Oxford University Press, 1998.
Mintz, Steven. *Moralists and Modernizers: America's Pre-Civil War Reformers.* Baltimore,
    Md.: Johns Hopkins University Press, 1995.
Mitchell, Henry H. *Black Church Beginnings: The Long-Hidden Realities of the First Years.*
    Grand Rapids, Mich.: Wm. B. Eerdmans, 2004.
Moyer, Anna Jane. *"A Young Man's Fancy: I, Samuel Simon, Take Thee, Mary Catherine . . . ,"*
    To Waken Fond Memory: Moments in the History of Gettysburg College. Gettysburg,
    Pa.: Friends of Musselman Library, Gettysburg College, 2006.
Murdoch, David A., ed., "Catherine May White Foster's Eyewitness Account of the Battle
    of Gettysburg." *Adams County History* 1 (1995): 45–67.
Nash, Gary B. and Jean R. Soderlund, *Freedom by Degrees: Emancipation in Pennsylvania
    and Its Aftermath.* New York: Oxford University Press, 1991.
Neely, Mark E., Jr., *The Civil War and the Limits of Destruction.* Cambridge, Mass.: Har-
    vard University Press, 2007.
Newhouse, Pam. *The Codori Family and Farm: In the Path of Battle.* Gettysburg, Pa.:
    Friends of the National Parks at Gettysburg, Inc., 1999.
Newman, Richard S. *Freedom's Prophet: Bishop Richard Allen, the AME Church, and the
    Black Founding Fathers.* New York: New York University Press, 2008.
Noll, Mark A. *The Civil War as a Theological Crisis.* Chapel Hill: University of North
    Carolina Press, 2006.

Nolt, Steven M. *Foreigners in Their Own Land: Pennsylvania Germans in the Early Republic*. University Park: Pennsylvania State University Press, 2002.

Nylander, Jane C. *Our Own Snug Fireside: Images of the New England Home, 1760–1860*. New York: Alfred A. Knopf, 1994.

Oblinger, Carl D. "In Recognition of Their Prominence: A Case Study of the Economic and Social Backgrounds of an Antebellum Negro Business and Farming Class in Lancaster County." *Journal of the Lancaster County Historical Society* 72 (Easter, 1968): 65–83.

Osborne, Christopher. "Invisible Hands: Slaves, Bound Laborers, and the Development of Western Pennsylvania." *Pennsylvania History* 72 (Winter 2005): 77–99.

O'Toole, James M. *The Faithful: A History of Catholic America*. Cambridge, Mass.: Belknap Press of Harvard University Press, 2008.

Pfanz, Harry W. *Gettysburg—The First Day*. Chapel Hill: University of North Carolina Press, 2001.

———. *Gettysburg—The Second Day*. Chapel Hill: University of North Carolina Press, 1987.

Rable, George C. *God's Almost Chosen Peoples: A Religious History of the American Civil War*. Chapel Hill: University of North Carolina Press, 2010.

Rael, Patrick. *Black Identity & Black Protest in the Antebellum North*. Chapel Hill: University of North Carolina Press, 2002.

———. "The Market Revolution and Market Values in Antebellum Black Protest Thought," *Cultural Change and the Market Revolution in America, 1789–1860*, ed., Scott C. Martin. Lanham, Md.: Rowman and Littlefield Publishers, 2005, 13–45.

Reily, John T. *Collections and Recollections in the Life and Times of Cardinal Gibbons*. Martinsburg, W.Va.: Herald Print, 1892–93.

———. *Conewago: A Collection of Catholic Local History*. Martinsburg, W.Va.: Herald Print, 1885. Reprint, Westminster, Md.: John William Eckenrode, 1970.

———. *Conewago: Centennial Celebration*. Martinsburg, W.Va.: Herald Print, 1887.

Richey, Russell E. *Early American Methodism*. Bloomington and Indianapolis: Indiana University Press, 1991.

Robertson, Stacey M. *Hearts Beating for Liberty: Women Abolitionists in the Old Northwest*. Chapel Hill: University of North Carolina Press, 2010.

Roeber, A. G. *Palatines, Liberty and Property: German Lutherans in Colonial British America*. Baltimore: Johns Hopkins University Press, 1993, 1998.

Rolfs, David. *No Peace for the Wicked: Northern Protestant Soldiers and the American Civil War*. Knoxville: University of Tennessee Press, 2009.

Ryan, Mary P. *Cradle of the Middle Class: The Family in Oneida County, New York, 1790–1865*. New York: Cambridge University Press, 1981.

Sappington, Roger E. *The Brethren in the New Nation: A Source Book on the Development of the Church of the Brethren, 1785–1865*. Elgin, Ill.: Brethren Press, 1976.

Schantz, Mark S. *Awaiting the Heavenly Country: The Civil War and America's Culture of Death*. Ithaca, N.Y.: Cornell University Press, 2008.

Schwartz, Sally. "A Mixed Multitude": The Struggle for Toleration in Colonial Pennsylvania. New York: New York University Press, 1987.

Shattuck, Gardiner H., Jr. *A Shield and a Hiding Place: The Religious Life of the Civil War Armies*. Macon, Ga.: Mercer University Press, 1987.

Sheads, J. M. "Carriage Making Industry in Gettysburg." Typescript, Carriage Industry File, Adams County Historical Society, n.d.

Sheldon, George. *When the Smoke Cleared at Gettysburg: The Tragic Aftermath of the Bloodiest Battle of the Civil War*. Nashville, Tenn.: Cumberland House Publishing, 2003.

Sherfy, Marcella. "The Brien Farm and Family," Typescript, June, 1972, Gettysburg National Military Park.

Sheriff, Carol. *The Artificial River: The Erie Canal and the Paradox of Progress, 1817–1862*. New York: Hill and Wang, 1996.

Slaughter, Thomas P. *Bloody Dawn: The Christiana Riot and Racial Violence in the Antebellum North*. New York: Oxford University Press, 1991.

Sloane, David Charles. *The Last Great Necessity: Cemeteries in American History*. Baltimore, Md.: Johns Hopkins University Press, 1991.

Smith, David G. "On the Edge of Freedom: The Fugitive Slave Issue in South Central Pennsylvania, 1820–1870." Ph.D. diss., Pennsylvania State University, 2006.

———. "Race and Retaliation: The Capture of African Americans during the Gettysburg Campaign." In *Virginia's Civil War*, edited by Peter Wallenstein and Bertram Wyatt-Brown, 137–51. Charlottesville: University of Virginia Press, 2005.

Smith, Merritt Roe. *Harpers Ferry Armory and the New Technology: The Challenge of Change*. Ithaca, N.Y.: Cornell University Press, 1977.

Smith, Timothy H. "The Sherfy House." Typescript, Civilian Accounts of the Battle of Gettysburg, May 10, 1995, Adams County Historical Society.

Smith, Timothy L., "The Ohio Valley: Testing Ground for America's Experiment in Religious Pluralism." *Church History* 60 (1991): 461–79.

Smylie, James H. *A Brief History of the Presbyterians*. Louisville, Ky.: Geneva Press, 1996.

Spangler, Aaron. "Pastors," *Register of the German Branch of the First Reformed Church of York and of Zion Reformed Church, 1852–1907*. York, Pa.: typescript, York County Historical Society, 1945.

Stanislow, Gail A. "Antislavery Sentiment and Opposition in Adams County, Pennsylvania." typescript, Adams County Historical Society, n.d.

"Staubs and Codoris." Typescript, Staub Farm and Sherfy Tenant House, File 2–16, Gettysburg National Military Park.

Stewart, Mary Margaret. "Black's Graveyard: A History." Typescript mss., Gettysburg Presbyterian Church, Gettysburg, Pa.

Stewart, Reid W. *History of Scottish Dissenting Presbyterianism in Adams County, Pennsylvania*. Lower Burrell, Pa.: Point Pleasant, 2003.

Stout, Harry S. *Upon the Altar of the Nation: A Moral History of the American Civil War*. New York: Viking, 2006.

Tangires, Helen. *Public Markets and Civic Culture in Nineteenth-Century America*. Baltimore, Md.: Johns Hopkins University Press, 2003.

Thompson, John W. IV. *Horses, Hostages, and Apple Cider: J. E. B. Stuart's 1862 Pennsylvania Raid*. Mercersburg, Pa.: Mercersburg Printing, 2002.

Trefousse, Hans L. *Thaddeus Stevens: Nineteenth-Century Egalitarian.* Chapel Hill: University of North Carolina Press, 1997.

Trotter, Joe William, Jr., and Eric Ledell Smith. *African Americans in Pennsylvania: Shifting Historical Perspectives.* University Park and Harrisburg, Pa.: Pennsylvania State University and Pennsylvania Historical and Museum Commission, 1997.

Trudeau, Noah Andre. *Gettysburg: A Testing of Courage.* New York: HarperCollins, 2002.

Valuska, David L., and Christian B. Keller. *Damn Dutch: Pennsylvania Germans at Gettysburg.* Mechanicsburg, Pa.: Stackpole Books, 2004.

Vermilyea, Peter C. " 'We did not know where our Colored friends had gone' ": The Effect of the Confederate Invasion of Pennsylvania on Gettysburg's African American Community." *Gettysburg Magazine,* 24 (2001): 112–28.

Walls, William J. *The African Methodist Episcopal Zion Church: Reality of the Black Church.* Charlotte, N.C.: A.M.E. Zion Publishing House, 1974.

Walters, Ronald G. *American Reformers, 1815–1860.* New York: Hill and Wang, 1978.

Wentz, Abdel Ross. *Pioneer in Christian Unity: Samuel Simon Schmucker.* Philadelphia: Fortress Press, 1967. Reprint, Gettysburg: Lutheran Theological Seminary, 1999.

Wert, Jeffry D. *Gettysburg: Day Three.* New York: Simon and Schuster, 2001.

Wert, J. Howard. *Episodes of Gettysburg and the Underground Railroad, As Witnessed and Recorded by Professor J. Howard Wert.* Edited by G. Craig Caba. Gettysburg, Pa.: G. Craig Caba Antiques, 1998.

Wigger, John H. *Taking Heaven by Storm: Methodism and the Rise of Popular Christianity in America.* New York: Oxford University Press, 1998.

Wilentz, Sean. *The Rise of American Democracy: Jefferson to Lincoln.* New York: W. W. Norton and Company, 2005.

Williams, William Henry. *The Garden of American Methodism: The Delmarva Peninsula, 1769–1820.* Wilmington, Del.: Scholarly Resources, Inc., 1984.

Wills, Garry. *Lincoln at Gettysburg: The Words that Remade America.* New York: Simon & Schuster, 1992.

Wilson, Charles Reagan. *Baptized in Blood: The Religion of the Lost Cause, 1865–1920.* Athens: University Press of Georgia, 1980.

Wilson, Harold F., and Arnold R Daum. *American Petroleum Industry: The Age of Illumination, 1859–1899.* Westport, Conn.: Greenwood Press, 1981; originally published by Northwestern University Press, 1959.

Wolf, Stephanie Grauman. *Urban Village: Population, Community, and Family Structure in Germantown, Pennsylvania, 1683–1800.* Princeton, N.J.: Princeton University Press, 1976.

Zuckerman, Michael W., ed. *Friends and Neighbors: Group Life in America's First Plural Society.* Philadelphia: Temple University Press, 1986.

Index

Brooks, John, 22
Buchanan, James, 7, 132, 160, 167
Buehler, David: antislavery of, 105–7, 111, 113, 116; on colonization, 114–15; nativism and, 93–95
buildings, church, 7, 22–23, 24, 36, 65, 92, 97, 121; hospitals as, 6, 146, 152; refinement and, 2, 8, 37–38, 54, 60–62; post-battle repair of, 154–55. *See also individual congregations*

Calvinism, 18, 22, 56, 80, 120, 173
Camp Letterman, 154, 155
camp meetings, 85, 87; Methodists and, 43, 44–45, 48, 80, 136, 172, 173
Carlisle, Pa., 24, 31, 125, 135; AME congregation in, 20, 124; Gettysburg campaign and, 137, 141
Cashtown, Pa., 134, 141
Catholics, 33, 41, 62, 156, 171, 181; African Americans and, 101, 102; diversity and, 3, 4, 26, 73, 87–97, 98, 174, 175; doctrine of, 3, 88–90, 174; and Dunkers, 97; ethnicity and, 3, 26, 91; German ethnicity and, 3, 24, 26, 74, 91, 97, 175; German language and, 3, 79, 173; nonconformity of, 3, 73, 87–90, 174; slavery and, 103–4; tolerance of, 26, 87, 90, 174. *See also* St. Francis Xavier Parish
cemeteries, 171; refinement and, 54, 55–59, 69; rural, 2, 55–59, 69, 171, 172
Cemetery Hill, 1, 5, 13, 144, 162
Cemetery Ridge, 145, 144, 146, 147–48, 149–51
Chambersburg, Pa., 7, 15, 24, 124, 125, 134, 162, 166; Gettysburg campaign and, 137, 138–39, 141; slave-catchers in, 31
Chester County, Pa., 29
choir masters, 1, 2, 63, 64–65
choirs, 60, 63, 64, 64–65, 67, 68, 122, 172
Christiana riot, 31–32, 180
Christ Lutheran, 23–24, 59, 93, 105, 132, 136; battle of Gettysburg and, 145, 146, 152, 154, 157–58; building of, 24, 60; debt of, 67–68; English and, 3, 23, 79, 174; fairs, 65–66; gas lights, 61–62; Pennsylvania College and, 40, 67, 158; pew rent, 66–67; refinement and, 41, 60; Schmucker sermon in, 92–93; seminary and, 27, 67, 136
church buildings. *See* buildings, church
Church of God, 26, 45, 87, 130
civil religion, 5, 6, 8, 159–67, 169, 172, 175; Dunkers and, 6, 164; jeremiads and, 163–64; Samuel Simon Schmucker and, 164–65
Civil War, 8, 131–69, 172; change and, 5–6, 131, 168–69, 175, 176; civil religion and, 6, 159–67, 169, 175, 176; home front during, 131–37, 168. *See also* Gettysburg, battle and campaign of
classes (Wesleyan), 19, 43, 45–46, 47, 48, 119, 158, 159

Codori, Antoine/Anthony, 70, 71, 142
Codori, Elizabeth Martin (wife of Nicholas), 70, 71, 144, 186
Codori farm, 71, 145, 149–50, 186
Codori family, 173, 186
Codori, George (son of Nicholas), 71, 186
Codori, Jean George, 70, 151, 186
Codori, Magdaleine (wife of Antoine/Anthony), 70, 71
Codori, Nicholas, 70–71, 141, 144, 173
Codori, Regina Wallenberger (wife of Jean George), 70, 71, 186
Cole, Abraham, 22, 141
colonization, 5, 21, 108, 114–16
Columbia, Pa., 25, 31, 124
The Compiler. See Republican Compiler
Confederacy, 135, 161, 162, 166, 180
Confederate army, 134, 171, 180; Antietam campaign and, 135–36; capture of blacks and, 6, 134, 138–39, 140, 155; Gettysburg campaign and, 137–51, 152, 153, 155, 159, 161, 163, 173
Conrad, F. W., 162–63
consumer revolution. *See* market revolution
Cotting, James, 24–25, 79, 87
counterculture. *See* nonconformity
Covenanters, 18, 19, 26
Cumberland County, Pa., 27, 32, 41

Democratic Party, 28, 71, 94, 104, 105, 117–18, 160, 166; Know Nothings and, 91–92, 96–97
Devan, Eden, 99, 117, 119
DeNeckere, Francis Xavier, 25, 87, 88–89
Dickinson College, 18
diversity, 1, 26, 98, 171–72, 173–74, 175, 187n4; American life and, 98, 176–78; Border North and, 73, 172; doctrinal, 3, 8, 59, 73, 80–98, 103, 173–74, 175; ethnic, 3, 4, 6, 8, 33, 59, 72, 73–80, 98, 103, 173, 176, 188n5; language and, 75–80, 98; racial, 4, 8, 12, 73, 175, 188n6. *See also various ethnicities and denominations*
Divit, Margaret "Mag," 99
Dobbin, Alexander, 18, 26, 27
Dosh, J. H. C., 41, 57–58, 59, 162, 172
Duffield, George, 81
Duncan, Catherine Schmucker, 145, 153, 154
Dunkers (Brethren), 3, 7, 49, 71, 95–96, 138; African Americans and, 101, 103, 17; buildings of, 25, 49–50, 51, 52, 84; Catholics, compared to, 97; civil religion and, 6, 164, 165–67; diversity and, 3, 4, 26, 73, 98, 174, 175; doctrine, 3, 84–87; English and, 75–76, 79–80; Love Feast, 69, 87, 97, 109, 174; music, 63–64; nonconformity, 3, 4, 48–52, 59, 68–69, 73, 84–87, 98, 118, 167, 172, 174; race and, 108, 111, 116; refinement and, 2, 38, 48–52, 68–69, 172, 173; Sherfy family and, 128–30, 185. *See also* Marsh Creek Dunkers

THE NORTH'S CIVIL WAR
Paul A. Cimbala, series editor

Anita Palladino, ed., *Diary of a Yankee Engineer: The Civil War Story of John H. Westervelt, Engineer, 1st New York Volunteer Engineer Corps.*

Herman Belz, *Abraham Lincoln, Constitutionalism, and Equal Rights in the Civil War Era.*

Earl J. Hess, *Liberty, Virtue, and Progress: Northerners and Their War for the Union.* Second revised edition, with a new introduction by the author.

William L. Burton, *Melting Pot Soldiers: The Union's Ethnic Regiments.*

Hans L. Trefousse, *Carl Schurz: A Biography.*

Stephen W. Sears, ed., *Mr. Dunn Browne's Experiences in the Army: The Civil War Letters of Samuel W. Fiske.*

Jean H. Baker, *Affairs of Party: The Political Culture of Northern Democrats in the Mid–Nineteenth Century.*

Frank L. Klement, *The Limits of Dissent: Clement L. Vallandigham and the Civil War.* With a new introduction by Steven K. Rogstad.

Lawrence N. Powell, *New Masters: Northern Planters during the Civil War and Reconstruction.*

John A. Carpenter, *Sword and Olive Branch: Oliver Otis Howard.*

Thomas F. Schwartz, ed., *"For a Vast Future Also": Essays from the* Journal of the Abraham Lincoln Association.

Mark De Wolfe Howe, ed., *Touched with Fire: Civil War Letters and Diary of Oliver Wendell Holmes, Jr.* With a new introduction by David Burton.

Harold Adams Small, ed., *The Road to Richmond: The Civil War Letters of Major Abner R. Small of the 16th Maine Volunteers.* With a new introduction by Earl J. Hess.

Eric A. Campbell, ed., *"A Grand Terrible Dramma": From Gettysburg to Petersburg: The Civil War Letters of Charles Wellington Reed*. Illustrated by Reed's Civil War sketches.

Herbert Mitgang, ed., *Abraham Lincoln: A Press Portrait*.

Harold Holzer, ed., *Prang's Civil War Pictures: The Complete Battle Chromos of Louis Prang*.

Harold Holzer, ed., *State of the Union: New York and the Civil War*.

Paul A. Cimbala and Randall M. Miller, eds., *Union Soldiers and the Northern Home Front: Wartime Experiences, Postwar Adjustments*.

Mark A. Snell, *From First to Last: The Life of Major General William B. Franklin*.

Paul A. Cimbala and Randall M. Miller, eds., *An Uncommon Time: The Civil War and the Northern Home Front*.

John Y. Simon and Harold Holzer, eds., *The Lincoln Forum: Rediscovering Abraham Lincoln*.

Thomas F. Curran, *Soldiers of Peace: Civil War Pacifism and the Postwar Radical Peace Movement*.

Kyle S. Sinisi, *Sacred Debts: State Civil War Claims and American Federalism, 1861–1880*.

Russell L. Johnson, *Warriors into Workers: The Civil War and the Formation of Urban-Industrial Society in a Northern City*.

Peter J. Parish, *The North and the Nation in the Era of the Civil War*. Edited by Adam L. P. Smith and Susan-Mary Grant.

Patricia Richard, *Busy Hands: Images of the Family in the Northern Civil War Effort*.

Michael S. Green, *Freedom, Union, and Power: The Mind of the Republican Party During the Civil War*.

Christian G. Samito, ed., *Fear Was Not In Him: The Civil War Letters of Major General Francis S. Barlow, U.S.A.*

John S. Collier and Bonnie B. Collier, eds., *Yours for the Union: The Civil War Letters of John W. Chase, First Massachusetts Light Artillery.*

Grace Palladino, *Another Civil War: Labor, Capital, and the State in the Anthracite Regions of Pennsylvania, 1840–1868.*

Christian B. Keller, *Chancellorsville and the Germans: Nativism, Ethnicity, and Civil War Memory.*

Sidney George Fisher, *A Philadelphia Perspective: The Civil War Diary of Sidney George Fisher.* Edited and with a new Introduction by Jonathan W. White

Robert M. Sandow, *Deserter Country: Civil War Opposition in the Pennsylvania Appalachians.*

Craig L. Symonds, ed., *Union Combined Operations in the Civil War.*

Harold Holzer, Craig L. Symonds, and Frank L. Williams, eds., *The Lincoln Assassination: Crime and Punishment, Myth and Memory.* A Lincoln Forum Book.

Earl F. Mulderink III, *New Bedford's Civil War.*

George Washington Williams, *A History of the Negro Troops in the War of the Rebellion, 1861–1865.* Introduction by John David Smith.

Randall M. Miller, ed., *Lincoln and Leadership: Military, Political, and Religious Decision Making.*

David G. Smith, *On the Edge of Freedom: The Fugitive Slave Issue in South Central Pennsylvania, 1820–1870.*

Andrew L. Slap and Michael Thomas Smith, eds., *This Distracted and Anarchical People: New Answers for Old Questions about the Civil War–Era North.*

Paul D. Moreno and Johnathan O'Neill, eds., *Constitutionalism in the Approach and Aftermath of the Civil War.*

Steve Longenecker, *Gettysburg Religion: Refinement, Diversity, and Race in the Antebellum and Civil War Border North.*